5/30/06 Stains
noted

# ALL ABOUT BONDS AND BOND MUTUAL FUNDS

## OTHER TITLES IN THE "ALL ABOUT..." FINANCE SERIES

*All About Options, 2nd Edition*
by Thomas McCafferty (0-07-045543-0)

*All About Stocks, 2nd editon*
by Esmé Faerber (0-07-134508-6)

*All About Futures*
by Thomas McCafferty and Russell Wasendorf (1-55738-296-4)

# ALL ABOUT BONDS AND BOND MUTUAL FUNDS

## The Easy Way to Get Started

**ESMÉ FAERBER**

## Second Edition

**McGraw-Hill**

New York  San Francisco  Washington, D.C.  Auckland  Bogotá
Caracas  Lisbon  London  Madrid  Mexico City  Milan
Montreal  New Delhi  San Juan  Singapore
Sydney  Tokyo  Toronto

**Library of Congress Cataloging-in-Publication Data**

Faerber, Esmé.
    All about bonds and bond mutual funds : the easy way to get
started / Esmé Faerber.—2nd ed.
        p.    cm.
    Rev. ed. of: All about bonds. 1993.
    ISBN 0-07-134507-8
    1. Bonds.   2. Bond funds.   3. Investments.   I. Faerber, Esmé.
All about bonds.   II. Title.
HG4651.F29   1999
332.63'23—dc21                                          99-28744
                                                           CIP

# McGraw-Hill

*A Division of The McGraw·Hill Companies*

*The sponsoring editor for this book was Stephen Isaacs, the editing supervisor was
Janice Race, and the production supervisor was Elizabeth J. Strange. It was set
in Palatino per the IPROF design specs by Joanne Morbit and Michele Pridmore of the
McGraw-Hill Desktop Publishing Unit, Hightstown, NJ.*

*Printed and bound by R. R. Donnelley & Sons Company.*

This publication is designed to provide accurate and authoritative information in
regard to the subject matter covered. It is sold with the understanding that the pub-
lisher is not engaged in rendering legal, accounting or other professional service.
If legal advice or other expert assistance is required, the services of a competent
professional person should be sought.

> —*From a Declaration of Principles Jointly Adopted by a Committee
> of the American Bar Association and a Committee of Publishers.*

McGraw-Hill books are available at special quantity discounts to use as premiums
and sales promotions, or for use in corporate training programs. For more information, please write to the Director of Special Sales, McGraw-Hill, 11 West 19th
Street, New York, NY 10011. Or contact your local bookstore.

This book is printed on recycled, acid-free paper containing a
minimum of 50% recycled de-inked paper.

# CONTENTS

**Chapter 12**

**Chapter 13**

# PREFACE

This new edition of *All About Bonds and Bond Mutual Funds* is, of course, updated, and it introduces many changes and improvements over the first edition. Most individuals investing in the different types of bonds use mutual funds over individual bonds. This practical guide is designed not only for practicing investors with some experience in mutual funds or the individual types of bonds but also for potential bond investors who have yet to get their feet wet. By understanding the underlying bond investments held by mutual funds, investors are able to better evaluate their choices of bond mutual funds. The purpose of this book is to introduce and explain as lucidly and simply as possible the information needed to purchase individual bonds and bond mutual funds. While the book covers the basics of investing in the different types of bonds, many sophisticated concepts also are included. These concepts may be difficult for beginning investors, but then the nature of determining the choices of different investments is not an easy matter.

The first chapter explains what bonds and bond mutual funds are, their characteristics, the terminology of bonds, the advantages of investing in bonds, how to buy and sell bonds, and how the bond markets function. A discussion of the differences of the investment classes of assets, such as stocks, bonds, and money market securities, has been added. How these would be included to achieve the investor's objectives as set out by an investment plan is also covered.

The second chapter evaluates the characteristics of bonds, their risks, rates of return, yield, liquidity, duration, and valuation.

The third chapter includes an overview of the economic influences which have a bearing on the valuation of bonds. Understanding the relationships between the economy and the bond markets is of great significance for bond investors. The second part of the chapter includes tables on how to read the different bond quotations listed in the newspapers. Beginning investors should read these first three chapters in their entirety.

Chapters four through ten discuss the different bond securities individually, namely, short-term instruments (money market mutual funds, Treasury bills, commercial paper, bankers' acceptances); corporate bonds and corporate bond mutual funds; Treasury securities, including the new Treasury inflation-indexed securities and inflation-indexed savings bonds, and Treasury mutual funds; government agency bonds and agency mutual funds; municipal bonds and municipal bond mutual funds; convertible bonds and convertible bond mutual funds; and zero-coupon bonds and zero-coupon mutual funds. These may be read in any order.

Chapters eleven and twelve include the general information on fixed-income mutual funds and closed-end funds. Each type of fund is analyzed as to how it works, the risks, how to buy and sell funds, the advantages, disadvantages, caveats, and whether this type of investment is suitable for you.

Chapter thirteen discusses the management of a bond portfolio.

Investing money is not easy, and the aim of this book is to make the task a little less difficult. Investors should invest in only those investments that they understand and feel comfortable with.

*Esmé Faerber*

# ACKNOWLEDGMENTS

The preparation of this book was greatly facilitated by the people at McGraw-Hill Publishing Company, most notably Stephen Isaacs, who was a pleasure to work with, and Donna Muscatello and Elizabeth Strange, who provided superb editorial assistance.

I would like to thank the following people for their assistance with computer software and hardware: Jennifer Faerber, Michael Faerber, and Bill McKenna. I am grateful for their help, which saved me many hours of trial and error on the computer.

I would like to thank James H. Gately and Tisha Findeison of the Vanguard Group for the information and materials that they so willingly provided.

A special note of thanks to my husband, Eric, and our children, Jennifer and Michael, for their continued support.

## CHAPTER 1

# Why Invest in Bonds and Bond Mutual Funds?

## KEY CONCEPTS

- Advantages of investing in bonds
- The stock market versus the bond market
- Investment planning
- Stocks, bonds, money market securities, and mutual funds
- A description of the bond markets
- What are bonds?
- The terminology of bonds and bond mutual funds
- What are bond mutual funds?
- How to buy and sell bonds

## ADVANTAGES OF INVESTING IN BONDS

People work hard for their money, and when they invest it, they expect to earn satisfactory rates of return. Money that is not spent is saved. This book is intended to assist savers with their investment options to earn satisfactory returns. There are a great number of investment alternatives, but many investors end up with the same few choices.

Investments are made to generate future purchasing power that will keep ahead of inflation and provide investors with a sense of financial security. However, if rates of return earned on these investments are meager, this sense of security can quickly turn to a sense of frustration. Rates of return need to exceed the rate of inflation and cover the taxes paid on the earnings to produce positive purchasing power for investors. Should rates of return not exceed those of inflation and the taxes paid, then the investments are earning negative rates of return and are losing future purchasing power.

After buying a house, the average investor's savings go into low-yielding bank savings accounts, money market funds, and certificates of deposit. The record bull market of the last three years has enticed many individual investors, who have never previously invested in stocks, to jump into the stock market. This is evidenced by the frenzy to invest in the Internet stocks, which have defied gravity in their ascent to dangerously high valuations. The staggeringly high returns earned in relatively short periods of time from these Internet stocks have prompted investors to disregard the risks of investing in these expensive stocks. Stocks that can rise over 20 points in one day have the potential to fall by that amount and more in a downturn. Ignoring the volatility of the stock market in pursuit of higher returns may be disastrous for investors who do not weigh the overall risks of their individual investments. On the other side of the spectrum, there are many investors who completely shun the stock market because of the volatility.

This book is about bond investments, and it will show how investors who cannot tolerate the risks of the stock market can increase their overall returns over low-yielding savings accounts and generate steady levels of income.

Investing the bulk of savings in low-yielding savings accounts translates into lower rates of return, higher income taxes, and the loss of capital appreciation (price growth). Bank accounts and money market mutual funds tend to pay interest at the low end of the yield scale without providing the tax advantages and capital appreciation opportunities of some of the other investment alternatives.

Despite these disadvantages of keeping money in low-yielding bank accounts, many investors persist with this strategy because they find the complexities of other investments such as stocks and bonds overwhelming. There is also the worry that with the increased volatility of the stock and bond markets, a downturn

## TABLE 1-1

### Comparison of Yields

| | |
|---|---|
| Passbook savings account | 1.80–2.00% |
| Interest-bearing checking accounts | 1.19% |
| Money market bank accounts | 2.49% |
| Money market mutual funds | 4.00–5.00% |
| 6-month certificate of deposit | 4.59% |
| 12-month certificate of deposit | 4.88% |
| 5-year certificate of deposit | 5.16% |
| 1-year Treasury bill | 5.407% |
| 10-year Treasury security | 6.00% |
| 10-year agency bond | 6.28% |
| 10-year high quality corporate bond | 6.66% |
| 30-year Treasury bond | 6.00% |

Source: *The Wall Street Journal*, May 1, 1998, p. C19, and *Barron's*, April 27, 1998, p. MW 104.

in either market could result in a loss of their savings. Therefore, these investors are paralyzed into keeping their money invested in low-yielding accounts.

Table 1-1 shows the rates that investors currently earn on different investments. Returns on bank savings accounts are now about 1.8 to 2 percent per annum, bank money market accounts 2.49 percent, and money market mutual funds between 4 and 5 percent per annum. A six-month certificate of deposit earns 4.5 to 5.5 percent, while 52-week Treasury bills only yield 5.407 percent. Investments with horizons of five, ten, and thirty years don't seem to be all that compelling when compared with these short-term rates. Investing in low-yielding bank accounts and money market funds is a conservative approach which focuses on not losing any principal. However, this riskless, low interest rate type of investment strategy will not help investors keep pace with rising costs and growing anxieties about funding retirement.

With interest rates at 20-year lows and the stock and bond markets at record high levels, it is a puzzling time for investors. If the Federal Reserve Bank raises interest rates or inflation rears its ugly head, then the stock and bond markets could plunge, causing investors losses in their principal. Consequently, many investors are reluctant to plunge into the stock and bond markets at this stage, afraid of the possibility of an erosion of their savings in the event of a correction or downturn in the markets. Yet, over long periods of time, bond and stock investments have outperformed the savings accounts. This is confirmed by a study done by Ibbotson and Sinquefeld (1991, p. 32) which reported the following average yearly returns for investments in the different portfolios of securities over the 64-year period from 1926 to 1990 (Faerber, 1995, p. 3).

|  | Nominal Average Returns | Standard Deviation of Returns | Real Average Returns |
|---|---|---|---|
| Common stocks of large companies | 12.1% | 20.8% | 9% |
| Common stocks of small companies | 17.1% | 35.4% | 14% |
| Long-term corporate bonds | 5.5% | 8.4% | 2.4% |
| Long-term government bonds | 4.9% | 8.5% | 1.8% |
| Intermediate-term government bonds | 5.1% | 5.5% | 2.0% |
| U.S. Treasury bills | 3.7% | 3.4% | 0.6% |

Had your grandparents invested in a diversified portfolio of the common stocks of large companies 64 years ago, the nominal average yearly rates of return earned would have been 12.1 percent per year. This would have been surpassed only by the returns earned by the common stocks of small companies, which averaged 17.1 percent per year. The real average rate of return, which is the nominal rate minus the rate of inflation, was 9 percent per year for common stocks of large companies and 14 percent for the common stocks of small companies. This surpasses by far the real returns earned on corporate bonds, 2.4 percent; long-term government bonds, 1.8 percent; and Treasury bills, 0.6 percent (Faerber, 1995, p. 3). The astute investor will immediately ask, "Why bother with other investments such as bonds and Treasury bills when you can get higher rates of return from investing in common stocks?"

There are a number of reasons, one of which has to do with the variability of the returns. The standard deviation of the returns measures the riskiness of the portfolios. Bonds have always been less risky than stocks, and this is shown by the standard deviation of the returns. Treasury bills have the least risk due to their relatively short maturities and the fact that there is almost no chance of default on them by the U.S. government. Risk increases for long-term government bonds, which surprisingly have almost the same risk as long-term corporate bonds. Generally, corporate bonds have greater risks of default than government bonds. The reason for this anomaly is that in the late 1970s and early 1980s, there were sharp increases in interest rates which had the effect of depressing the prices of the lower-yielding government bonds more than the higher-yielding corporate bonds.

The greatest risks are those experienced by portfolios of large company stocks (20.8 percent) and small company stocks (35.4 percent). This means that stocks are the riskiest of the above investment classes in terms of volatility, despite the fact that stocks are expected to earn the highest real rates of return over time. Investing in common stocks over long periods of time will produce higher returns because the variability of the returns can be averaged out. This is confirmed by the Ibbotson study of the 64-year time frame between 1926 and 1990, in which common stocks produced negative returns in 18 of the 64 years, compared with only one year for Treasury bills (Petty, 1993, p. 118).

Ken Gregory, a money manager in San Francisco, estimates that the risk of losing money on an investment in a basket of common stocks resembling the Standard & Poor's (S&P) Index diminishes over time: 30 percent over a one-year period versus 15 percent over a three-year period and 3 to 4 percent over a ten-year period (Gottschalk and Donnelly, 1989, C1).

## THE STOCK MARKET VERSUS THE BOND MARKET

Despite the fact that stocks have historically outperformed bonds over long periods of time and the spectacular gains of the U.S. stock markets in recent years, the following discussion will show why investors should consider bonds as part of a portfolio. Comparing the characteristics of stocks and bonds gives a clearer picture.

Common stocks represent ownership in a corporation, whereas bonds are IOUs and bondholders are debtholders, or creditors. Investors in common stock are the owners of a corporation. They have a claim on income and assets and are entitled to voting rights. As to their claim on income and assets, common stockholders stand last in line in their right to a share. Shareholders are only entitled to receive dividends after the bondholders and preferred stockholders have been paid. Similarly, in bankruptcy, the claims of bondholders are settled first, and common stockholders are last in line for the collection of any remaining proceeds from the liquidation of assets.

Bonds have a maturity date, at which time the bond is paid back at par value, $1000 per bond. For longer maturity bonds, the risks increase. Thirty-year corporate bonds, for example, are riskier than 30-year U.S. Treasury bonds because the interest and principal payments for the Treasury bonds are backed by the U.S. Treasury. Anything could happen within a 30-year period to force a corporation into bankruptcy before the bonds are redeemed. However, in the event of a default, the corporate bondholder still has a priority claim over the common stockholder, and the bondholders' claims would have to be paid before any proceeds are paid to the common stockholders.

Investors in common stocks are not guaranteed dividends. Dividends on common stocks are declared at the discretion of the company's board of directors. If the board decides to use the money for other purposes or earnings go down, dividends may be reduced or may not be declared. By contrast, investors in bonds can count on a steady stream of interest income. Thus, investors who cannot tolerate a reduction or termination of current income should not buy common stock.

Investors are greatly attracted to common stocks for their ability to provide for capital growth over long periods of time, as confirmed by the Ibbotson study. Bonds also offer the potential for capital appreciation (an increase in the selling price of the bond or stock over the purchase price), but investors invest in bonds primarily for current income.

The above comparison of the characteristics of stocks and bonds highlights some of the following reasons why investors should also consider investing some of their portfolio in bonds:

- Due to the higher volatility of stocks over bonds, investors might not want to be 100 percent invested in stocks. According to the Ibbotson study, stocks have been three times more volatile than bonds in the 64 years since 1926. The worst year for U.S. intermediate-term bonds was 1994, when they fell 5.1 percent in value. The worst year for stocks was 1991, when stock prices fell by 43.3 percent (Zuckerman, 1998, C1). By diversifying and investing some of their portfolios in bonds, investors may lower their risks of loss stemming from a stock market downturn.

- In the current economic climate, bonds offer positive real rates of return. Bonds offer a steady stream of income, whereas stockholders are not guaranteed the receipt of dividends. If inflation remains low, around the current 1.5-percent annual rate, and bonds continue to yield nominal returns between 5 and 6 percent, then bonds can still provide positive real rates of return of around 4 percent, which exceed those of bank accounts and Treasury bills. The S&P dividend yield for stocks is currently around 1.5 percent, which means that bond returns exceed those of common stocks with regard to income. Stocks of small companies generally pay no dividends.
- Investors who are risk-averse and/or have shorter investment horizons might shun stocks in favor of bonds to protect against possible downturns in the stock market, which would cause losses in principal.
- With the recent excessively high valuations in the stock market, it may be a good time to take some profits in some of these stocks and put the money into bonds.
- Investors in high tax brackets may be able to reduce their federal, state, and local taxes by investing in municipal bonds and government bonds.

Table 1-2 summarizes some of the conditions favoring the choice of stocks over bonds and vice versa. Investing in the stock market provides for the long-term growth of a portfolio. Investors who have long time horizons (longer than 5 to 10 years) and who do not need the income from the investments should stick with stocks. Investing in the bond markets provides for current income. These investments are more suitable for investors who are risk-averse and who have shorter time horizons for needing the money.

**TABLE 1-2**

Stocks versus Bonds

| Stocks | Bonds |
|---|---|
| 1. Provide long-term growth. | 1. Provide current income. |
| 2. Need a long time horizon. | 2. Require a shorter time horizon. |
| 3. Are more suitable for investors who do not need the principal from the stock investments to live on. | 3. Require low current and future inflation rates. |
| 4. Take an investor who can withstand volatility of the stock markets. | 4. Are more suited to the risk-averse investor. |
| 5. Provide potential for capital gains, which are taxed at lower tax rates than current income. | 5. Can lower federal, state, and local taxes, in the case of municipal bonds and government bonds. |
| 6. Provide a store of value. | |

## INVESTMENT PLANNING

Before making investment decisions, investors should assess their financial situations and then devise an investment plan.

The first step in any investment plan is to determine your financial net worth (what you own minus what you owe), because then you will know how much you can afford to invest. A portion of these funds should be kept in liquid investments—bank money market accounts, money market mutual funds, Treasury bills, and other money market securities, for example—for living expenses and for any emergencies. The amount to keep in these liquid investments for your emergency/living-expense fund will vary according to individual circumstances. An examination of your personal assets will determine how much to keep. A conservative rule of thumb is to keep three- to six-months' worth of expenses in liquid investments. Keeping too much in these liquid investments is not a good idea, since it may result in a loss of current and future purchasing power (see Table 1-1).

Included in your monthly expenses should be premiums for life, health, and disability insurance. It is especially important for families for the breadwinner to have adequate life and disability insurance. Health insurance is important for all members of the family. Similarly, home and auto insurance premiums should be included in your monthly expenses.

Once an emergency fund has been created, an investment program should be started for both the medium and the long term. Even on a modest starting salary, consistently setting aside a small portion for savings can make a difference over time. The secret is to pay yourself first. At the beginning of the month, write a check to your investment account. Certain mutual funds allow investors to deposit amounts as small as $25 per month on a regular monthly basis. See Figure 1-1 for the steps in the investment-planning process.

**FIGURE 1-1**

Investment Planning

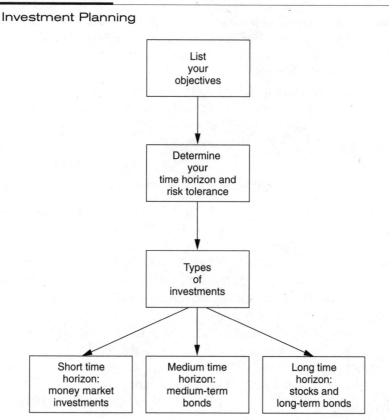

## List Your Objectives

List your goals and objectives for your medium- and long-term investment plan. This will determine how much you need to invest to reach your goals and the appropriate type of investments to make. For example, the following objectives have a time horizon:

- Buy a car in two years.
- Save for a down payment on a house in five years.
- Fund a college education in ten years.
- Accumulate a retirement fund in twenty-five years.

## Determine Your Time Horizon and Risk Tolerance

Once you have your objectives, the types of investments can then be geared to the time horizons of these objectives. The first two objectives are short- to medium-term time horizons, which means that the investments chosen should focus on generating income and preserving principal. Investing the money set aside for the purchase of a car in two years in the stock market would be risky; over a short period of time, the risk of losing money in the stock market is quite high and diminishes over time.

## Types of Investments

Investments for your emergency fund should be *liquid*, which is the ability to convert them into cash without losing very much of your principal in the conversion. Examples of these are U.S. Treasury bills, commercial paper, bankers' acceptances, money market mutual funds, short-term (six-month) certificates of deposit, money market bank deposits, and savings and checking accounts. These are discussed in Chapter 4.

Investments for short- and medium-term horizons should produce higher yields than money market investments, and the maturities should match the time period when you need the money invested. Investments in 2-year and 5-year U.S. Treasury notes, for example, will provide current income with virtually no risk of default on the interest and principal amount invested. Other options for these shorter maturities are U.S. government agency notes, short-term U.S. Treasury bonds, and short-term bond mutual funds.

Investing options to fund a college education in 10 years are greater and could include a mixture of common stock and bonds. With a 25-year time horizon, the mix of investments should be weighted more heavily toward stocks than bonds. This is because over long periods of time, stocks have outperformed bonds and most other investments, which means that if the past is a reflection of the future, you can expect average yearly returns of 10 percent for stocks versus 4 to 5 percent for bonds. Investors who are nervous about stock market corrections or crashes might consider investing some of their retirement savings in 30-year U.S. Treasury bonds. As you will read in Chapter 2, bonds are not immune from risk, and the degree and type of risk varies depending on the quality and the issuer of the bonds. Before investing in bonds, stocks, or mutual funds, you should be aware of the risks and factors affecting them.

The key to building a large portfolio is to get your finances in order. Table 1-3 provides some guidelines.

## TABLE 1-3

### Guidelines to Building an Investment Portfolio

1. Pay off all high-interest credit card debts first and then make extra payments to your mortgage account.
2. Cut all frivolous spending to increase amounts saved.
3. Pay yourself first at the beginning of the month.
4. Open up an automatic investment plan to encourage regular savings.
5. Contribute to retirement plans.
6. Map out your investment plan, listing all your objectives.
7. Determine the level of risk that you are comfortable with for your investments.
8. Increase the rates of return on your investments within comfortable levels of risk.
9. Review your investment strategy with regard to taxes. High-tax-bracket investors should increase their municipal bond holdings.
10. Review your investment plan once or twice a year.

# DESCRIPTION OF THE BOND MARKETS

Fixed-income securities are divided into two major markets: the money markets and the capital markets.

## Money Markets

The key distinction between money market securities and capital market securities is the length of time to maturity. Money market securities all mature within one year or less. This means that money market securities consist of bonds, notes, and other fixed-income instruments with maturities of one year or less, in addition to such traditional short-term securities as U.S. Treasury bills and commercial paper. Table 1-4 lists some of the money market securities. These money market securities are discussed in Chapter 4.

Large institutional borrowers, such as the U.S. government, corporations, and financial institutions, raise money by selling their short-term securities in the money markets. The money market does not have a specific location like the New York Stock Exchange for common stocks, for example. Instead, it consists of a collection of markets in a variety of locations, such as New York, Tokyo, London, and other financial capitals around the world. The major participants in the money markets are:

### TABLE 1-4

Money Market Securities

- U.S. Treasury bills
- Commercial paper
- Bankers' acceptances
- U.S. government agency notes
- Municipal notes
- Repurchase agreements
- Bank certificates of deposit
- Federal funds
- Call loans

- The primary dealers, about 38 in number, in U.S. Treasury securities
- Large money center banks in the financial centers around the world
- Commercial paper dealers
- Dealers in bankers' acceptances
- Other money market brokers

There are many advantages to money market securities, most notably the short maturities of one year or less, the high liquidity, and, hence, the relatively low risk of default. Money market mutual funds have enabled individual investors to participate in these money market securities. Similarly, the Federal Reserve has made it easier for individual investors to buy Treasury bills, commission-free (see Chapter 4). And with the active *secondary market* for these securities, investors are able to sell them before maturity. The secondary market is where already-issued securities are traded. Dealers will buy and sell these securities from their own inventories.

## Capital Markets

In the capital markets, securities with maturities of longer than a year are traded, and these markets are where capital is raised for the issuers of these securities. Capital market securities consist of stocks and bonds. Table 1-5 lists the capital market securities. The capital market bonds are covered in Chapters 5 through 10.

### TABLE 1-5

Capital Market Securities

- Common and preferred stocks of domestic and foreign corporations
- Bonds of domestic and foreign corporations
- U.S. Treasury notes and bonds
- Federal agency notes and bonds
- Municipal notes and bonds issued by state and local governments
- Foreign government notes and bonds.

The issues with longer maturities are traded in the *bond markets*, which are differentiated by the types of issues: the U.S. Treasury bond market, the municipal bond market, the corporate bond market, the government agency market, the Eurobond market, etc. These markets are not located in a central place like the New York Stock Exchange. Instead, they are made up of dealers in the different financial centers. These dealers sell bonds from their own accounts to institutional buyers and broker/dealers. They also buy for their own accounts. Markets which are made up of dealers are referred to as *over-the-counter markets*. However, the New York and American Stock Exchanges do list a small number of corporate bonds.

Individual investors are not able to compete with the institutions which trade in large blocks of bonds (in the millions of dollars). Individual investors typically trade in small quantities, usually called *odd lots*, and thus face greater dealer/broker markups. Individuals are also at a disadvantage in their access to specific bond issues. Brokerage firms may not have inventories of a particular issue; hence the broker may try to convince the investor to buy a similar but different bond issue.

Most individual investors use bond mutual funds to invest in bonds, which helps to overcome some of these disadvantages.

## WHAT ARE BONDS?

Before describing the characteristics of bonds, we need to answer the question, What are bonds?

Bonds bear certain similarities to savings accounts. When an investor deposits money in a savings account, in effect, that investor is lending the bank money. The bank pays the investor interest on the deposit. Similarly, the investor who buys bonds lends the issuer money in return for interest payments. When the bonds mature (come due), the investor will receive the principal amount of the bonds back, as he would have had he withdrawn the amount from the savings account. A bond is an IOU.

The major difference between savings accounts and bonds is that investors can sell their bonds before they mature to other investors. Savings accounts cannot be sold to other investors. Thus, bonds are negotiable IOUs. Savings accounts are not.

## THE TERMINOLOGY OF BONDS

In examining bonds, we need to understand the basic terminology that is used.

### Par Value

The par value is also known as the *face value* of the bond, which is the amount that is returned to the investor when the bond matures. For example, if a bond is bought at issuance for $1000, the investor bought the bond at its par value. At the maturity date, the investor will get back the $1000. The par value of bonds is usually $1000, although there are a few exceptions.

### Discount

Bonds do not necessarily trade at their par values. They may trade above or below their par values. Any bond trading below $1000 is said to be trading at a discount. For example, General Motors Acceptance Corporation bonds, which have a coupon rate of $5\frac{1}{2}$ percent and mature in the year 2001, are currently trading at a discount, $975 per bond.

### Premium

Bonds may trade at a premium, that is, more than the $1000 par value. IBM's $7\frac{1}{2}$ percent bonds maturing in the year 2013 are currently trading at $1086.50 per bond. This is an $86.50 premium per bond.

### Coupon Interest Rate

The coupon rate is the interest rate that the issuer of the bond promises to pay the bondholder. If the coupon rate is 5 percent, the issuer of the bonds promises to pay $50 in interest on each bond per year (5% $\times$ $1000).

Many bonds pay interest semiannually. If the issuer pays 5 percent semiannually, the bondholder would receive $25 per bond every six months. Some bonds have adjustable, or floating, interest rates, which are tied to a particular index. This means that the coupon payment will fluctuate based on the underlying index.

## Maturity

The maturity of a bond is the length of time until the bond comes due and the bondholder receives the par value of the bond.

## Market Rates of Interest

Market rates of interest affect bond prices. This is illustrated with the following example. Suppose you bought a bond last year with a coupon rate of 5 percent, when market rates of interest were also 5 percent, and you paid $1000 per bond. This year, market rates of interest have risen to 6 percent.

What price would you get if you tried to sell this bond? Obviously, a buyer would not pay $1000 for a bond yielding 5 percent when the buyer could buy new bonds with current coupon rates of 6 percent for $1000. The buyer would expect to get at least 6 percent, which means that this bond will sell at a discount (less than $1000) in order to be competitive with current bonds.

Conversely, if market rates of interest fall below the coupon rate, investors will be willing to pay a premium (above $1000) for the bond. Thus, bond prices are vulnerable to market rates of interest as well as other factors, which are discussed in Chapter 2.

## Call Provision

Many bonds have a call provision, which means that the issuer of the bonds can call, or redeem, the bonds at a specified price before their scheduled maturity.

Issuers exercise the call provision when market rates of interest fall well below the coupon rate of the bonds.

## Bid Price

Bonds are quoted on a bid and ask price. The bid price is the highest price buyers will pay for the bonds.

## Ask Price

The ask price is the lowest price offered by sellers of the issue.

## Spread

The spread is the difference between the bid and the ask price of the bond, part of which is a commission that goes to the broker or dealer. A large spread indicates that the bonds are inactively traded.

## Basis Point

A basis point is one hundredth of a percentage point. For example, if the yield on a bond falls from 5.25 percent to 5.20 percent, then the yield has declined by five basis points. Basis points are used to measure the differences in bond yields.

# WHAT ARE BOND MUTUAL FUNDS?

A mutual fund pools the money from investors and then uses it to make investments on behalf of those investors. The types of investments that the mutual fund invests in depend on the objectives of that particular fund. For example, if the objective of a mutual fund is to provide short-term income from money market securities, then this fund would invest in money market instruments. Similarly, there are stock mutual funds of various types and bond mutual funds of various types.

Mutual funds give investors the flexibility of investing in stocks, bonds, and money market investments without having to buy investments (stocks, bonds, and money market instruments) individually. Mutual funds are particularly popular with investors who do not have the expertise, knowledge, or time to research individual investment alternatives. Mutual funds are discussed in greater detail in Chapter 11, and there are specific sections on mutual funds in each of the bond instrument chapters.

# HOW TO BUY AND SELL BONDS

There are many more complexities involved in buying and selling bonds than there are for other investments. Certainly investors can buy and sell bonds through their brokerage firms as they do with common stocks. And for certain bonds, such as U.S. Treasury bonds, investors can bypass their brokers and deal directly with the Federal Reserve Bank. However, there are significant differences in buying and selling bonds, which, if appreciated, can reduce the transaction costs and increase the investor's overall return.

Investors can find the prices of listed common stocks on the New York and American Stock Exchanges and over-the-counter markets in the daily newspapers. This is not so for all bonds. Only a small percentage of the listed corporate bond issues and only the major government agency issues are quoted daily in *The Wall Street Journal*. Price quotes for municipal bonds can be found in a costly publication entitled *The Blue List of Current Municipal Offerings*. Thus individual investors do not have ready access to the majority of daily bond price quotes as they do for common stocks.

Prices of bonds vary from broker to broker and dealer to dealer. This price variance is due to many factors: availability of the bonds, size of the order, the markup on the bonds, the commission costs, and so forth.

By understanding the process behind the buying and selling of the different types of bonds, investors will be able to reduce the amount of commissions that they are charged.

Suppose an investor wants to buy a particular corporate bond. If that investor's brokerage firm does not have inventories of that bond, the brokerage firm will have to buy those bonds from a dealer. Hence, the price quoted to that investor for those bonds may be higher than that quoted by another brokerage firm that has existing inventories of that particular bond.

Individual investors should shop around at different brokerage firms to get the best prices. It can never hurt to negotiate with the brokers for a better price. When comparing prices, investors should compare the bid/ask prices, because the difference, or spread, between the bid and ask price represents the commission. Needless to say, this spread varies from broker to broker (and dealer to dealer). The spread also varies for the different types of bonds. For example, spreads on government agency bonds and municipal bonds are wider than those for U.S. Treasury bonds. This is because the former two bonds are not as actively traded. Similarly, spreads are wider for thinly or inactively traded issues of all types.

Dealers make their money from buying and selling bonds; therefore, they would not want to buy an inactively traded issue at a price at which they would lose money when they resell. Consequently, they will quote a wider spread. Investors should be cautious in buying bonds with large spreads—4 percent or more (Thau, 1992), because this is an indication that they may have difficulty selling the bond. In general, large spreads may also indicate that the creditworthiness of the bond issuer may be low. There are many other reasons to which a wide spread may be attributed. They are discussed in later chapters.

The importance of the discussion so far is to highlight some of the reasons why bond prices vary so that investors know to shop around at different brokerage firms to get the best price when they buy and sell their bonds. Even if the differences in price per bond appear to be small, when multiplied by the total number of bonds bought and sold, it can amount to quite a substantial savings. Keep these savings in your pocket rather than in your broker's.

With this brief discussion of the advantages of bonds, the subtleties of buying and selling, and the mechanics of the bond markets, the investor will want to evaluate bonds with regard to their liquidity, risk, and return. Chapter 2 discusses these issues and the evaluation process.

# REFERENCES

**Faerber, Esmé:** *Managing Your Investments, Savings, and Credit,* McGraw-Hill, New York, 1992.

**Faerber, Esmé:** *All About Stocks,* McGraw-Hill, New York, 1995.

**Gottschalk, Earl C., Jr., and Barbara Donnelly:** "Despite Market Swings, Stocks Make Sense," *The Wall Street Journal,* October 1989, p. C1.

**Ibbotson, Roger G., and Associates:** *Stocks, Bonds, Bills and Inflation: Historical Return,* Ibbotson Associates, Chicago, 1991.

**Petty, William J., et al:** *Basic Financial Management,* Prentice-Hall Inc., Englewood Cliffs, NJ, 1993.

**Thau, Annette:** *The Bond Book,* McGraw-Hill, New York, 1992.

**Zuckerman, Gregory:** "Bonds Pitched as Alternative to Wild Stocks," *The Wall Street Journal,* May 8, 1998, p. C1.

## CHAPTER 2

# Evaluating Bond Characteristics

## KEY CONCEPTS

- Short-term debt securities
- Long-term debt securities
- The risks of bonds
- Rate of return
- Different types of yield
- What rate of return to expect
- Taxes and returns
- Liquidity
- Duration and how it can help lessen volatility
- Valuation of bonds
- The yield curve and how to use it
- Why bonds fluctuate in price

All debt securities have the following similar characteristics:

- A *maturity date,* which is the date when the bond must be paid off
- *Interest payments,* which the issuer promises to pay in return for the use of the money loaned
- *Repayment of principal,* which the issuer promises to pay back at the maturity date

All bond issues have a master loan agreement, called a *bond indenture,* which contains the information for the issue. The following terms of a bond issue would be included in the indenture:

- The amount of the bond issue.
- The coupon rate.
- Frequency of interest payments (annual or semiannual).
- Maturity date.
- Call provision, if any. This provision allows the issuer of the bonds to call them in and repay them before maturity.
- Refunding provision, if any. This provision allows the issuer to obtain the proceeds with which to repay the bondholders when the issue matures by issuing new securities.
- Sinking fund provision, if any. This provision offers bondholders greater security in that the issuer sets aside earnings to retire the issue.
- Put option, if any. This provision allows the bondholders to sell the bonds back to the issuer at par value.

The main advantages of investing in bonds, as pointed out in Chapter 1, are that investors can count on a steady stream of interest income, and if the bonds are held to maturity, investors will receive the face value of the bonds back. However, with the wide fluctuations in market rates of interest in the past two decades, bond markets have become more volatile. Investors should become more cautious regarding the types of bonds they choose and the timing of their buying and selling. There are many different types of bonds to choose from, each with its own set of characteristics. For instance, bonds vary in their safety, marketability, return, liquidity, tax treatment, maturity, and the frequency with which interest is paid.

Investors can improve their returns and lessen their risk of loss by examining and understanding the varying characteristics of bonds before investing. A good starting point is to match bond maturities to financial needs, which can limit the loss of principal. Maturities of bonds range from less than a year to 50 years. For example, an investor who has funds to invest for six months would not want to invest in 30-year U.S. Treasury bonds because if interest rates rise during that period, the investor will lose a portion of his principal as bond prices of existing issues go down. However, if interest rates go down during that period, the investor will be able to sell the bonds at a profit because prices of existing bonds will rise. By matching the bond maturities to financial needs, investors can limit their losses due to market interest rate fluctuations.

## SHORT-TERM DEBT SECURITIES

Generally, the longer the maturity of the investment, the higher the yield for the investor. This higher yield is due to the uncertainty of interest rates, inflation, and the credit risk of the issuer in the future. By investing in shorter maturity issues, investors generally receive lower yields, but the risk of loss of principal is limited as well. Bear in mind that there are occasions when short-term interest rates exceed longer-term interest rates. The structure of interest rates, which determines the yield curve, will vary according to economic conditions, which is discussed later in this chapter.

There are many different short-term IOUs which are negotiable and actively traded in the money market. The money market is a collection of markets consisting of brokers and dealers who trade in billions of dollars of short-term securities—Treasury bills, bankers' acceptances, negotiable certificates of deposit, and commercial paper, among others. There is a market for newly issued securities and an active secondary market where issues that have already been issued trade.

The primary money market instruments are as follows:

*Treasury bills* are sold by the U.S. Treasury to finance some of the federal government's expenditures. Their maturities are for 13, 26, or 52 weeks.

*Bankers' acceptances* are promissory notes which are used mainly to finance international trade transactions. Their maturities are nine months or less.

*Commercial paper* is issued by the most creditworthy companies as a source of short-term credit and is, in essence, an unsecured promissory note. Maturities are 270 days or less.

*Negotiable certificates of deposit* are deposits of $100,000 or more deposited in commercial banks at a specific rate of interest. These can be bought and sold in the open market.

*Repurchase agreements* are contracts that involve the sale of money market securities with the simultaneous agreement to buy the securities back at an agreed-on price in the future.

*Money market mutual funds* invest in a diversified portfolio of short-term securities such as those described above.

These short-term securities are relatively safe from default and are also fairly liquid thanks to the active secondary markets. These short-term debt instruments are discussed in greater detail in Chapter 4.

By tailoring your investment options to your financial needs, you can build stability into your financial program. Short-term money should be matched with short-term securities, and longer-term funds should be invested in longer-term maturities.

## LONG-TERM DEBT SECURITIES

There are medium-term notes and bonds with maturities from one to ten years and long-term bonds maturing from ten to fifty years after issuance. These are referred to as *capital market securities*. However, there isn't always a clear distinction between short-term and long-term debt instruments. For example, there are municipal bond issues with maturities of less than a year and U.S. Treasury bonds and notes that are about to mature which are considered to be money market securities.

Long-term debt securities which make regular interest payments include U.S. Treasury notes and bonds, U.S. agency issues, municipal bond issues, and corporate issues. Zero-coupon bonds and convertible bonds are hybrid debt securities. They have different characteristics but are also considered to be capital market securities.

The U.S. Treasury issues two types of long-term securities: *Treasury notes* have maturities of less than 10 years, and *Treasury bonds* have maturities in excess of 10 years.

U.S. governmental agencies sell long-term debt issues to finance various activities. Although they are not backed by the full credit of the U.S. government, these *U.S. agency issues* are considered to be of good investment quality. There are many different agencies selling obligations with varying maturities, liquidity, and marketability.

*Municipal bonds* are issues sold by states, counties, and cities. The main advantage of municipal bonds is their special tax treatment. The interest received from municipal bonds is exempt from federal income tax and from state and/or local tax if issued in that state and county.

*Corporate bonds* are debt obligations of corporations and vary considerably in their features and their risk.

Among the hybrids, *zero-coupon bonds* pay no periodic interest but are issued at a deep discount and are redeemed at face value ($1000) at maturity. *Convertible bonds* are debt securities which can be exchanged for the common stock of the issuing company at the option of the bondholder.

Each of these long-term securities differs in risk, return, taxability, liquidity, and marketability. Investors should analyze the characteristics of the different types of bonds before investing.

Instead of investing in these individual long-term bonds, investors may invest in the various bond mutual funds. There are Treasury bond mutual funds, U.S. government agency mutual funds, corporate bond mutual funds, zero-coupon mutual funds, and convertible bond mutual funds.

The advantages of investing in long-term maturities are the higher yields and the potential to ride out price fluctuations.

## THE RISKS OF BONDS

Investing in bonds is not without risk. All bond instruments carry risk, but the degree of risk varies with the type of debt and the issuer. There is always the risk that if you try to sell a bond before maturity, you could lose money on it if market rates of interest have risen. This does not mean that you should resort to stashing your money under the mattress, because that too involves a risk of loss. There are different types of risk, and you should be aware of how these affect your bond investments.

### Interest Rate Risk

*Interest rate risk* refers to the changes in market rates of interest, which have a direct effect on bond investments. The prices of fixed-income securities move inversely with changes in interest rates.

During periods of rising interest rates, investors holding fixed-income securities will find that the market prices of their bonds will fall, because new investors in these bonds will want a competitive yield. Similarly, in periods of declining interest rates, prices of fixed-income securities will rise. The longer the time to maturity, the greater the potential interest rate risk.

Interest rate risk can be lessened by reducing the maturities and also by staggering bond investments with different maturities. Interest rate risk is minimized if investors hold onto their bonds until maturity.

## Risk of Default

Another risk of bonds revolves around the creditworthiness of the issuer of the debt. *Creditworthiness* is the ability of the issuer to make the scheduled interest payments and to repay the principal when the bonds mature. Credit risk varies with bond issuers. U.S. Treasury issues carry virtually no risk of default. We would all be in a sorry state of affairs if the U.S. Treasury defaulted on its interest and principal repayments.

U.S. agency debt has a slightly increased risk of default. Bonds issued by state and local governments depend on the financial health of the particular issuer and the ability to raise revenue. For corporate issuers, credit risks are linked to their balance sheets, income statements, and their earnings capacities.

There are independent ratings services that evaluate the credit risk of municipal and corporate bonds. See Table 2-1 for a list of credit ratings. These range from the best credit quality for the issuers with the strongest financial status to the lowest ratings for issuers in default.

Moody's and Standard & Poor's (S&P) are two of the best-known ratings agencies, and their ratings are similar, though not identical. Ratings of AAA, AA, A, and BBB from S&P are considered to be investment-grade quality. Bonds with ratings below BBB are considered to be junk bonds and are speculative. These junk bonds' lower ratings mean that the issuers have a greater likelihood of default on their interest and principal repayments. Before buying a bond issue, investors should ask their brokers for the ratings on that issue.

**TABLE 2-1**

Bond Ratings

| Moody's | Standard & Poor's | Interpretation of Ratings |
|---------|-------------------|---------------------------|
| Aaa | AAA | Highest-quality obligations. |
| Aa | AA | High-quality obligations. |
| A | A | Bonds that have a strong capacity to repay principal and interest but may be impaired in the future. |
| Baa | BBB | Medium-grade quality. |
| Ba | BB | Interest and principal are neither |
| | B | highly protected nor poorly secured. Lower ratings in this category have some speculative characteristics. |
| B | CCC | Speculative bonds with great |
| Caa | CC | uncertainty. |
| Ca | C | |
| C | DDD | In default. |
| | DD | |
| | D | |

Individual investors should stick to issues with ratings of BBB and above to ensure against sleepless nights. However, these ratings provide only a relative guide for investors, because the financial status of the issuer could deteriorate over time and result in the issue being downgraded to a lower rating. A downgrading usually causes a decline in the market price of the bond. The opposite occurs when a bond issue is upgraded. The same issuer with many different bond issues outstanding could have different ratings for each issue. For example, in May 1999, Moody's Investors Service downgraded ContiFinancial Corporation's senior unsecured debt from B1 to Caa1.

Investors need not be duly alarmed if their bonds are downgraded from AAA to A, for example, because this still indicates good quality. However, if the issue is downgraded below BBB, an investor should review whether to continue owning that bond.

Credit risk can be minimized by buying quality bonds with investment-grade ratings of A and above by S&P, which have a reduced likelihood of default, and by diversifying investments. In other words, instead of investing all your money in the bonds of one issuer, buy bonds of different issuers.

## Call Risk

Bonds with a call provision have *call risk*. Many corporate and municipal bond issues are callable by their issuers. This means that the issuers can repurchase their bonds at a specified (call) price before maturity. This is beneficial to the issuer and detrimental to the investor because when interest rates drop below the coupon rate of the bond, the issuer can call the bonds. The issuer can then reissue bonds at a lower coupon rate.

Call risk poses a potential loss of principal when the bonds are purchased at a premium and the call price is less than the premium price. Call risk can be anticipated by estimating the level to which the interest rates must fall before the issuer would find it worthwhile to call the issue. As will be explained in a later chapter, the call provision of a bond makes the duration of the bond uncertain.

To minimize call risk, examine the call provisions of the bond and choose bonds which are unlikely to be called. This is particularly important if you are contemplating the purchase of bonds that are trading above their par values (at a premium).

## Purchasing-Power Risk

Purchasing-power risk affects bonds. Bond coupon, or interest, payments are generally fixed amounts; thus the value of the payments is affected by inflation. When the rate of inflation rises, bond prices tend to fall because the purchasing power of the coupon payments is reduced. So to say the least, bonds are not a good hedge against inflation. Bond prices react favorably to low rates of inflation. When the monthly announcement of the consumer price index or producer price index (measures of inflation in the economy) is less than anticipated, bond prices rise.

To combat purchasing-power risk, invest in bonds whose rates of return exceed that of anticipated inflation. If you anticipate inflation in the future, invest in floating-rate bonds, whose coupon rate adjusts up and down with market interest rates.

## Reinvestment Rate Risk

All coupon bonds are subject to reinvestment rate risk. Interest payments received may be reinvested at a lower interest rate than the coupon rate of the bond, particularly if market rates of interest decline or have declined. Zero-coupon bonds, which make no periodic interest payments, have no reinvestment risk.

## Foreign Currency Risk

If you decide to escape it all by investing in foreign bonds, these are subject to foreign currency risk. A rise in the dollar against a foreign currency can decimate any returns and result in a loss in principal when the bond matures.

It is evident that risk cannot be avoided, not even with the most conservative investments, savings accounts and Treasury bills. Even stashing money under the mattress entails risk. However, through diversification, which is investing in different types of bonds rather than investing completely in one bond issue, certain levels of risk can be minimized. By understanding and recognizing the different levels of risk for each type of bond, the total risk can be better managed in the construction of a bond portfolio.

There is a direct correlation between risk and return. The greater the risk in an investment, the greater the return to entice investors. However, in most cases investing in bonds with the greatest rate of return, therefore the greatest risk, can lead to financial ruin if the odds do not pan out.

# RATE OF RETURN

Investors invest in bonds to earn interest income or achieve capital appreciation (when the face value of the bond at maturity, or the sale price, is greater than the purchase price), or both. The simple definition of total return includes both income and capital gains or losses.

Why is calculating a rate of return so important? There are a number of reasons. First, it is a measure of the growth or decline of your wealth. Second, it is a yardstick with which to evaluate the performance of your bond investments against your objectives. The total rate of return can be calculated as follows:

Rate of return = [(ending value − beginning value)
+ income] ÷ gross purchase price

Spreads and commissions should be included in the calculations. For example, if the gross purchase price of a bond bought at the beginning of the year is $850 and the bond is sold for $950 at the end of the year, minus a commission of $25 and with interest of $50, the rate of return is:

Rate of return = [(925 − 850) + 50] ÷ 850 = 14.71%

This is not the most accurate rate of return, since it ignores the time value of money. A more comprehensive measure of the rate of return of a bond is the yield to maturity, which takes into account the time value of money. The *time value of money* is a concept that recognizes that a dollar today is worth more in the future because of its earnings potential. A dollar invested at 5 percent for one year would equal $1.05 at the end of the year. Similarly, a dollar to be received at the end of one year would be worth less than a dollar at the beginning of the year.

The average rate of return of 14.71 percent in the example does not take into account the earnings capacity of the interest received. In other words, the $50 of interest received would be reinvested, which would increase the rate of return above 14.71 percent.

## DIFFERENT TYPES OF YIELD

This section explains the three basic types of yields, which may be confusing to investors.

### Coupon Yield

The *coupon yield*, as noted in Chapter 1, is the stated yield of the bond issue. This is the specified amount of interest that the issuer of the bond promises to pay the bondholder each year. This annual amount of interest may be stated as a percentage of the par value of the bond or as a dollar amount. For instance, a bond with a par value of $1000 that pays $80 of annual interest has an 8 percent coupon yield.

The coupon yield is fixed through the life of the bond issue, unless it is a variable-interest coupon, which fluctuates through the life of the loan.

## Current Yield

Another type of yield is the current yield. The current yield is determined as follows:

$$\text{Current yield} = \frac{\text{Coupon interest amount}}{\text{purchase price of the bond}}$$

For example, if a bond is purchased at par, $1000, and the coupon is 5 percent (interest will be $50 per year), then the current yield is 5 percent (same as the coupon yield). However, on the secondary market most bonds trade above or below par. For a bond purchased at $1100 with a 5-percent coupon, the current yield is 4.54 percent (50/1100).

There is a relationship between bond prices, current yields, and coupon rates. Bonds trading at a discount to their par values have current yields which are higher than their coupon rates. Bonds trading at a premium to their par values have current yields which are lower than their coupon rates. For investors who are concerned with high current income, the current yield is a useful measure.

## Yield to Maturity

The *yield to maturity* is the discount rate calculated by mathematically equaling the cash flows of the interest payments and principal payments with the price of the bond. This is also referred to as the *internal rate of return* of the bond.

The yield to maturity can be solved easily with the use of a financial calculator, which has built-in financial tables. For example, a bond that was purchased for $770.36, pays a coupon of 5 percent ($50 annually), and has a maturity of 10 years has a yield to maturity of 8.5 percent:

The process on the financial calculator would be:

1. The purchase price of $770.36 is entered into the PV (present value) button.

2. The coupon payment of $50 is entered into the PMT (payment) button.

3. The maturity value ($1000 par value) is entered into the FV (future value) button.

4. The time to maturity is entered into the $n$ (number of payment periods per year multiplied by the number of years) button.

5. Press the $i$ (interest/yield to maturity) button, and the calculator will solve the yield to maturity for you.

If you don't have a financial calculator, you can use the following formula, which will approximate the yield to maturity (YTM):

$$\text{YTM} = \frac{\left( \text{coupon payment} + \dfrac{1000 - \text{purchase price}}{\text{years to maturity}} \right)}{\left( \dfrac{1000 + \text{purchase price}}{2} \right)}$$

$$= \frac{\left( 50 + \dfrac{(1000 - 770.36)}{10} \right)}{\left( \dfrac{1000 + 770.36}{2} \right)}$$

$$= 8.24\%$$

Using the approximation formula, the yield of 8.24 percent understates the true yield to maturity calculated with a financial calculator.

The yield to maturity can also be calculated with pencil, paper, and financial tables. You would solve the following equation for $r$ (which is the yield to maturity).

$$\text{Purchase price of bond} = \Sigma \frac{\text{coupon}}{(1 + r)^n} + \frac{1000}{(1 + r)^n}$$

where $\Sigma$ is the summation and $n$ is the number of years to maturity. For the above:

$$770.36 = \Sigma \frac{50}{(1 + r)^{10}} + \frac{1000}{(1 + r)^{10}}$$

Solving this equation can be a tedious task since you have to use a trial-and-error approach to determine the value of $r$. Choose a value for $r$ and plug it into the calculation. If this value does not equate the right side of the equation to the left-hand side, choose another value until you find the right one. (This is not a calculation recommended for investors who get squeamish at the thought of adding three figures together.)

The yield to maturity incorporates the compounding effects of the interest payments, but it also hinges on two assumptions:

1. That the investor holds the bond to maturity
2. That the investor reinvests the interest payments received at the same yield-to-maturity rate

If the bond is not held to maturity, then the internal rate of return of the bond can be calculated by substituting the sale price of the bond for the maturity value.

Similarly, when the bond has a call feature, investors can calculate the *yield to call* by substituting the call price for the maturity price in the equation.

The yield-to-maturity rate assumes that the investor will reinvest the interest received at the same yield to maturity. If this does not occur, the investor's actual rate of return will differ from the quoted yield-to-maturity rate. For example, if the interest received is spent and not reinvested, the interest does not earn interest, and the investor will earn much less than the stated yield to maturity. Similarly, if the stated yield to maturity is 8 percent and the investor reinvests the interest at lesser (or greater) rates, then the 8 percent will not be achieved.

In reality, it is difficult to match the yield-to-maturity rate for the interest received because interest rates are constantly changing. The interest received is usually reinvested at different rates from the stated yield-to-maturity rate.

Some readers may throw in the towel at this stage because the yield to maturity can't even convey a dependable rate of return for a bond.

The yield to maturity is useful, however, in comparing and evaluating different bonds of varying quality with different coupons and prices (Thau, 1992, p. 49). For example, by comparing the yield to maturity of an AAA-rated bond with a BBB-rated bond, the investor can easily see how much the increment in yield would be in choosing the lower-rated bond. The investor can also see the yield differential between bonds with different maturities.

The yield to maturity does not indicate the price volatility of different coupon bonds with different maturities. When comparing different bonds with different maturities, investors will want to know which bond's price will fall more when interest rates rise. This can be answered by calculating the bond's duration.

## WHAT RATE OF RETURN TO EXPECT

Overall, the rate of return of a bond depends on the type of bond, the levels of risk, and the time period to maturity. For instance, as pointed out earlier, U.S. agency bonds have slightly increased risk of default over U.S. Treasury bonds of the same maturity. Similarly, a junk bond with an S&P rating of CCC would have to pay a considerably higher yield than a bond with an A rating to entice investors.

The question that is always asked by investors is: What rate of return should I expect?

Although there is no obvious answer, you need to take the following factors into account:

1. The spectrum of rates for the different types of fixed-income securities
2. The levels of risk that will give you the comfort of being able to sleep well at night
3. The maturities that match your financial needs and objectives

Market rates of interest have been falling over the past decade, which means that bond investors currently may not be able to match the double-digit returns of the 1980s. Table 2-2 lists the yields of the different types of maturities at the time of this writing.

By increasing the level of risk and extending the maturities of bonds, investors can increase their rates of return. However, basing investments on the greatest yield may be disastrous. Going for higher yields and ignoring risk does not guarantee high returns over a period of time. For example, investing in lower-quality corporate bond issues which go into default translates into a loss of principal and negative returns. Investors must decide whether the additional returns warrant the additional risk. This is known as the *risk-return tradeoff.* Choose the level of risk that you feel comfortable with.

## TABLE 2-2

| Treasuries | |
|---|---|
| 30-year U.S. Treasury bonds | 5.832% |
| 10-year U.S. Treasury bonds | 5.559% |
| 5-year U.S. Treasury bonds | 5.573% |
| 2-year U.S. Treasury bonds | 5.553% |
| *U.S. Agency Issues* | |
| 30-year FNMA bonds | 6.74% |
| 15-year FNMA bonds | 6.26% |
| *Municipal Issues* | |
| 22+ year revenue bonds (A) | 5.14% |
| 12–22-year government obligation bonds (AA) | 5.01% |
| 7–12-year government obligation bonds (AA) | 4.65% |
| *Corporate Bonds* | |
| 10+ year AAA–AA rated | 6.54% |
| 10+ year A–BBB | 6.84% |
| 1–10-year AAA–AA | 6.06% |
| 1–10-year A–BBB | 6.33% |
| *Money Market Securities* | |
| 3-month Treasury bill | 5.02% |
| 3-month bank certificate of deposit | 4.04% |
| 90-day commercial paper | 5.49% |

On the other hand, by playing it too safe and investing in securities with minimal risk, you are assured of low, minimal returns. To get higher returns, you have to accept greater risk.

As was pointed out earlier, extending the maturities on your investments without regard for your financial needs can result in a loss in principal due to interest rate risk. The other extreme is just as bad: investing every cent of one's savings in short-term bank accounts and money market funds. This approach ensures the safety of principal but produces low yields. Currently, the spread between short- and long-term interest rates is low, less than 1 percent between 30-year Treasury bonds and 3-month Treasury bills (Table 2-2). This narrow spread still presents opportunities for investors. For example, instead of investing everything in savings accounts currently yielding around 2 percent, some money can be invested in 3-month Treasury bills or money market mutual funds, both of which are yielding around 5 percent. Increasing the rate of return by three percentage points by investing in U.S. Treasury bills or money market mutual funds, which still fall within acceptable risk levels, enhances the overall value for the investor. Consider the future value of two investments if $1000 is invested in each:

|  | End of Year 1 | End of Year 5 | End of Year 10 |
| --- | --- | --- | --- |
| Bank savings account at 2% | $1020.00 | $1104.10 | $1219.00 |
| Money market mutual fund at 5% | $1050.00 | $1276.30 | $1628.90 |

Over a 10-year period, by investing in money market mutual funds with an additional yield of 3 percent, an investor can increase his investment by $409.90 ($1628.90 − $1219.00) for each $1000 of principal invested.

The optimal approach is to ladder your investments in terms of yields and maturities. Cash and funds needed currently for living expenses and contingencies (medical expenses and emergencies) can be invested in money market funds and bank accounts where there is little risk. Savings to fund longer-term objectives can be invested in higher-yield, longer-maturity investments such as U.S. Treasury notes and bonds, U.S. agency bonds, and municipal and corporate bonds with compatible levels of risk. See How to Use the Yield Curve later in this chapter to determine how far into the future to extend maturities of bond investments.

There are two important factors which affect the rates of return earned on investments. These are inflation and taxes. If an investment earns 4 percent per year and inflation is 3 percent for the same period, the real rate of return is only 1 percent. If inflation rises to 4 percent or above, investors holding fixed-income securities yielding 4 percent will not be jumping for joy at the prospect of earning zero or negative returns. This is why market prices of long-term bonds decline so rapidly when the inflation rate rises, because bondholders receive fixed amounts of interest. Market prices of existing bonds on the secondary markets will go down in price (to include the rate of inflation) in order to make their rates of return more competitive and entice investors to buy them.

If you anticipate inflation, you should choose investments that will yield rates of return which will cover the rate of inflation. In times of rising inflation, investors tend to avoid long-term fixed-income securities and invest in short-term investments (money market accounts and Treasury bills) so that rates of return can increase with the rates of inflation.

## TAXES AND RETURNS

Taxes also diminish investors' rates of return. Interest income is taxed at ordinary rates at the federal level. Currently, capital gains are taxed at lower marginal tax rates if the securities are held for the required length of time to qualify. If the securities are held for less than the prescribed time, then the capital gains on bonds are taxed at the higher ordinary tax rates.

Since taxes (federal, state, and possibly local) are levied on income and capital gains, the *after-tax returns* of different bonds should be compared. The after-tax return is calculated as follows:

After-tax return = (1 − tax rate)(rate before taxes)

For example, an investor in the 39.6 percent marginal tax bracket who invests in a corporate bond yielding 6.8 percent has an after-tax return of 4.107 percent:

After-tax return = (1 − 0.396)(0.068) = 4.107%

This can be compared to the rate of return of a municipal bond, which is tax-free at the federal level. In many cases, taxes affect the choice of investments, and effective tax planning can reduce the level of taxes paid.

Rates of return are diminished by inflation, taxes, and commissions (spreads), and investors should consider these factors to ensure that their investments yield positive returns after these have been deducted. This is particularly important during periods when inflation rates are high or interest rates are low.

## LIQUIDITY

*Liquidity* is defined as the ability to convert an investment into cash without losing a significant amount of the funds invested. Funds which are to be used in a short period of time should be invested in assets which are high in liquidity (savings accounts, certificates of deposit, Treasury bills, money market funds). A Treasury bill can be sold very quickly with a slight concession in selling price, whereas a 20-year-to-maturity junk bond may not only take time to sell but may also sell at a significant price concession. This is especially true for bonds that are thinly traded, i.e., where relatively few are traded and the trades take place only with large spreads between the bid and the ask prices. In other words, thinly traded bonds are not *marketable*. That means they can't be sold quickly.

All bonds have different characteristics and vary with regard to risk, return, tax status, marketability, and liquidity. To make the appropriate choices of bonds for your portfolio, you must understand these factors, which also determine the value of the bond.

## DURATION AND HOW IT CAN HELP LESSEN VOLATILITY

Bonds, as pointed out at the beginning of this chapter, are subject to the following risks:

- Risk of default by the issuer
- Loss of purchasing power through inflation
- Fluctuations in market rates of interest

Investors can lessen the risk of default by investing in a diversified portfolio of bonds, in other words, by not putting all their money into the bonds of one issue or a few issues; and by buying better-quality bond issues. There is not much that an investor can do to reduce inflation in the economy, but the investor can purchase bonds with yields that exceed the current and expected future rates of inflation. Similarly, investors may be able to lessen the impact of interest rate risk through the concept of *duration*.

Duration is defined as the average time that it takes for a bondholder to receive the total interest and principal. It is the point in time in the life of the bond where the bond's return remains unchanged despite the movement of market rates of interest. For example, the duration on a $1000 face value bond, coupon of 6 percent, maturing in three years, market price of $973.44, and current market rate of interest of 7 percent can be calculated using the following formula (Mayo, 1991).

$$\text{Duration} = \frac{(1 + y)}{y} - \frac{(1 + y) + n\,(c - y)}{c\,[(1 + y)^n - 1] + y}$$

where c = coupon rate
    y = yield to maturity
    n = number of years to maturity

Substituting the figures in the example:

$$\text{Duration} = \frac{(1 + .07)}{.07} - \frac{(1 + .07) + 3\,(.06 - .07)}{.06\,[(1 + .07)^3 - 1] + .07}$$

$$= 2.83 \text{ years}$$

Another method of determining the duration of a bond is to use the time-value-of-money concept. Using the same example above, a bond with a coupon of 6 percent, maturing in three years, market price of $973.44, and current market rate of interest of 7 percent, duration is determined as follows:

| Time Period of Payment | | Payment Amount (Coupon & Principal) | | Present Value Interest Factor | | Present Value of Time-Weighted Payments |
|:---:|:---:|:---:|:---:|:---:|:---:|:---:|
| 1 | × | $ 60 | × | 0.9346 | = | $ 56.08 |
| 2 | × | $ 60 | × | 0.8734 | = | $ 104.80 |
| 3 | × | $1060 | × | 0.8163 | = | $2595.83 |
| | | | | | | $2756.71 |

$$\text{Duration} = \frac{\text{summation of present value of time-weighted payments}}{\text{market price of the bond}}$$

$$= \frac{\$2756.71}{\$\ 973.44}$$

$$= 2.83 \text{ years/periods}$$

Duration is a time-weighted average of the summation of the present values of the coupon and interest payments, multiplied by the time periods of the payments, which is then divided by the market price of the bond. The present value is the opposite of the future or compound value in the time-value-of-money concept. A dollar today is worth more in the future because of its earnings potential. Similarly, a dollar in the future can be discounted to today's value and is worth less now than in the future.

The duration of 2.83 means that the bondholder will collect the average of the coupon and the principal payments of this particular bond in 2.83 years.

Bonds with different maturities and different coupons will have different durations. Bonds with higher durations experience greater price volatility as market rates of interest change, and bonds with smaller durations have lower price volatility. Different bonds with the same durations have price fluctuations similar to changes in market rates of interest.

This is explained in Table 2-3, which shows the prices of the bond with the different maturities when market rates of interest change.

When market rates of interest decline below the 6 percent coupon rate to 5 percent, the price of the bond increases above par value. Correspondingly, as the maturities increase from 2 years to 20 years, so do the prices of the bond. The opposite is true when market rates of interest rise to 7 percent, above the coupon rate of 6 percent, as shown in Table 2-3. Bond prices fall below par and decline further as maturities extend into the future.

Following are some generalizations with which duration can be better explained:

1. The longer the maturity of a bond, the greater the price volatility.
2. There is an inverse relationship between bond prices and market rates of interest: When market rates of interest rise, bond prices fall; when market rates of interest fall, bond prices increase.

As pointed out in the discussion, a bondholder with a coupon of 6 percent and a maturity of 30 years will face greater price volatility than a similar coupon bond with a shorter maturity. A lower coupon bond (for example, 4 percent) with the same maturities will experience even greater price volatility with changes in

## TABLE 2-3

Impact of Market Fluctuations in Interest Rates on a Par Value Bond with a Coupon Rate of 6 Percent with Different Maturities

| Maturity | 5% Market Rate of Interest | 7% Market Rate of Interest |
| --- | --- | --- |
| 2 years | $1018.56 | $981.88 |
| 5 years | $1042.27 | $959.01 |
| 10 years | $1077.21 | $929.72 |
| 20 years | $1124.63 | $894.04 |

market rates of interest. This is because with the lower coupon bond, the bondholder will receive lower cash flows ($40 per year through maturity versus $60 per year), which, when reinvested, will produce lower future values. The longer the maturity of the bond, the longer the bondholder will have to wait to receive the face value of the bond. Hence, the present value of the par value of the bond would be discounted to a lesser amount than the present value of the par value of a bond maturing earlier.

Duration accounts for this investment rate risk, the coupon rate, and the term to maturity of a bond as follows:

- The lower the coupon, the higher the duration.
- The higher the coupon, the lower the duration.
- The longer the term to maturity, the higher the duration.
- The shorter the term to maturity, the lower the duration.
- The smaller the duration, the smaller the price volatility of the bond.
- The greater the duration, the greater the price volatility of the bond.

Duration explains why a zero-coupon bond has the same duration as its term to maturity. With a zero-coupon bond, there are no coupon payments, and only the principal is received at maturity. Except for zero-coupon bonds, the durations for all other bonds are less than their terms to maturities.

Duration is a tool that can be used to manage interest rate risk and the maturity of the bonds with the timing of the investor's need for the funds. By matching the duration of bonds with the timing of the funds, investors can lessen their risk of loss on their bonds.

## VALUATION OF BONDS

Bond prices fluctuate up and down due to the relationship between their coupon and market rates of interest, their creditworthiness, and the length of time to maturity. After bonds are issued, they rarely trade at their par values ($1000) in the secondary markets because interest rates are always changing. Certain bonds sell at premiums and others sell at discounts.

There is a mathematical formula for determining the price of a bond, but bear in mind that this is conceptual. The market price of a bond depends on the stream of the bond's coupon payments and the principal repayment in the future. Using the time value of money, this stream of future payments is discounted at market rates of interest to its present value in today's dollars. It is the same formula used in the financial calculator for yield to maturity, except you solve for PV (present value) and input *i* (yield to maturity) that reflects market rates of interest and a risk premium.

For example, a bond which pays coupon interest of $100 per year and matures in three years time, with market rates of interest projected at an average of 6 percent per year, will have a price of $1107.30 according to the calculation. Thus, the price of the bond is linked to the coupon yield, market rates of interest, discount rate, and the length of time to maturity.

If we compare the price of a U.S. Treasury note with the same coupon rate and maturity as that of a corporate bond, we find that their prices will differ. The Treasury note will trade at a higher price than that of the corporate bond because there is a greater risk of default with the corporate bond and the price will thus be calculated with a higher discount rate (or yield to maturity). Investors will require a greater yield on the corporate bond for assuming greater risk of default. This confirms why an AAA rated corporate bond will trade at a higher price than a BBB rated corporate bond if the coupon and maturity are the same. The difference in yield between the AAA- and BBB-rated bonds is referred to as the *excess yield,* which issuers must pay for the extra grade of credit risk.

Bond prices fluctuate depending on investors' assessment of their risks. The greater the risk, the greater the yield (and the lower the market price).

## THE YIELD CURVE AND HOW TO USE IT

*Yield* is defined as the potential return on a bond. There are several different measures of yield, which were discussed earlier in this chapter.

The *yield curve* depicts the relationship between the yield and the length of time to maturity of bonds with the same level of risk. Figure 2-1 shows the yield curve for U.S. Treasury securities for June 3, 1998. Yields for the 3-month, 6-month, 1-year, 2-year, 5-year, 10-year, and 20-year Treasury securities are plotted. The graph shows a relatively flat yield curve, with a slightly upward-sloping curve.

**FIGURE 2-1**

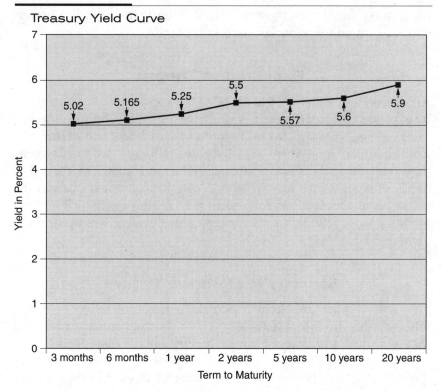

Treasury Yield Curve

The spread between the 3-month Treasury bill, with a yield of 5.02 percent, and the 30-year Treasury bond, with a yield of 5.83 percent, is 81 basis points (or 0.81 percent). This is a narrow spread between the 3-month maturity and a 30-year maturity. One would expect an upward-sloping curve because the longer the maturity, the greater the bondholder's exposure to risk. Hence, bond issuers tend to pay more to compensate investors for the risk.

What a relatively flat yield curve means is that by extending maturities, investors are taking greater risk for very small additional returns.

Historically, there have been a few occasions when the yield curve has had a downward slope, i.e., where short-term yields have exceeded long-term yields. In other words, yields declined as maturities increased. This happened in 1979, 1981, and 1982.

The shape of the yield curve changes daily with the changes in yield due to fluctuations in market rates of interest. There are a number of theories which explain the shape of the yield curve. The three most quoted are the expectation theory, the liquidity preference theory, and the market segmentation theory.

## Expectation Theory

According to this theory, the shape of the yield curve is determined by expected future interest rates. If investors expect future interest rates to rise, they will invest their funds in short-term maturities. Consequently, long-term security rates will rise as prices come down to make them more attractive to investors. On the other hand, if expectations are for lower long-term interest rates in the future, investors will buy long-term maturities now to lock into the higher yields. This will push prices of these securities up and the yields will go down.

## Liquidity Preference Theory

This theory adds the element of risk to the expectation of future interest rates. Investors generally prefer short-term maturities, and they will invest in longer-term maturities only if they expect long-term interest rates to rise enough to compensate them for the risk of the expected fluctuations in future interest rates. In other words, investors require an additional amount of return, called a *risk premium*, in order to expose themselves to the future uncertainties of longer-term interest rates. If they do not expect to receive this additional risk premium, they will continue to invest in short-term maturities and roll them over at maturity into new short-term securities.

## Market Segmentation Theory

This theory is based on the preferences of institutional investors for particular types of maturities, which would then determine the yield curve through supply and demand of these securities. For example, life insurance companies generally invest more in longer maturity bonds, whereas banks stick to short- and medium-term maturities.

## How the Yield Curve Can Help Investors

The yield curve can assist investors in choosing the maturities of their fixed-income securities. By examining the current yield curve, investors have information on the yields at the different maturities, which can help them make decisions as to maturity.

Figure 2-1 shows a relatively flat yield curve with a small spread between the 3-month Treasury bill of 5.02 percent and a 30-year Treasury bond of 5.83 percent. With this kind of curve, investors are not receiving very much more yield for the risk they are taking by extending their maturities. In fact, the 20-year Treasury bond is currently earning a greater yield than the 30-year. This anomaly could be explained by the fact that the 20-year bond is not as actively traded as the 30-year bond. In other words, it costs more to buy the 30-year bond, which pushes the yield down.

To assess the risk of extending maturities, yield curves can be constructed for other types of bonds besides Treasury securities.

## WHY BONDS FLUCTUATE IN PRICE

To sum up, bond prices fluctuate in price for the following reasons:

1. Changes in risk assessment by the market: the lower the quality, the lower the price; the greater the quality, the higher the price.
2. The length of time to maturity: the longer the maturity, the more volatile the fluctuations in price.
3. The coupon rate relative to market rates of interest. When market rates of interest rise and exceed the coupon rate of a bond, the price of the bond will decline in order to relate the current yield to the market rate of interest. When interest rates fall, the price of the bond will rise.

## REFERENCES

**Mayo, Herbert B.**: *Investments*, 3d ed., Dryden Press, New York, 1991.
**Thau, Annette**: *The Bond Book*, McGraw-Hill, New York, 1992.

## CHAPTER 3

# How to Read the Financial Pages

## KEY CONCEPTS

- The relationship between the economy and the financial markets
- Monetary policy and the financial markets
- Fiscal policy and the markets
- The dollar and the financial markets
- Why you should read the credit market columns
- The bond markets
- How to read bond quotations
- How to read bond mutual fund quotations

The easy years of earning 30 percent annual returns on stocks (1995–May 1999) and double-digit returns on bonds (the 1980s and early 1990s) seem to be over. Instead, returns on these investments appear to be coming back to the normal annual levels of 7 to 10 percent for stocks and 5 percent for bonds. This means that investors are going to have to be more careful in the selection of their investments. By understanding the relationships between the economy and the bond and stock markets, investors will be better able to make decisions as to the types of investments to have in their portfolios.

Portions of this chapter have been previously published by Esmé Faerber in *Managing Your Investments, Savings, and Credit,* McGraw-Hill, New York, 1992, and in *All About Stocks,* McGraw-Hill, New York, 2000.

The aim of this chapter is to explain and make sense of some of the economic and financial jargon with regard to the bond markets that is contained in the financial pages of the newspapers. This is not meant to be a comprehensive guide to understanding macroeconomics and finance. Instead, this chapter will help investors understand some of the key relationships between the economy and the bond markets.

For many people, the financial pages of the newspaper are difficult to read. There is an abundance of confusing interrelationships between economic events and the bond and stock markets. Terms like CPI, GNP, S&P 500 Index, M-1, M-2, and Barron's Confidence Index are bandied about like the codes of a secret society. In fact, economic data can be extremely esoteric, and the same data can be used by different economists and financial analysts to come up with different conclusions about the state of the economy and the financial markets.

To better explain the relationship between bond prices and the influence of the economic environment, the first part of this chapter will include a brief overview of some of the key terms which are used to measure the economy and their effects on the bond markets. The latter part of the chapter will focus on bond indices and the different bond price quotations in the newspapers.

The double-digit returns from both the bond and stock markets during the 1980s and early 1990s have made investing in bonds and stocks very glamorous and exciting. In the coming years, it may not be as easy to repeat those successes, and investors may have to be more discriminating in their choices of investments to equal their earlier stellar returns.

The clearest picture of the economy and financial markets is gained through hindsight, but after-the-fact information is too late for investment decisions. By interpreting economic and financial market indicators, investors are looking for early signs of changes in the direction of the stock and bond markets. On the other hand, the astute reader will observe that if economists and financial analysts can't agree on the state of the economy, how is the lay individual to come up with any more definitive answers?

For individual investors, it is not important if the forecasted numbers are not in agreement because after all, economists and analysts all base their forecasts on the same information. What is important, however, is to be able to use either their forecasts or the key statistical indicators to predict changes in the direction of the economy and the financial markets. An understanding of the economic indicators can help you make timely decisions in the stock and bond markets.

The previous chapter detailed the different characteristics of bonds and pointed out that the value of a bond is determined by the interest payments and the investor's required rate of return, both of which are related to the economy. If interest rates and levels of risk are influenced by the state of the economy, it then becomes important to understand the relationship between the bond markets and the economy.

## THE RELATIONSHIP BETWEEN THE ECONOMY AND THE FINANCIAL MARKETS

If you are an investor in the bond or stock markets, your investments are affected by the state of the economy. The U.S. economy is currently growing at an average annual rate of 4.2 percent (for 1998), but corporate profits in the U.S. are expected to fall due to weakness in Asia and Latin America. This weakness affects the large multinational corporations and all other companies that do business in Asia and Latin America.

Changes in the economy have a large impact on interest rates and inflation, which both directly affect the stock and bond markets.

Interest rates are currently low, which means that investors will not be able to add significant wealth to their nest eggs by leaving their funds in bank accounts and money market funds. With increasing taxes, concerns about job security, and rising tuition for higher education added to these low interest rates, investors will need to take on more risk in their investment strategies. This means placing a greater emphasis on longer-term securities, which offer higher yields. Investors must then contend with the gyrations of bond prices in the credit markets, which react to different economic and political events.

Investors are better equipped to plan their investment strategies if they are able to understand and forecast the state of the economy. This section outlines the effects of the most common economic indicators, which can then be used to identify trends in the economy.

*Gross domestic product* (GDP) is a measure in dollar value of the economy's total production of goods and services. Comparing the current GDP with previous periods indicates the economy's rate of growth (or lack of it). An increasing GDP indicates that the economy is expanding. GDP grew around 3.5 percent in 1994, slowed to around 2 percent in 1995, and accelerated to 4.2 percent in the first quarter of 1998. The expectation for GDP is to slow somewhat into the future. Slower economic growth is expected to slow corporate profits, which will impact inventories. With slower sales, companies experience a buildup in inventories, which means that they will slow down their production to adjust for this buildup. However, the state of the economy is far more complex than the mere correlation of two variables. To better assess the state of the economy, many measures—the inflation rate, unemployment rate, national income, international trade, and manufacturing capacity, among others—need to be considered.

Inflation distorts the accuracy of this measurement of growth, so there is a measure of the real growth of an economy's output, referred to as "real" GDP. Real GDP is adjusted for price-level changes and measures each period's growth in goods and services using prices which prevailed in a selected base year. A comparison of real GDP figures with those of prior periods provides a more accurate measurement of the real rate of growth. Gross domestic product is therefore a measure of the economic health of a country. In the U.S., inflation has been low recently and has not significantly detracted from real GDP.

A more narrowly focused measure of a nation's output is *industrial production*, which measures manufacturing output. The manufacturing sector generally leads the economy's short-term swings. Currently, factory production is down, again due to weakness in Asia and Latin America.

The *unemployment rate* is the percentage of the nation's labor force that is out of work, and it is another indicator of the economy's strength (or lack of it). Currently, the United States has a tight labor market, with an unemployment rate that dropped to 4.3 percent in April 1998, the lowest in 28 years. A growing economy and a low unemployment rate in combination have traditionally fueled inflation. Concern arises when rates for labor rise faster than productivity gains. This is why the bond and stock markets pay so much attention to the utterances of the Federal Reserve Chairman's speech to Congress about interest rates. When there is even a shadow of inflation on the horizon, the Federal Reserve will raise short-term interest rates.

The other side of the coin is a high unemployment rate. Governments become concerned when the unemployment rate rises above a certain level (about 7 percent), and they will stimulate the economy (through fiscal and monetary policies) to reduce the unemployment rate. These actions may also stimulate inflation.

In the early 1980s, the U.S. experienced high rates of both unemployment and inflation. The government dealt with the inflation first by pursuing restrictive economic policies. This sent the economy into a recession and the unemployment rate increased further. In 1992, the U.S. experienced low inflation but high unemployment. The government's approach was to stimulate the economy by lowering interest rates (through the Federal Reserve Bank).

*Inflation* is defined as the rate at which the prices for goods and services rise in an economy. Inflation often characterizes a growing economy, in which the demand for goods and services outstrips production, in turn leading to rising prices. In other words, there is too much money chasing too few goods and services. At the time of this writing, there appears to be no inflation on the short-term horizon of the U.S. Some economists expect the rate to go below 2 percent, while others argue for a future increase due to rising wages in a tight job market and increases over the existing low levels of commodity prices.

The *Consumer Price Index* (CPI) is one measure of inflation. It is calculated monthly by the Bureau of Labor Statistics. The Bureau monitors the changes in prices of items (such as food, clothing, housing, transportation, medical care, entertainment) in the CPI. It is a gauge of the level of inflation and is more meaningful when it is compared to the CPIs of previous periods.

Some economists believe that the CPI fuels inflation, similar to a cat chasing its tail. Social Security payments and many cost-of-living increases in employment contracts are tied to increases in the CPI. The CPI may, in fact, exacerbate the level of inflation.

When the level of inflation is high (relative to previous periods), governments will pursue restrictive economic policies to try and reduce the level of inflation.

The *Producer Price Index* (PPI) is announced monthly and monitors the costs of raw materials used to produce products. The PPI is a better predictor of inflation than the CPI, because when prices of raw materials increase, there is a time lag before consumers experience these price increases.

Another key indicator is the Commodity Research Bureau's *commodity price index*, which measures prices of raw materials. When this index rises significantly over a six-month period, it is a warning that inflation is on the horizon.

The *Leading Inflation Index,* developed by Columbia University's Center for Business Cycle Research, is an index that anticipates cyclical turns in consumer price inflation. When it moves up with commodity prices, it is a clear signal that inflation is ahead.

When an economy is in recovery, the *manufacturing capacity utilization rate* becomes a key indicator to watch. This indicator measures how much of the economy's factory potential is being used. Economists worry about inflation when the nation's factory capacity rises above 82.5 percent. For example, when a recovery is robust and the economy is growing rapidly, with interest rates remaining low, there will be a decline in unemployment, which will give rise to increasing wage pressures and increasing prices of goods.

Inflation has a detrimental effect on both the bond and stock markets as well as on the economy. When the level of inflation increases, real GDP falls (in 1980 in the U.S.). Similarly, when inflation declines, real GDP increases (in 1983 in the U.S.). This inverse relationship may not always hold up, as evidenced by the economy in the mid 1990s. Despite lower levels of inflation, real GDP showed insignificant growth, which translated into the economy taking a long time to move out of recession.

*Housing starts* are released monthly and show the strength in housing production. An increase in housing starts relative to previous months indicates optimism about the economy as more people are buying homes. Thus, strength in housing starts shows consumer confidence in the economy.

Economists have designed an index of *leading indicators* to forecast economic activity. This index includes data series ranging from stock prices, new building permits, and average work week to changes in business and consumer debt. By analyzing this monthly index, economists hope to be able to forecast economic turns and be able to give advance warning of a turn in the stock market, which can impact the bond markets. In reality, however, when the leading indicators forecast an economic turn, the stock market has already reacted to the change.

## The Impact of the Economy on the Bond Markets

Those are some of the pieces to the overall economic picture. By examining such indicators and statistics, investors are better able to fine-tune their opinions and forecasts of the economy. I am not suggesting that with a brief overview of some economic terms, you are now an expert who can dispense with all the economists' forecasts. On the contrary, it is difficult to predict economic behavior; economists are notorious for differing in their forecasts of economic growth, inflation, and unemployment. This highlights the complexities of the economy, but it does not mean that the investor should throw in the towel and discount the economy. Instead, by using a consensus of economic forecasts, investors are better prepared in deciding how to invest their funds.

Generally, the bond markets tend to react to the economy in the following way:

- An expanding, growing economy may have a negative effect on the bond markets, because expansion may be perceived to be inflationary.
- A sluggish economy is good news for the bond markets owing to the fact that interest rates and inflation would tend to be low.

This is because a bond pays a fixed amount of interest at the stated coupon rate. With rising inflation, the purchasing power of this interest is eroded and the price of this bond will go down. In these circumstances, issuers of new bonds must, therefore, increase their coupon rates to make it conducive for investors to buy them. Similarly, if inflation is expected to fall, prices of existing bonds will go up because bondholders will receive greater *real rates of return*. The real rate of return on a bond is determined as follows:

Real rate of return = bond yield or coupon rate − rate of inflation

For example, if inflation is around 2.6 percent and the bond yield is 5 percent, the real rate of return is 2.4 percent:

Real rate of return = 5% − 2.6% = 2.4%

Besides getting a sense of the state of the economy and inflation, before purchasing bonds, investors need to determine the direction of interest rates. Buying bonds when interest rates are rising can cause paper losses, or capital losses if they are sold before maturity. As we have seen from earlier chapters, there is an inverse relationship between bond prices and market rates of interest. When market rates of interest go up, prices of existing bonds go down; when market rates of interest go down, prices of existing bonds go up.

Investors will want to follow the actions of the Federal Reserve Bank, which impact interest rates and the bond and stock markets.

## MONETARY POLICY AND THE FINANCIAL MARKETS

Monetary policy can have a substantial impact on the economy and, thus, the financial markets. The Federal Reserve Bank (the Fed) is the central bank of the United States and works with the government to maintain financial stability and to devise and implement monetary policy. In addition, the Federal Reserve regulates the nation's banks and provides financial services to the U.S. government. The stability of the monetary system depends upon the supply of money in the economy. By regulating the supply of credit and money in the economy, the Federal Reserve Bank can affect the country's economic growth, inflation, unemployment, production, and interest rates.

### How the Federal Reserve Changes the Supply of Money

The Federal Reserve Bank can increase or decrease the nation's money supply to provide a stable currency value, a reasonable level for interest rates, and sufficient money to fund transactions in the economy. The principal tools used by the Federal Reserve Bank to change the supply of money are:

- Open market operations
- Reserve requirements
- Discount rate

#### Open Market Operations

The Federal Reserve buys and sells securities (mostly U.S. Treasury bills and repurchase agreements, discussed in Chapter 4) in the open market to change the money supply and the reserves of commercial banks. Table 3-1 illustrates the process when the Federal Reserve expands the money supply by buying securities on the open market. The Federal Reserve purchases the securities on the open market, which then expands their inventory of securities. Payment is made within three days by check, which is deposited in the commercial banks, expanding their deposits. This increases the reserves of the commercial banks and the reserves of the commercial banks at the Federal Reserve. The banks are then able to lend more money, which expands the nation's credit and money supply.

When the Federal Reserve wants to contract the money supply, it will sell securities from its portfolio in the open market. This has the effect of siphoning off money from the nation's money supply. Commercial banks' reserves are reduced, therefore reducing banks' ability to lend money. Table 3-2 illustrates the contraction of the money supply by the Fed.

These open market operations are conducted by the Federal Open Market Committee (FOMC), which is composed of the president of the Federal Reserve Bank of New York, the board of

**TABLE 3-1**

Transactions When the Fed Buys Securities on the Open Market

| Federal Reserve Bank | | Commercial Banks | |
|---|---|---|---|
| Inventory of securities increases when the Fed buys securities | Reserves of the commercial banks increase | Reserves of the banks increase, which allows banks to issue more credit | Demand deposits increase when the Fed pays the sellers of the securities |

**TABLE 3-2**

Transactions When the Fed Sells Securities on the Open Market

| Federal Reserve Bank | | Commercial Banks | |
|---|---|---|---|
| Inventory of securities decreases when the Fed sells securities | Reserves of the commercial banks decrease | Reserves of the banks decrease, which reduces banks' ability to issue more credit | Demand deposits are decreased when the Fed is paid by the buyers of the securities |

governors, and the presidents of the other Federal Reserve Banks on a rotating basis. This committee meets every two weeks, and the minutes of their meetings are released to the public six weeks after each meeting. However, Federal open market transactions are reported in the newspapers the day after they occur. Bond traders are acutely aware of the Fed's actions with regard to buying, selling, or refraining from open market transactions.

## Reserve Requirements

The Federal Reserve Bank requires banks to maintain reserves with the Fed. The percentage of banks' deposits held as reserves is determined by the Fed and is called the *reserve requirement*. The Fed can increase the money supply by reducing the reserve requirement: banks will need to keep less in reserve and can, therefore, increase their lending. The reverse is true when the Fed increases the reserve requirements, which increases interest rates.

Not only does the money supply increase or decrease due to changes in the reserve requirements, but there is also a multiplier effect on the money supply. This can be illustrated with a simple example.

Suppose you deposit $100 in Bank X and the reserve requirement is 10 percent. Bank X now has $100 on deposit, of which $10 is kept on reserve and $90 is lent to Corporation A. Corporation A deposits this $90 check in its bank, Bank A. Bank A keeps $9 on reserve and lends the remaining $81. This process is repeated, which shows how the original $100 is increased through the banking system to expand the money supply. Figure 3-1 illustrates the multiplier process graphically.

The Fed can stimulate the multiplier effect by lowering reserve requirements, which correspondingly increases banks' capacities to lend.

The Fed does not pay interest on the reserves of the banks. Banks with excess reserves lend to banks that need to add to their reserves. These funds are called *federal funds* and are mostly provided on a short-term (one-day) unsecured basis, although there are occasions when these funds are provided on a longer-term basis. The rate that banks pay for these funds is called the *federal funds rate*, which is reported in the financial newspapers. The Fed can alter the money supply by changing the Fed funds rate, and these changes to both the federal funds rate and reserve requirements are widely reported in the newspapers.

**FIGURE 3-1**

The Multiplier Process

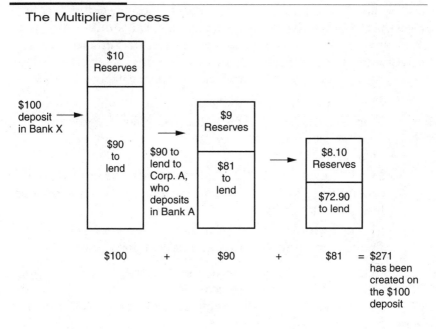

## Discount Rate

The discount rate is the Fed's third tool. The discount rate is the rate of interest that the Fed charges banks when they borrow from the Fed. When the discount rate is too high, banks are discouraged from borrowing reserves from the Fed. When the discount rate is low or lowered, banks are encouraged to borrow. So, by changing the discount rate, the Fed can expand or contract the money supply. Changes in the discount rate are reported in the newspapers.

Monitoring the changes in open market transactions, reserve requirements, and discount rates give you a better feeling for the future direction of interest rates.

## Defining the Money Supply

Before looking at the relationship between the money supply and the financial markets, we need to define the different measures of the money supply. This can be likened to measuring your own personal money supply, although that is somewhat more finite by comparison!

How much cash do we have? We have the cash in our pockets, wallets, under the mattress, and in our checking accounts. However, savings accounts, money market funds, and some investments can be easily converted into cash. Similarly, the narrowest measure of the nation's money supply is referred to as M-1, a broader definition as M-2, and the broadest category as M-3.

- M-1 consists of the nation's cash, coins, travelers' checks, checking accounts (NOW accounts, which are interest-bearing checking accounts, are included), and demand deposits.
- M-2 includes M-1 but also adds savings and time deposit accounts (e.g., CDs and money market deposit accounts of less than $100,000).
- M-3 includes M-1 and M-2 as well as time deposits and financial instruments of large financial institutions.

Which is the best measure of the economy's money supply? That is hard to answer because economists continue to debate this point. The Federal Reserve's preferred measure is M-2, which is America's broad money supply.

Interest rate changes explain this discrepancy. Short-term interest rates have fallen prompting investors to move their savings out of low-yielding bank deposits (included in M-2) into higher-yielding bonds, since long-term rates have remained relatively high. Economists argue that portfolio shifts make the definitions of the money supply unreliable as indicators of the state of the economy. For example, you can see at once that M-1 could increase when people transfer money from their savings accounts to checking accounts without affecting M-2. There will be discrepancies between the classifications of the money supply from week to week, but investors should be more concerned with the overall changes over a period of time so they can see trends. By monitoring the Fed's open market transactions, changes in the reserve requirements and the discount rate, and the rate of growth or decline in the money supply, investors are better able to make their investment decisions.

In short, evidence suggests that changes in the money supply have an influence on nominal economic activity, but the influence on real economic growth is still hotly contested.

## Impact on the Financial Markets

When the Fed pursues a restrictive monetary policy, it may sell securities on the open market to siphon money from the money supply; and/or raise the reserve requirements, which reduces banks' capacity to lend money, and/or raise the discount rate to discourage banks from borrowing money.

These changes in monetary conditions will have an effect on corporate earnings. When the money supply is decreased, interest rates go up, making it more costly for companies and individuals to borrow money. This causes them to delay purchases and leads to reduced sales. With lowered sales and higher credit costs, companies will have decreased earnings, which translates into lower stock prices and lower prices of existing bonds.

When interest rates are rising, investors earn more by investing in fixed-income securities and money market instruments. Therefore, many investors take their money out of the stock markets and invest in liquid short-term securities and longer-term debt securities, which puts more downward pressure on stock prices. Higher interest rates also translate into higher borrowing costs for margin investors. These investors will move their money to debt instruments to justify their higher interest costs.

Monetary policy has a direct effect on interest rates, and interest rates and the stock market are strongly correlated. Rising interest rates tend to depress stock market prices, and falling interest rates have the opposite effect. Stock market investors move into bonds when interest rates go up and out of bonds when interest rates go down.

The open market operations of the Fed have a direct impact on interest rates and the bond markets. When the Fed buys Treasury securities on the open market, it competes with other buyers, thus driving up prices and causing a decrease in Treasury yields. This creates a rate discrepancy between the yields on government debt and corporate debt. As a result, investors will purchase corporate debt, causing prices to increase and yields to decrease. The reverse is true when the Fed sells government securities on the open market.

This suggests that if investors anticipate changes in monetary policy, they can make the appropriate changes to their investment strategies.

# FISCAL POLICY AND THE MARKETS

The goals of both monetary and fiscal policy are the same: the pursuit of full employment, economic growth, and price stability. The government uses fiscal policy to stimulate or restrain the economy. The tools of fiscal policy are taxation, government expenditures, and the government's debt management, whereas monetary policy uses changes in the money supply to pursue the same objectives. Changes in fiscal policy can affect the financial markets.

## Taxation

The federal government uses *taxation* to raise revenue and also to reduce the amount of money in the economy. Taxation policies can stimulate or depress the economy and the stock markets. When taxes are increased, consumers have less money to invest and spend on goods and services, and corporations have reduced earnings, which leads to lower dividends.

Tax cuts, however, have the opposite effect. Individuals will have more money to spend and invest, and corporations will experience the benefits of greater consumer spending along with lower corporate taxes, which generally leads to higher sales and higher earnings.

## Government Spending

A tax cut has an effect similar to an increase in government spending. A tax cut has a favorable effect on savings and investments, whereas government spending has a greater effect on the goods and services produced in the economy. Therefore, government spending can also be used as a tool to stimulate or restrain the economy.

## Debt Management

When the government's revenues are less than its expenditures, it runs a deficit. Deficit spending can have a significant effect on the financial markets in general and the stock market in particular. The government can finance its deficit in either of two ways, by borrowing in the financial markets or by increasing the money supply.

*Borrowing in the Financial Markets*   By borrowing in the financial markets, the government drives up yields on the bond markets, which has a depressing effect on the stock market. By selling securities on the market, prices of government securities go down, which increases their yields. To counter the rate differential (between corporate and government securities), investors will invest in government securities rather than in corporate securities, which reduces the prices of corporate bonds, which leads to increased yields (on corporate bonds). Thus, borrowing in the market by the government has the effect of depressing bond prices and increasing interest rates. The opposite is true of the government buying securities in the market: bond prices are pushed up and interest rates are lowered.

When a government is faced with financing an increasing deficit, it will have to pay high rates of interest to attract buyers to invest in all its securities. This leads to higher interest rates in the economy. This has a depressing effect on stock prices and tends to drive up yields. The announced reduction in the budget deficit in 1998, for example, had the effect of a downward pressure on bond yields and increasing bond prices.

*Increasing the Money Supply*   If the government increases the money supply, inflation may raise its ugly head, and inflation has a negative effect on the economy and particularly on the bond markets.

In summary, when a government is unable to reduce the growth of its deficit spending, there is an effect on the bond and stock markets. When a government is able to reduce its deficit spending, it is able to reduce its borrowing and pay down its debt, which lowers interest rates in the economy. Investors are constantly looking for policies or budgets that can effectively change the direction of growth of the deficit.

Increased government spending can be inflationary and can bring an immediate response from bondholders. Due to computerized global trading, bondholders can unload millions of dollars of U.S. Treasuries within hours and can send bond prices plummeting and long-term yields soaring. This is especially true for the U.S. Treasury bond market, which attracts a large amount of foreign investment due to the perception of the dollar as a "safe haven" currency.

Fiscal policies affect the securities markets, and by anticipating changes in the policies, you can better formulate your investment strategy.

# THE DOLLAR AND THE FINANCIAL MARKETS

Great attention is paid to the relative value of the dollar, the trade deficit, and whether the Japanese and the Europeans will continue to fund the budget deficit through the Treasury auctions. The financial markets react to these financial events. In fact, by now you have come to realize that the financial markets react on a daily basis to almost all economic, political, and financial announcements. In some cases, the markets anticipate the news. For example, the bond markets may go up or down in anticipation of the announcement of the balance of trade figures for the quarter.

## International Trade and the Dollar

There is a relationship between the markets, international trade, and the relative value of the currency. Readers of the financial press will come across an assortment of terms—balance of payments, trade deficit (not the same as a budget deficit), current account surplus, and foreign portfolio investment, for example—and wonder how these can guide (or misguide) economic policymakers. Great care should be used in interpreting balance of payments figures because of the complexities and ramifications involved.

*Balance of payments* is an accounting of all the transactions that take place between the residents of a country and the rest of the world. The balance of payments shows whether a country is a net importer or exporter of goods and services, whether foreigners are net investors in that country or whether that country is a net exporter of capital, and the changes in the country's reserves.

*Balance of trade* shows whether a country imports or exports more merchandise. The balance of trade is, therefore, the difference between a country's exports and its imports of merchandise. A balance of trade surplus indicates that the country exports more goods than it imports. A deficit indicates the opposite (imports more goods than it exports).

A balance of trade deficit is not necessarily a bad financial omen and should not be judged in isolation from the rest of the country's balance of payment figures. For example, Switzerland has had balance of trade deficits, but it also has surpluses in its balance of services account. As long as a country can finance its balance of trade deficit through its other current accounts and capital accounts, it is economically acceptable.

*Current account* is the first major section of the balance of payments, and it includes all the country's imports and exports of merchandise (balance of trade), services (balance of services), and transfers (which includes foreign aid). A country with a current account surplus is able to contribute to its capital and reserve accounts. A country with a current account deficit has to finance it from capital inflows from abroad or run down its reserves.

*Capital account* indicates whether the country is a net importer or exporter of capital. In other words, has the rest of the world invested more in this country or has this country invested more in the rest of the world? A country with a current account deficit needs to finance this deficit with imported capital or it will be forced to run down its reserves.

*Reserve account* includes liquid assets, such as gold, foreign currencies, special drawing rights (SDRs), and the country's reserve position at the International Monetary Fund. All of these can be converted into foreign currencies to settle the country's international claims.

International trade, investments, and the country's actual or relative reserves affect the value of its currency. When Americans buy goods from abroad, they pay in U.S. dollars, which are exchanged at the going rate into the foreign currency. Since 1973, most of the currencies of the industrialized nations have been allowed to float against each other. That means the value of one currency is measured against the value of other currencies through the forces of supply and demand. When there is great demand for a currency, it appreciates in value relative to other currencies. When demand is low, the currency may experience a loss in value. Prices of currencies are determined on the foreign exchange markets, which are composed of international banks and foreign exchange traders.

Inflation and interest rates are important economic factors which influence a currency's value.

*Inflation*   High inflation in a country causes the currency in that country to depreciate. For example, if inflation rises in the U.S., the price of goods that originally cost $100 will increase in price, say, to $105. As a result, American consumers may prefer to buy imported goods for the equivalent of $100. This increases demand for foreign currencies and puts downward pressure on the dollar. The *theory of purchasing power parity* addresses this issue by stating: If the prices of goods go up in one country relative to another, then in order to keep parity in prices of goods between the two countries, the currency must depreciate.

Inflation also has a detrimental effect on foreign investments, since foreigners will not invest in financial assets that lose value. Therefore, higher inflation puts upward pressure on interest rates to attract foreign investors.

Rising interest rates exert downward pressure on the bond markets because investors may sell their long-term bonds and invest in shorter-term securities whose yields will increase as interest rates go up.

*Interest Rates*   When interest rates are higher in one country relative to another, foreigners will then invest in that country's T-bills, CDs, and other higher-yielding investments. This means a greater demand for that country's currency and, theoretically, an appreciation in value of that currency. The opposite holds true for low interest rates and lower rates of inflation.

The relationships between interest rates, inflation, and the value of a currency all add an important dimension to international investments.

This discussion points to the overall relationship between economic activity and the financial markets. Generally, if companies are experiencing greater earnings, an expanding economy may be accompanied by a booming stock market.

However, economic expansion can also spook the bond markets, which react to fears of inflation. Great care should be taken in not oversimplifying the relationships. A declining bond market can have a detrimental effect on the stock market during economic expansion because of fears of inflation and the anticipation of higher interest rates. Similarly, a declining economy can be associated with a rising bond market because of lower interest rates, which would have a positive effect on the stock markets. By forecasting the direction of the economy, investors can anticipate the direction of the bond market.

## WHY YOU SHOULD READ THE CREDIT MARKET COLUMNS

Bond investors and potential bond investors can benefit from reading the credit market columns in the newspapers. Not only do you get a feeling for bond-related happenings, you also get access to:

- How bond professionals view the bond markets
- Discussions of the future direction of interest rates
- Upcoming bond issues
- Summaries of the previous day's bond sales and auctions
- Foreign bond markets and issues
- Summaries of yields for the different types of bonds and the maturities

By reading the credit market columns, you will get a better feeling for the bond markets and which types of bonds to purchase.

## THE BOND MARKETS

Bonds are issued by corporations, the federal government, agencies of the federal government, municipal governments, and foreign corporations and governments.

### Exchanges

It is relatively easy for investors to buy and sell bonds, especially since most bonds trade on the exchanges and the over-the-counter markets. After a bond is brought to the market, it trades in the *secondary markets,* which include the exchanges and the over-the-counter (OTC) markets.

A large number of corporate bonds are listed on the New York Bond Exchange and the American Bond Exchange. The price quotes of these bonds are listed in the bond tables of the financial newspapers. There are many other corporate bonds which are not listed on these exchanges, but which are traded in the over-the-counter markets among bond traders.

U.S. government securities, government agency bonds, and municipal bonds are traded in the OTC markets.

There is an active secondary market for Treasury bills, notes, and bonds. The secondary market is where buyers can buy the securities when the Treasury is not selling them and where sellers can sell their securities before they mature. Security dealers make up this market. The Federal Reserve Bank will buy and sell Treasury securities as part of its open market operations.

There is also a secondary market for government agency bonds, such as FNMAs (Federal National Mortgage Association), and GNMAs (Government National Mortgage Association);

municipal bonds, such as state and local government issues and those of highway authorities; and foreign bonds.

The OTC markets consist of thousands of brokers and dealers, who are not located in any single place but are spread throughout the country. They use computers and telephones for their transactions.

These brokers and dealers can buy for their own accounts or on behalf of their customers, in which case they are acting as agents or brokers. In this latter type of transaction, the agent/broker receives a commission for placing the order. When acting as dealers, they (the firms acting as the dealers) do not receive commissions, but they will add a markup on sales and a markdown on purchases.

Many broker/dealers specialize in certain securities. In other words, they "make a market" in buying and selling certain securities. How this works with respect to orders from individual investors is as follows:

- An individual investor calls in an order to the brokerage firm.
- If the brokerage firm is a market maker for that particular bond, the firm will sell it to the customer.
- If the brokerage firm is not a market maker for this security, the firm will negotiate with a firm that is a market maker.

### Indices

Bond market indices differ from equity market indices in two respects. First, bond market indices are not followed as extensively as stock market indices. Second, bond market indices focus on rates of return or bond prices, whereas equity indices focus only on price movements. There are several indices for assessing the behavior of the bond markets.

The *Dow Jones Bond Average* consists of 10 utility bonds and 10 industrial bonds. The focus is on the closing prices of these bonds, and the average shows the percent of face value at which these bonds would sell.

The *Lehman Indices* are more extensive than the Dow Jones Bond Average. They include:

- The *Corporate Bond Index* includes all the publicly issued debt of industrial, finance, and utility companies whose issues are nonconvertible and have a fixed rate. Only bonds with maturities of at least one year or more and a minimum outstanding principal balance of $25 million are included.

- The *Government Bond Index* includes all the publicly issued debt of the federal government and its agencies whose issues are nonconvertible and have fixed rates. Only issues with a maturity of one year or more and with a principal balance of $25 million are included.
- The *Treasury Bond Index* includes debt issues of the U.S. Treasury.
- The *Mortgage Backed Securities Index* includes all the fixed-rate debt issues which are backed by the mortgages of the GNMA, FNMA, and the Federal Home Loan Corporation.
- The *Yankee Bond Index* includes U.S. dollar bonds registered with the Securities and Exchange Commission which are issued or backed by governments other than the U.S.
- The *Government-Corporate Bond Index* combines the Government Bond Index and the Corporate Bond Index. This is the most representative of all the bond market indices.

*Barron's Confidence Index* is the ratio of Barron's average yield of 10 high-grade corporate bonds to the yield on the more speculative Dow Jones average of 40 bonds. This index shows the yield spread between high-grade bonds and more speculative bonds.

Users of the index believe that during periods of optimism, investors will invest more in speculative bonds (to get the higher rate of return), which will push their prices up and thus lower their yields. This causes the confidence index to increase.

The opposite happens when investors are pessimistic. They will invest in high-quality bonds, which increases the yield differential between low-quality and high-quality debt and the confidence index declines.

Other notable bond indices include the *Salomon Brothers Indices*, the *Bond Buyer Municipal Index*, and the *Merrill Lynch Corporate Index*.

Although bond market indices are not as widely known or used as are the stock market indicators, the bond indices are becoming more important. More investors have been investing in bonds and fixed-income mutual funds during the 1980s and 1990s, and these indices are excellent yardsticks for investors to evaluate the performance of their fixed-income investments.

## HOW TO READ BOND QUOTATIONS

### Corporate Bonds

The daily quotations of listed bonds on the New York and American Exchanges can be found in the financial newspapers. For example, a typical listing of a corporate bond from the financial pages would appear as follows:

| Bonds | Cur Yld | Vol | Close | Net Chg |
|---|---|---|---|---|
| ATT 7s 05 | 6.7 | 30 | 104 $\frac{7}{8}$ | +$\frac{1}{2}$ |

Reading from left to right:

- After the name of the bond, AT&T, is the coupon yield of 7 percent (i.e., each bond holder will receive $70 in interest each year until maturity). The s following the coupon yield means that the interest is paid semiannually, i.e., $35 twice a year. The 05 is the maturity date for this bond. It matures in the year 2005.
- The current yield is 6.7 percent. This is determined by dividing the annual interest received, $70, which is the coupon rate, by the market price at the close of the day, which is $1048.75 (70/1048.75 = 6.7%).
- The volume indicates the number of bonds traded, which was 30 for that day, or $30,000 in terms of the face value of the bonds.
- Close indicates the closing price of $1048.75 per bond. Bonds are quoted in 100s; i.e., the last digit is dropped, so a $1000 face value bond is quoted as $100. Bonds under 100 are selling at a discount, and those over 100 are selling at a premium.

- The net change column shows the change from the previous day's close. In this case, AT&T was up by one-half point from the previous day's close.

## Corporate Convertible Bonds

These are listed on the same exchanges and read the same way as corporate bonds. A *cv* in the current yield column would signify that it is a convertible bond, as in the following example:

| Bonds | Cur Yld | Vol | Close | Net Chg |
|-------|---------|-----|-------|---------|
| Oryx 7.5 14 | cv | 50 | 100 | -$\frac{1}{2}$ |

- The name of the convertible bond is Oryx, and the coupon yield is 7.5 percent (the bondholder will receive $75 in interest each year until maturity). The next number, 14, means the maturity date is 2014.
- The *cv* in the current yield column indicates that this bond is a convertible bond: it may be converted into a specified number of shares of the company's common stock or preferred stock. The cv in this column does not mean that convertible bonds do not have current yields. The current yield is the coupon rate divided by the closing price.
- The volume indicates the number of bonds traded, which was 50 for that day, or $50,000 in terms of the face value of the bonds.
- Close indicates a closing price of $1000, or face value.
- The net change column shows that the Oryx convertible bond was down by a half point from the previous day's close.

## Zero-Coupon Bonds

There are zero-coupon corporate bonds and zero-coupon municipal bonds, which are quoted in different publications. Zero-coupon corporate bonds that are listed on the exchanges are quoted in the same tables as corporate bonds. A *zr* following the name of the bond signifies that it is a zero-coupon bond. In this case, there is no coupon rate because zero-coupon bonds pay no periodic interest. Following is an example of a corporate zero-coupon bond as quoted in the financial newspapers:

| Bonds | Cur Yld | Vol | Close | Net Chg |
|-------|---------|-----|-------|---------|
| Pep Boys zr 11 | ... | 25 | 55¼ | +¼ |

- The issuer of this bond is Pep Boys. After the *zr*, the indication that this is a zero-coupon bond, is the maturity date, 11, standing for 2011.
- Since zero-coupon bonds do not pay periodic interest, there is no current yield. The returns on zero-coupon bonds are measured by their yield to maturity, which is discussed in Chapter 10.
- The volume indicates that 25 of these bonds were traded on that day.
- The closing price on that day for this bond was $552.50. Zero-coupon bonds are issued at a deep discount to their face value and are redeemed at maturity at their face value, $1000 per bond.
- The net change column shows that this bond closed up a quarter of a point from the previous day's close.

## Municipal Bonds

The financial newspapers list some municipal bond quotes, but the most complete list is found in the *Blue List*, a daily brochure published by Standard & Poor's. It is appropriately printed on blue paper and with blue ink. Tax-exempt bonds are listed in the newspapers as follows:

| Issue | Coupon | Mat | Price | Chg | Bid Yld |
|-------|--------|-----|-------|-----|---------|
| LI Pwr Auth NY | 5.125 | 12-01-22 | 98¾ | +¼ | 5.21 |

- The issue is the Long Island Power Authority.
- The coupon rate is the percentage of par value that is paid in interest. These bonds pay 5.125 percent of par ($1000), which is $51.25 in interest per bond per year.

- The maturity date is the date that the bonds will be paid back, in this case December 1, 2022.
- The next column is the dollar price of the bond, which is $987.50 (per bond).
- The change indicates the difference from the previous day's price. Here, the bonds increased by a quarter of a point from the previous day's closing price.
- The last column is the bid yield. If investors bought these bonds at the closing price of $987.50 per bond and held them until maturity (12-01-22), their return would be 5.21 percent. So the bid yield is the percentage yield of a bond if held for its full term.

## Treasury Bonds and Notes

There is a separate table in the financial newspapers listing Treasury bonds and notes. The issues are listed in order of maturity. The following is an example of a Treasury note:

| Rate | Maturity Mo/Yr | Bid | Asked | Chg | Ask Yld |
|------|----------------|--------|--------|-----|---------|
| 7½   | Oct 99n        | 102:15 | 102:17 | -2  | 5.53    |

- The rate in the first column signifies the percentage of par value that is paid in interest. This note pays interest of $75 per note per year.
- The maturity date is when the note matures, October 1999. An *n* after the date signifies that it is a Treasury note rather than a Treasury bond.
- Treasury notes and bonds are quoted on a bid-and-asked basis. The bid price is the highest price buyers of this issue will pay. They are willing to pay $102$^{15}/_{32}$, or $1024.69 per note.
- The asked price is the lowest price offered by sellers. Here, sellers are asking $102$^{17}/_{32}$, or $1025.31 per note.
- The change shows the change in 32ds of a point between the bid price as quoted above and the bid price as quoted the previous day. This issue decreased by $^{2}/_{32}$ of a point from the previous day's bid price.

■ The ask yield is the return investors would get if they paid the asked price for the note and held it until maturity. The return for this note if held to maturity is 5.53 percent.

## Government Agency Bonds

These are listed in the government agency section of the bond listings, which includes quotes of FNMA issues, Federal Home Loan Bank issues, and bonds of the other government agencies. They are listed in order of maturity, and the quotes are based on large transactions, usually $1 million or more. Following is an example of a Federal National Mortgage Association (FNMA) issue:

| Rate | Mat | Bid | Asked | Yld |
|------|------|--------|--------|------|
| 6.35 | 8-99 | 100:22 | 100:25 | 5.62 |

■ The rate in the first column signifies the percentage of par value that is paid in interest. The FNMA issue pays interest of $63.50 per bond per year.
■ The maturity date is August 1999.
■ These issues are bought on a bid-and-asked basis. The bid price is $1006.875 per bond and is the highest price that buyers of this issue will pay.
■ The asked price is the lowest price offered by sellers. Sellers this time are asking $100$^{25}/_{32}$, or $1007.8125 per bond.
■ The yield is the return investors would get if they paid the asked price for the bond and held it to maturity. The yield to maturity is 5.62 percent.

## Treasury Bills

Treasury bills are quoted separately in a section marked Treasury bills in most financial newspapers. They are listed in order of maturity. The following is an example of a Treasury bill quote:

| Maturity | Date to Mat. | Bid | Asked | Chg | Ask Yld |
|----------|--------------|------|-------|-----|---------|
| Nov 19 98 | 150 | 5.16 | 5.14 | ... | 5.33 |

- Treasury bills are short-term securities, so all listed T-bills will mature within one year, in this case on November 19, 1998.
- There are 150 days from the date of this quote until maturity of the issue.
- Treasury bills are sold at a discount, which is less than the par, or face amount, of $1000 and then redeemed at par at maturity. This difference is attributed to interest. The bid discount of 5.16 percent is the discount (price) that buyers are willing to pay for this bill on this day, and the asked discount of 5.14 percent is the discount at which sellers are willing to sell this security on this day.

The dealer's selling price can be calculated as follows:

$$\text{Selling price} = \text{par value} - \text{par value (asked discount)} \frac{\text{days to maturity}}{360}$$

$$= \$100 - 100 \ (0.0514) \frac{150}{360}$$

$$= \$97.8584, \text{ or } \$978.584 \text{ per T-bill}$$

The dealer's purchase price can be calculated as follows:

$$\text{Purchase price} = \text{par value} - \text{par value (bid discount)} \frac{\text{days to maturity}}{360}$$

$$= \$100 - 100 \ (0.0516) \frac{150}{360}$$

$$= \$97.85, \text{ or } \$978.50 \text{ per T-bill}$$

The spread between the bid and the asked price is $0.08 per T-bill.

- The ask yield is 5.33 percent, the return an investor would get on this issue if bought at the ask price.

## HOW TO READ BOND MUTUAL FUND QUOTATIONS

There are many different types of bonds, and correspondingly, there are many matching types of mutual bond funds. For example, there are money market mutual funds of various types, taxable and tax-free funds, Treasury bond funds, GNMA mutual funds, high-yield corporate bond mutual funds, convertible bond funds, municipal bond funds, and so on.

## Mutual Fund Indices

Individual investors can track how well their particular bond mutual funds are doing against the *Lipper Indexes* of mutual funds, which are published in the financial newspapers, such as *The Wall Street Journal*, on a daily basis. These bond indices are based on the largest funds with the same investment objectives.

Below is a listing of two examples from the *Lipper Indexes* of bond mutual funds as reported in *The Wall Street Journal*, June 26, 1998, p. C17:

|  | *Lipper Indexes* | | | |
|  |  | *Percentage Chg Since* | | |
| **Bond Indexes** | **Close** | **Prev** | **Wk Ago** | **Dec 31** |
| Corp. A Rated Debt | 776.82 | −.03 | +.24 | +3.66 |
| U.S. Government | 292.34 | −.03 | +.19 | +3.35 |

- The Corporate Bond A Rated Index is composed of the largest A-rated corporate bond mutual funds.
- The close for this index on June 25, 1998, was 776.82.
- The next column shows a loss of 0.03 percent from the previous day's close.
- The next column shows a gain for the period of a week of 0.24 percent.
- The last column shows that this bond fund index has increased by 3.66 percent since December 31, 1997.

These indices for bond mutual funds provide yardsticks with which investors can evaluate the performance of their particular bond mutual funds. However, with this advice come two caveats for investors:

- You should not be tempted to use your bond mutual funds as trading vehicles, constantly buying and selling when your mutual funds underperform or outperform the indices over short periods of time.
- Evaluate the performance of your bond mutual funds against the indexes over longer periods of time.

There is the "Mutual Fund Scorecard," also published in *The Wall Street Journal,* which lists the 15 top-performing mutual funds in each objective investment category over different periods of time.

## Money Market Mutual Funds

Money market funds are divided into taxable and tax-free funds. The investments in the taxable money market funds include Treasury bills, commercial paper, repurchase agreements (repos), domestic and foreign bank obligations, and time deposits. Money market funds have fixed net asset values (NAVs) of $1 per share. Following is a listing of a taxable money market fund as quoted from *Barron's:*

| Money Market Fund | Net Assets (Mil $) | Avg. Mat. | 7 day Yld (%) | 30 day Yld (%) | 7 day Comp (%) |
|---|---|---|---|---|---|
| Vanguard MMR/Fed Portfolio | 3735.8 | 59 | 5.23 | 5.23 | 5.37 |

Reading from left to right:

- The money market fund is the Vanguard Money Market Federal Portfolio, which invests primarily in short-term federal securities.
- The net assets column shows the size of the assets under investment for the fund, which is $3735.8 million.
- The average time to maturity of the investments carried in the fund is 59 days.
- The seven-day yield (for the past week) is 5.23 percent on an annualized basis.
- The 30-day yield (for the past 30 days) is also 5.23 percent on an annualized basis.
- The last column shows the compound annualized yield, which is the effective rate of return. It is 5.37 percent for the past seven days. This return includes the compounding effect of any dividends paid out within the period.

## Bond Mutual Fund Quotations

Bond mutual fund quotations are found in the daily newspapers. Unlike money market funds, which have constant $1-per-share prices, prices or net asset values of bond funds fluctuate on a daily basis. Following are two examples from the Vanguard Group of funds:

| Name | N.A.V. | Net Chg | YTD % Ret |
|------|--------|---------|-----------|
| Vanguard Fds | | | |
| GNMA | 10.42 | ... | +3.2 |
| MuInt | 13.38 | ... | +2.1 |

- In the Vanguard Group of funds, the GNMA (Ginnie Mae) fund has a net asset value of $10.42 per share. The Municipal Intermediate Term Bond Fund has a share price of $13.38 per share.
- The share prices for both funds did not change overnight, as indicated by the three dots for both in the net change column.
- The year-to-date percentage return for the GNMA fund is 3.2 percent, and 2.1 percent for the Municipal Intermediate Term Fund.

The following chapters explain the basics behind each of the different types of bonds and bond mutual funds.

## REFERENCES

Antilla, Susan: "Comparing Stocks with Boring Bonds," *The New York Times*, September 20, 1992.

Faerber, Esmé: *Managing Your Investments, Savings, and Credit*, McGraw-Hill, New York, 1992.

Faerber, Esmé: *All About Stocks*, McGraw-Hill, New York, 1995

## CHAPTER 4

# Short-Term Fixed-Income Securities

## KEY CONCEPTS

- Money market mutual funds
- Treasury bills
- Commercial paper
- Bankers' acceptances
- Other short-term fixed-income securities

Short-term fixed-income securities are liquid, safe investments and are used by investors for their emergency and short-term needs. Examples of these types of investments are certificates of deposit, money market mutual funds, Treasury bills, commercial paper, bankers' acceptances, and repurchase agreements. These investments are also used as temporary, short-term cash substitutes. In other words, idle cash can be invested in these to earn a return. The characteristics of these short-term investments are low risk of default and high liquidity and marketability.

The easiest parking places for short-term funds are money market mutual funds. Even though money market funds offer investors a convenient way to invest short-term, it is also useful to understand some details of the separate short-term investments—T-bills, commercial paper, bankers' acceptances, repurchase agreements—for two reasons:

1. Money market mutual funds invest their pooled funds in these individual short-term fixed-income securities. By

understanding how these securities work, investors are better able to assess the risks and returns of the different money market mutual funds.

2. There are times when these individual securities offer greater advantages than using a money market mutual fund.

## MONEY MARKET MUTUAL FUNDS

Money market funds compete directly with bank deposit accounts, and over the years money market funds have grown considerably at the expense of bank accounts. Money market mutual funds are offered by banks, brokers, and investment companies. Brokerage firms compete with the investment companies to offer money market funds and alternative short-term parking places for cash. However, many of the investment products from the brokerage houses have higher fees, sales commissions (loads), and in the case of short-term bond funds, additional risk. Brokers and financial advisors are motivated to move you away from the investment companies' money market mutual funds to their own products, for which they are compensated through sales commissions, also called *loads*. Table 4-1 shows the effects of front-end load on a short-term bond fund compared to a no-load money market mutual fund. In addition, operating expenses for these brokerage funds may be higher.

The majority of the money market mutual funds are offered by investment companies. These money market funds provide an

**TABLE 4-1**

Load versus No-Load Fund

| Load Fund of 3% | | No-Load Fund | |
|---|---|---|---|
| Amount invested | $10,000 | Amount invested | $10,000 |
| 3% load charge | (300) | No-load | 0 |
| Funds available | $ 9,700 | Funds available | $10,000 |

This is an illustration of a *front-end load*, which is a charge taken off the initial amount of the funds invested. There is also a *back-end load*, which is a charge taken out of the proceeds when shares are sold.

alternative parking place for cash and short-term funds and offer lower risk than investing in stocks and bonds. Investment companies managing money market funds pool investors' money and issue shares to the investors. They then invest the money in short-term securities like Treasury bills, commercial paper, bankers' acceptances, CDs, Eurodollars, repurchase agreements, and government agency obligations.

There are three types of money market funds:

- *General purpose funds* invest in a wide range of money market securities, from T-bills, commercial paper, and bankers' acceptances to certificates of deposit, repurchase agreements, and short-term off-shore securities.
- *U.S. government funds* invest in short-term Treasury securities and U.S. agency obligations.
- *Tax-exempt money market funds* invest in short-term municipal securities. The income from these securities is exempt from federal income tax.

## How Safe Are Money Market Funds?

Money market mutual funds do not carry the FDIC insurance carried by bank money market deposit accounts. The safest money market funds invest in U.S. Treasury securities only, as these are backed by the full faith and credit of the U.S. government. However, all money market funds are relatively safe because (1) their investments are in securities issued by governments, their agencies, and large corporations and (2) the maturities of these securities are short-term, which lowers the risk. Large institutions are unlikely to default on securities issued for a short period of time, and the prices of short-term securities will not fluctuate widely.

If you are still concerned about the risk of default, limit your investments to high-quality funds and U.S. government funds.

Before investing, read the prospectus; it lists the types of securities that the money market mutual fund invests in. The risk of default has been zero to very low for Treasury bills, certificates of deposit, bankers' acceptances, and commercial paper. Although the risk of default on commercial paper is low, a few companies have defaulted, which affected money market funds holding those issues. However, the investment companies running the funds absorbed the losses instead of the investors in the fund.

This does not mean that there are no high-risk short-term securities. Higher-yielding, high-risk short-term securities do exist, and some aggressive money market funds will invest in these to raise yields. The prospectus for a fund outlines the investment restrictions for that fund. If the stated objectives are to invest in low-risk securities, the Securities and Exchange Commission (SEC) will monitor and regulate the investment company's adherence to the stated objectives.

Fraud is another concern of investors. What if someone in the fund steals or embezzles their savings from their accounts? This, of course, could happen with all investments, but there are certain safeguards with money market funds, namely:

- The investment company does not physically handle the funds. Instead, there is a custodial bank which makes the deposits into and transfers from the investors' accounts in the funds.
- The custodial bank is bonded and has insurance in the event of theft or loss due to embezzlement or fraud.

Money market funds, then, have the same safeguards against fraud as other short-term investments, such as savings accounts, and this should allay investors' fears somewhat.

## How to Invest in Money Market Funds

Money market funds sell shares, which generally do not fluctuate in value as stock and bond mutual funds do. Money market funds typically have a constant share price of $1 (due to the short maturities of their investments), and this constant price is maintained by the investment company. It offers investors the advantage of being able to add and withdraw funds from these accounts without incurring any tax consequences. By comparison, short-term mutual bond funds do not have constant share prices, which means that when shares are sold, there will be capital gains or losses when the purchase and sale share prices differ.

This is one of the major reasons you would not want to invest your short-term funds in a short-term bond fund rather than a money market mutual fund. Brokers and financial advisors may encourage investors to park their cash in short-term bond funds over money market mutual funds, because they (the brokers and financial advisors) can earn more from the sales loads than they can from recommending money market mutual funds (Schultze, 1998, C1).

The other reason you would not want to choose a short-term bond fund as a parking place for your cash is the potential risk of loss. If market rates of interest rise, the share price of the short-term bond fund will fall, which means that you would lose part of your invested funds if you have to sell.

To invest in a money market fund, call the fund (most have 800 telephone numbers) or write for a prospectus and application form. The Internet provides a comprehensive list of all the mutual fund families. One of the Websites is *www.moneymarketmutual-funds.com*. Mutual fund companies are required by the SEC to send the prospectus either by mail or through the Internet to new investors. The prospectus includes such information about the fund as:

- The minimum dollar investment necessary to open an account
- How the investor can withdraw funds from the account
- The investment objectives and policies as well as the investment restrictions
- Who manages the fund, the fees charged by the management company, and an outline of the operating expenses and other charges
- The fund's financial statements

Read the prospectus before filling out the application form. The completed form can be sent back with a check to open the account. Investors will then receive monthly statements showing the number of shares in their accounts, their deposits, withdrawals, and dividend income. Most funds have a minimum amount (usually $100) for additional investments.

Investors can withdraw money on demand from their money market funds in several ways, which vary from fund to fund, including:

- Through check-writing (if check-writing is available for that fund)
- Wire transfers from the fund to a bank account
- Checks written by the fund and mailed to the account holder in response to a written request
- Money transfers to other funds within the same investment company's family of funds
- Systematic withdrawal plans (SWP), in which the investor may request the fund to send a periodic check to the investor, a third party, or a bank

## How to Select a Money Market Fund

There are hundreds of money market funds to choose from, and you may want to read the prospectus for the following criteria before choosing:

- If there is a selling commission or load charge, eliminate that fund. Most, if not all, money market funds today are no-load (NL) funds, which means that all of your investment is being invested in the fund.
- Know your own objectives to determine which type of money market fund you want to invest in. If you want a high-quality fund, make sure the one you choose invests in top-grade securities. If you are looking for federally tax-exempt income, choose funds that invest in short-term, tax-exempt municipal bonds.
- Examine the return of the fund. The yield, or return, depends on the earnings of the fund and the fees and operating charges deducted by that fund. Generally, the safer the fund, the lower the yield. U.S. government securities (T-bills) have lower yields than commercial paper and repurchase agreements, but the U.S. government will not default on its obligations.
- Picking a fund which earns a higher yield may not give a higher overall return after operating expenses are deducted. Those costs may be considerably higher for

higher-yield funds than for other money market funds. Unfortunately, investors are at a disadvantage in comparing yields because of two factors:

1. Some funds use the cost basis to calculate yields, whereas others use the market value approach. This makes a comparison of yields misleading. Investors can find a list of the seven-day yields in the financial newspapers.
2. There is variability in funds' management fees and operating expenses.

- So, choosing a fund on yield alone can be misleading. However, *Donaghue's Money Letter*, a newsletter published by the Donaghue organization, lists the yields of the money market funds so that they are comparable. The Internet also offers various Websites where yields on money market mutual funds can be compared.
- Compare the features that the funds offer, such as check-writing and whether the fund provides free check-writing privileges; the number of funds within that investment family; whether there are limitations on the number and amount of transfers within the family of funds; and the minimum dollar amount to open a fund (it typically varies from $500 to $2000).
- A comparison of these features will guide you in your choice of a money market fund.

## Advantages of Money Market Funds

The advantages of money market funds are:

- They offer high liquidity, relative safety of principal, and competitive money market rates of return.
- They can be used as a parking place for funds between financial transactions or investments.
- They earn daily income on your money, which can be used for paying bills.
- It is easy to open a money market account, and the small minimum investment amount required to open an account makes this type of fund accessible to small investors.
- There are no tax consequences when adding and withdrawing funds from money market mutual funds.

## Disadvantages

- Interest income on regular money market funds is fully taxed at the federal level, and state and local levels, if applicable.
- Sometimes investors can earn greater yields by investing directly in money market instruments than indirectly through money market funds.

## Caveats

- Choose a money market fund from an investment company which has a wide range of different funds. This allows you greater flexibility in your transfers to other types of investment funds.
- Avoid funds that have sales charges, redemption fees, and high management and expense ratios.
- Avoid keeping too much money in money market funds. Over the long term, real rates of return from money market funds are unlikely to exceed the rate of inflation.
- Avoid choosing a short-term bond fund over a money market mutual fund as a parking place for your cash for short periods of time. You could experience losses in principal if the share price falls below the purchase price.

# TREASURY BILLS

Treasury bills (T-bills) are slightly more difficult to purchase directly than money market funds, but many investors prefer to invest in T-bills directly rather than indirectly through money market funds. After money market mutual funds, Treasury bills are the most popular of the short-term investments.

## What Are Treasury Bills?

Treasury bills are short-term safe-haven investments which are issued by the U.S. Treasury and fully backed by the U.S. government. The risk of default is extremely low. In fact, if the U.S. government defaulted on any of its obligations, all investments in the

U.S. would be suspect. Treasury bills are considered to be the safest of all fixed-income investments.

Treasury bills are negotiable, non-interest-bearing securities which mature in three months, six months, or one year. They are available in minimum denominations of $10,000 and multiples of $1000 above that. See Table 4-2 for details on the different Treasury bill issues. The 13- and 26-week bills are auctioned every week, and the 52-week bills are auctioned every four weeks. The announcements for the auctions generally are made two weeks before each auction.

T-bills are issued at a discount from their face value. The amount of the discount depends on the prices bid in the Treasury bill auctions. At maturity, the bills are redeemed at full face value. The difference between the discount value and the face value is treated as interest income.

As there is no stated rate of interest, the yield on Treasury bills can be determined as follows:

$$\text{Yield} = \frac{\text{face value} - \text{price paid}}{\text{price paid}} \times \frac{365}{\text{days to maturity}}$$

For example, a six-month Treasury bill purchased for $9600 and redeemed at face value has an annual yield of 8.33 percent:

$$\text{Yield} = \frac{\$10,000 - \$9600}{\$9600} \times \frac{365}{182.5}$$

$$= 8.33\%$$

To make matters more complex, however, bids submitted to the Federal Reserve Banks are not quoted on an annual basis,

**TABLE 4-2**

Treasury Bills

| Term | Minimum | Multiples | Auction | Auction Time | Issue Date |
|------|---------|-----------|---------|--------------|------------|
| 13 week | $10,000* | $1000 | Weekly | Monday | Thursday |
| 26 week | $10,000* | $1000 | Weekly | Monday | Thursday |
| 52 week | $10,000 | $1000 | Every four weeks | Thursday | Thursday |

*Treasury allowed investors to buy these in denominations of $1000 in the August 10, 1998, auction.

as above, but on a *bank discount basis,* which is computed as follows:

$$\text{Yield} = \frac{\text{face value} - \text{price paid}}{100^*} \times \frac{360^{**}}{\text{days to maturity}}$$

*Yield is quoted for each $100 of face value.
**Note the use of 360 as opposed to 365 days.

Using the same example as above, for the T-bill selling at $96 per $100 face value with a maturity of six months, the discount is $4. Rerunning the calculation this way, you get:

$$\text{Bank discount yield} = \frac{100 - 96}{100} \times \frac{360}{180}$$

$$= 8\%$$

Thus, the bank discount yield is always less than the annual yield.

## How to Buy and Sell Treasury Bills

New issues of Treasury bills can be bought either directly from any of the Federal Reserve Banks or indirectly through banks and brokerage firms. The easiest way to buy T-bills is through banks and brokerage firms, who charge commissions for their services. Buying newly issued Treasury bills on the primary market directly from the Federal Reserve Bank saves on these commissions. For already existing T-bills there is an active secondary market where dealers buy and sell these securities.

## Buying T-Bills at Banks and Brokers

New T-bills and those already existing can be bought and sold through banks and brokerage firms, who charge fees for their services ranging from $20 to $60 per T-bill. Smaller banks that are not dealers in government securities will generally charge higher fees (these banks will have to purchase the T-bills from their correspondent banks, who are dealers). Similarly, small brokerage firms who are not dealers in T-bills will charge higher commissions (to cover their purchases of these securities from dealers).

Of course, the payment of fees or commissions reduces your yields due to the increased amount that you have to pay for the buying or selling of T-bills. For a little extra effort, you can buy T-bills directly from Federal Reserve Banks and eliminate the fees and commissions charged by banks and brokers.

## Direct Purchase

You can buy directly from the Treasury by opening an account and then submitting a tender form. See Figures 4-1, 4-2, and 4-3 for a list of the offices of the Federal Reserve Banks where you can obtain the forms, a copy of a new account request form, and a copy of a tender form for a Treasury bill. Along with the new account registration form and tender form, there is a booklet "Buying Treasury Securities at the Federal Reserve Banks," which can be obtained at no charge from the Federal Reserve Banks.

The first step is to fill out the new account request form (Figure 4-2) to establish an account with the Department of the Treasury. Besides your name, address, and social security or employer identification number, you will need to fill in your bank or savings and loan association information so that payments by the Treasury can be made by direct deposit to your account. The routing number on the form is the identifying number of your financial institution. It can be found on the bottom line of one of your checks before your account number or on your deposit slip before your account number. It is a nine-digit number.

After submitting this form to the Federal Reserve Bank branch in your geographic area, you will receive confirmation of the establishment of your account and your own account number. All your purchases of Treasury securities will be recorded in this account, which is free up to the amount of $100,000 of securities. Over this amount, the Federal Reserve charges $25 to maintain the account. You are now ready to fill in the tender form to buy Treasury bills directly from the Federal Reserve Bank. See Figure 4-3 for a copy of the tender form.

New issues of Treasury bills are auctioned on a weekly basis by the Federal Reserve Bank, and investors may submit their bids either on a competitive or noncompetitive basis.

Using *competitive bids*, investors must submit their bids on a bank discount basis, with two decimals. For example, if an investor wanted to buy $100,000 of six-month Treasury bills and pay $96,000, the competitive bid submitted to the Federal Reserve Bank would be 8.00 percent. The Federal Reserve will then accept

## FIGURE 4-1

### List of Federal Reserve Banks and Treasury Servicing Offices

|  | When you call or visit: | When you write: |
| --- | --- | --- |
| FRB<br>Atlanta | 104 Marietta Street, NW<br>Atlanta, Georgia<br>404-521-8657 (Recording)<br>404-521-8653 | Securities Service Dept.<br>104 Marietta Street, NW<br>Atlanta, GA<br>30303 |
| FRB<br>Baltimore | 502 South Sharp Street<br>Baltimore, Maryland<br>410-576-3500 (Recording)<br>410-576-3300 | P.O. Box 1378<br>Baltimore, MD<br>21203 |
| FRB<br>Birmingham | 1801 Fifth Avenue, North<br>Birmingham, Alabama<br>205-731-8702 (Recording)<br>205-731-8708 | P.O. Box 830447<br>Birmingham, AL<br>35283-0447 |
| FRB<br>Boston | 600 Atlantic Avenue<br>Boston, Massachusetts<br>617-973-3800 (Recording)<br>617-973-3810 | P.O. Box 2076<br>Boston, MA<br>02106 |
| FRB<br>Buffalo | 160 Delaware Avenue<br>Buffalo, New York<br>716-849-5158 (Recording)<br>716-849-5000 | P.O. Box 961<br>Buffalo, NY<br>14240-0961 |
| FRB<br>Charlotte | 530 East Trade Street<br>Charlotte, North Carolina<br>704-358-2424 (Recording)<br>704-358-2100 | P.O. Box 30248<br>Charlotte, NC<br>28230 |
| FRB<br>Chicago | 230 South LaSalle Street<br>Chicago, Illinois<br>312-786-1110 (Recording)<br>312-322-5369 | P.O. Box 834<br>Chicago, IL<br>60690 |
| FRB<br>Cincinnati | 150 East Fourth Street<br>Cincinnati, Ohio<br>513-721-4794 Ext. 334 | P.O. Box 999<br>Cincinnati, OH<br>45201 |
| FRB<br>Cleveland | 1455 East Sixth Street<br>Cleveland, Ohio<br>216-579-2490 (Recording)<br>216-579-2000 | P.O. Box 6387<br>Cleveland, OH<br>44101 |
| FRB<br>Dallas | 2200 North Pearl Street<br>Dallas, Texas<br>214-922-6100<br>214-922-6770 (Recording) | Box 655906<br>Dallas, TX<br>75265-5906 |

**FIGURE  4 - 1**   Continued

| | When you call or visit: | When you write: |
|---|---|---|
| FRB<br>Denver | 1020 16th Street<br>Denver, Colorado<br>303-572-2475 (Recording)<br>303-572-2470 or 2473 | P.O. Box 5228<br>Denver, CO<br>80217-5228 |
| FRB<br>Detroit | 160 West Fort Street<br>Detroit, Michigan<br>313-963-4936 (Recording)<br>313-964-6157 | P.O. Box 1059<br>Detroit, MI<br>48231 |
| FRB<br>El Paso | 301 East Main<br>El Paso, Texas<br>915-521-8295 (Recording)<br>915-521-8272 | P.O. Box 100<br>El Paso, TX<br>79999 |
| FRB<br>Houston | 1701 San Jacinto Street<br>Houston, Texas<br>713-659-4433 | P.O. Box 2578<br>Houston, TX<br>77252 |
| FRB<br>Jacksonville | 800 West Water Street<br>Jacksonville, Florida<br>904-632-1178 (Recording)<br>904-632-1179 | P.O. Box 2499<br>Jacksonville, FL<br>32231-2499 |
| FRB<br>Kansas City | 925 Grand Avenue<br>Kansas City, Missouri<br>816-881-2767 (Recording)<br>816-881-2883 | P.O. Box 419033<br>Kansas City, MO<br>64141-6033 |
| FRB<br>Little Rock | 325 West Capitol Avenue<br>Little Rock, Arkansas<br>501-324-8274 (Recording)<br>501-324-8272 | P.O. Box 1261<br>Little Rock, AR<br>72203 |
| FRB<br>Los Angeles | 950 South Grand Avenue<br>Los Angeles, California<br>213-624-7398 | P.O. Box 2077<br>Terminal Annex<br>Los Angeles, CA<br>90051 |
| FRB<br>Louisville | 410 South Fifth Street<br>Louisville, Kentucky<br>502-568-9240 (Recording)<br>502-568-9238 | P.O. Box 32710<br>Louisville, KY<br>40232 |
| FRB<br>Memphis | 200 North Main Street<br>Memphis, Tennessee<br>901-523-9380 (Recording)<br>901-523-7171 Ext. 423 | P.O. Box 407<br>Memphis, TN<br>38101 |

**FIGURE 4-1** Continued

| | When you call or visit: | When you write: |
|---|---|---|
| FRB Miami | 9100 NW Thirty-Six Street Miami, Florida 305-471-6257 (Recording) 305-471-6497 | P.O. Box 520847 Miami, FL 33152 |
| FRB Minneapolis | 250 Marquette Avenue Minneapolis, Minnesota 612-340-2051 (Recording) 612-340-2075 | 250 Marquette Ave. Minneapolis, MN 55480 |
| FRB Nashville | 301 Eighth Avenue, North Nashville, Tennessee 615-251-7236 (Recording) 615-251-7100 | 301 Eighth Ave., N. Nashville, TN 37203-4407 |
| FRB New Orleans | 525 St. Charles Avenue New Orleans, Louisiana 504-593-5839 (Recording) 504-593-3200 | P.O. Box 52948 New Orleans, LA 70152-2948 |
| FRB New York | 33 Liberty Street New York, New York 212-720-5823 (Recording) 212-720-6619 | Federal Reserve P.O. Station New York, NY 10045 |
| FRB Oklahoma City | 226 Dean A McGee Avenue Oklahoma City, Oklahoma 405-270-8660 (Recording) 405-270-8652 | P.O. Box 25129 Oklahoma City, OK 73125 |
| FRB Omaha | 2201 Farnam Street Omaha, Nebraska 402-221-5638 (Recording) 402-221-5636 | 2201 Farnam Street Omaha, NE 68102 |
| FRB Philadelphia | Ten Independence Mall Philadelphia, Pennsylvania 215-574-6580 (Recording) 215-574-6680 | P.O. Box 90 Philadelphia, PA 19105 |
| FRB Pittsburgh | 717 Grant Street Pittsburgh, Pennsylvania 412-261-7988 (Recording) 412-261-7802 | P.O. Box 867 Pittsburgh, PA 15230-0867 |
| FRB Portland | 915 S.W. Stark Street Portland, Oregon 503-221-5931 (Recording) 503-221-5932 | P.O. Box 3436 Portland, OR 97208-3436 |

**FIGURE  4 - 1**  Continued

| | When you call or visit: | When you write: |
|---|---|---|
| **FRB** **Richmond** | 701 East Byrd Street Richmond, Virginia 804-697-8355 (Recording) 804-697-8372 | P.O. Box 27622 Richmond, VA 23261 |
| **FRB** **Salt Lake City** | 120 South State Street Salt Lake City, Utah 801-322-7844 (Recording) 801-322-7882 | P.O. Box 30780 Salt Lake City, UT 84130-0780 |
| **FRB** **San Antonio** | 126 East Nueva Street San Antonio, Texas 210-978-1330 (Recording) 210-978-1303 or 1305 | P.O. Box 1471 San Antonio, TX 78295 |
| **FRB** **San Francisco** | 101 Market Street San Francisco, California 415-974-3491 (Recording) 415-974-2330 | P.O. Box 7702 San Francisco, CA 94120 |
| **FRB** **Seattle** | 1015 Second Avenue Seattle, Washington 206-343-3615 (Recording) 206-343-3605 | P.O. Box 3567 Seattle, WA 98124 |
| **FRB** **St. Louis** | 411 Locust Street St. Louis, Missouri 314-444-8703 | P.O. Box 14915 St. Louis, MO 63178 |
| **Public Debt\*** **Washington, DC** | Capital Area Servicing Center 1300 C Street, S.W. Washington, DC 202-874-4000 Device for hearing impaired: 202-874-4026 | Capital Area Servicing Center Bureau of the Public Debt Washington, DC 20239-0001 Mail Tenders to: Capital Area Servicing Center Bureau of the Public Debt Department N Washington, DC 20239-1500 |

\*This servicing office only serves customers residing in the metropolitan Washington, D.C. area.

## FIGURE 4-2

New Account Request Form to Open an Account

PD F 5182
Department of the Treasury
Bureau of the Public Debt
(Revised September 1994)

**TREASURY DIRECT®**

OMB NO. 1535-0069

**NEW ACCOUNT REQUEST**

### INVESTOR INFORMATION

ACCOUNT NAME

ADDRESS

CITY                STATE        ZIP CODE

**FOR DEPARTMENT USE**

DOCUMENT AUTHORITY

APPROVED BY

DATE APPROVED

EXT REG ☐

FOREIGN ☐

BACKUP ☐

REVIEW ☐

### TAXPAYER IDENTIFICATION NUMBER

1ST NAMED OWNER

SOCIAL SECURITY NUMBER

OR

EMPLOYER IDENTIFICATION NUMBER

CLASS ☐

### TELEPHONE NUMBERS

( ) -     WORK

( ) -     HOME

### DIRECT DEPOSIT INFORMATION

ROUTING NUMBER

FINANCIAL INSTITUTION

ACCOUNT NUMBER

ACCOUNT NAME

ACCOUNT TYPE
(Check One)

☐ CHECKING

☐ SAVINGS

### AUTHORIZATION

I submit this request pursuant to the provisions of Department of the Treasury Circulars, Public Debt Series Nos. 2-86 (31 CFR Part 357), and 1-93 (31 CFR Part 356).

Under penalties of perjury, I certify that the number shown on this form is my correct taxpayer identification number and that I am not subject to backup withholding because (1) I have not been notified that I am subject to backup withholding as a result of a failure to report all interest or dividends or (2) the Internal Revenue Service has notified me that I am no longer subject to backup withholding. I further certify that all other information provided on this form is true, correct and complete.

SIGNATURE                                              DATE

# FIGURE 4-3

## Treasury Bill, Note, and Bond Tender Form

PD F 5381
Department of the Treasury
Bureau of the Public Debt

OMB No. 1535-0069

**TREASURY DIRECT®**

**TREASURY BILL, NOTE & BOND TENDER**

For Tender Instructions, See PD F 5382

TYPE OR PRINT IN INK ONLY – TENDERS WILL NOT BE ACCEPTED WITH ALTERATIONS OR CORRECTIONS

**1. BID INFORMATION** *Tender amount must meet or exceed the minimum for the term selected below. (Must Be Completed)*

| DEPARTMENT USE |
| TENDER NO. |

Par Amount:

Bid Type: *(Fill in One)*
- ○ Noncompetitive
- ○ Competitive at ⌐_____.____⌐ %
  *(Bill bids must end in 0 or 5.)*

$ _____

RECEIVED BY/DATE

**2. TREASURY DIRECT ACCOUNT NUMBER** *(If NOT furnished, a new account will be opened.)*

**3. TAXPAYER ID NUMBER** *(Must Be Completed)*

⌐_____⌐-⌐__⌐-⌐_____⌐ OR ⌐__⌐-⌐_____⌐
Social Security Number (First-Named Owner)     Employer ID Number

ENTERED BY

APPROVED BY

**4. TERM SELECTION** *(Fill in One)*
*(Must Be Completed)*

*Treasury Bill*
$10,000 Minimum    Circle the Number of Reinvestments
- ○ 13-Week..........0  1  2  3  4
                    5  6  7  8
- ○ 26-Week..........0  1  2  3  4
- ○ 52-Week..........0  1  2

*Treasury Note/Bond*
$5,000 Minimum
- ○ 2-Year Note
- ○ 3-Year Note

- - - - - - - - - - - - - - - - -

$1,000 Minimum
- ○ 5-Year Note
- ○ 10-Year Note
- ○ 30-Year Bond
- ○ Inflation-Indexed
                    Term

**5. ACCOUNT NAME** Please Type or Print! *(Must Be Completed)*

**6. ADDRESS** *(For new account or if changed.)*  ○ New Address?

City     State     ZIP Code

ISSUE DATE

CUSIP 912794-

CUSIP 912827-

CUSIP 912810-

FOREIGN ☐

BACKUP ☐

**7. TELEPHONE NUMBERS** *(For new account or if changed.)*  ○ New Phone Number?

Work ( ___ ) ___ - _____     Home ( ___ ) ___ - _____

**8. DIRECT DEPOSIT INFORMATION** *(For new account only.)*  Changes? Submit PD F 5178.

Routing Number ⌐_____⌐

Financial Institution Name _____

Account Number ⌐_____⌐

Name on Account _____

Account Type: *(Fill in One)*  ○ Checking  ○ Savings

**9. PURCHASE METHOD**
*(Must Be Completed)*

- ○ Automatic Withdrawal
  *(Existing Treasury Direct Account Only)*
- ○ Cash:  $ _____
- ○ Checks:  $ _____
                $ _____
- ○ Securities:  $ _____

Total Payment Attached:  $ _____
CHECKS ARE DEPOSITED IMMEDIATELY

REVIEW ☐

CHECK #

**10. AUTHORIZATION** *(Must Be Completed – Original Signature Required)*
**Tender Submission:** I submit this tender pursuant to the provisions of Department of the Treasury Circulars, Public Debt Series Nos. 2-86 (31 CFR Part 357) and 1-93 (31 CFR Part 356), and the applicable offering announcement. As the first-named owner and under penalties of perjury, I certify that the number shown on this form is my correct taxpayer identification number and that I am not subject to backup withholding because (1) I have not been notified that I am subject to backup withholding as a result of a failure to report all interest or dividends, or (2) the Internal Revenue Service has notified me that I am no longer subject to backup withholding. I further certify that all other information provided on this form is true, correct and complete.

**Automatic Withdrawal:** (If using this purchase method.) I authorize a debit to my account at the financial institution I designated in TREASURY DIRECT to pay for this security. I understand that the purchase price will be charged to my account on or after the settlement date. I also understand that if this transaction cannot be successfully completed, my tender can be rejected and the transaction canceled. If there is a dispute, a copy of this authorization may be provided to my financial institution.

_____     _____
Signature(s)     Date

SEE BACK FOR PRIVACY ACT AND PAPERWORK REDUCTION ACT NOTICE

those bids which have the lowest discount rates (the highest prices) from all the bids received. Thus, for the accepted bids, there is a range of yields, from the lowest to the highest, known as the *stop-out yield*, which the Federal Reserve will pay. Investors who have their bids accepted at the stop-out yield or close to it will receive greater returns than those whose bids are accepted at the lowest yields.

The yields that investors bid depend upon the money market rates that are currently being offered by competing short-term instruments as well as expectations of what current short-term rates for T-bills will be. By studying these rates, an investor has a better chance of submitting a bid that will be accepted. In a competitive bidding, however, investors face the risk of not having their bids accepted if they are above the stop-out yields.

Less expert investors, who may not want to work out their bids, or those who want to be assured of purchasing T-bills can submit *noncompetitive bids*. With noncompetitive bids, investors are able to buy T-bills at the average accepted competitive bid in the auction. In general, all noncompetitive bids of up to $1 million per investor per auction are accepted, which means that investors are assured of their purchases.

Tender forms to submit bids may be sent by mail or carried in person to the Federal Reserve Banks and branches before the close of the auction. Competitive bids must be received by the time designated in the offering circular. Noncompetitive bids that are mailed must be postmarked no later than midnight the day before the auction and received on or before the issue date of the securities.

Payment must accompany the tender form. Check the type of payment: cash, check, securities, or other. The amount of the payment should be no less than the amount of the tender for a noncompetitive bid. For a competitive bid, it should be no less than the bid amount. If the payment amount is not correct, the tender will be rejected and returned.

On acceptance of your bid, you will receive a confirmation receipt from the Federal Reserve and a payment, which is the difference between the tender amount you submitted and the discounted price of the T-bills. You can stipulate on the tender form whether you want the Federal Reserve to reinvest the T-bills when they mature. If you do not choose the reinvestment option, the

Federal Reserve will credit your account for the face value of the Treasury bills at maturity.

Treasury bills purchased directly through the Federal Reserve system are held in the Treasury direct book-entry system, which is designed primarily for investors who hold their securities to maturity. Should you decide to sell your T-bills before maturity, you have to fill out a transfer request form (PD 5179), which transfers your account to the commercial book-entry system. Then your T-bills can be sold. The commercial book-entry system records those Treasuries bought through financial institutions and government securities dealers. Information on Treasury bills can be obtained from the government's Website, *www.publicdebt.treas.gov.*

The advantages of buying T-bills directly from the Federal Reserve and holding them to maturity is that the investor avoids paying commissions or fees.

## The Advantages of Treasury Bills

- T-bills provide investors with a flexible range of maturities along with near-complete safety for the repayment of principal and interest.
- T-bills offer excellent liquidity (probably the most liquid of all short-term money market instruments).
- Interest income on T-bills is exempt from state and local taxation.
- Treasury bills may be bought directly from the Federal Reserve Bank without incurring any charges or commissions.

## The Disadvantages of Treasury Bills

- You need a minimum of $10,000 to invest directly in Treasury bills.
- Although Treasury bill yields are benchmarks upon which the yields of other instruments are based, they tend to be less than those on certificates of deposit for similar maturities and money market mutual funds.

- Treasury bills are subject to interest rate risk. If market rates of interest go up, the price of existing Treasury bills will go down, which may result in capital losses for Treasury bill owners who are forced to sell before maturity. (If market rates of interest go down, investors who sell before maturity may realize capital gains.)
- T-bills do not protect against moderate to high inflation.

### Caveats

- When buying T-bills through banks or brokers, shop around for the lowest fees and commissions.
- When submitting competitive bids, there is always the possibility that your bid will not be accepted due to unanticipated fluctuations of money market interest rates on the day of the auction.
- Although submitting a noncompetitive bid assures the investor of a purchase, there is the possibility that the investor could receive yields well below current yields if there is an unexpected drop in short-term interest rates.

## COMMERCIAL PAPER

Despite the fact that commercial paper is difficult for individual investors to buy, it is a widely held indirect investment in money market funds. By understanding what commercial paper is all about, investors are better able to assess the risks of their money market funds.

### What Is Commercial Paper?

Commercial paper is an unsecured, short-term promissory note (IOU) issued by the largest and most creditworthy financial and nonfinancial corporations. Simply stated, the borrowing corporation promises to pay back the lender an amount of money in a short period of time. The commercial paper is sold at a discount to the amount of money the corporation will pay back at maturity. Commercial paper is generally issued with maturities of less than 270 days (in order to avoid registration with the Securities and

Exchange Commission (SEC), which is required for maturities in excess of 270 days). Denominations for commercial paper are large, ranging from $5000 to $5,000,000, with most being for $100,000 and over (Kolb and DeMong, 1988, p. 687).

## How to Buy Commercial Paper

Commercial paper is sold to investors either through dealers or directly by issuers.

### Dealer Paper

Dealers buy commercial paper and then immediately resell it in large amounts to institutional investors, charging relatively small margins ($\frac{1}{8}$ of one percent per annum) (Stigum and Fabozzi, 1987, p. 53). Even if individual investors have large amounts to invest ($150,000), dealers will not sell commercial paper to individual investors. The SEC has stated that commercial paper should only be sold to sophisticated investors, and dealers consider all individual investors to be unsophisticated. Thus, individual investors may buy dealer paper through brokers, who offer the paper in smaller amounts ($25,000 and over) and charge commissions, which can be significant on small purchases (Stigum and Fabozzi, 1987, p. 58).

### Direct Issue

Individual investors may buy commercial paper directly from the issuers in relatively small amounts ($25,000). They can telephone or write to well-known finance companies, such as GMAC (General Motors Acceptance Corp.), Chrysler Financial Corp., Sears, and the like, to find out their terms, rates, and maturities. When investors decide which paper to buy, they can mail their checks and have the company register the paper in their names and mail the paper securities to them. Buying directly from the issuer is the cheapest way, since no costs are involved other than telephone calls and postage. Investors can redeem their paper at maturity for cash by mailing the paper security certificates before they mature to the issuer (or to the bank that handles the collections for the issuer).

The investor also has the option of rolling over the paper when it matures. After a direct purchase from an issuer, a renewal form is routinely sent, and the investor should fill it out and send it back to the issuer before maturity. At maturity, the issuer will send the new commercial paper security and a check for the difference between the maturity value of the old paper and the discounted price of the new commercial paper (Stigum and Fabozzi, 1987, p. 60).

Commercial paper may also be bought through a bank, for which the bank will charge a small fee for its efforts.

Most small investors are indirect holders of commercial paper through their ownership of shares in money market mutual funds that purchase commercial paper as investments for the funds.

## The Advantages of Commercial Paper

- Commercial paper offers a higher yield than Treasury bills.
- Except for Penn Central's default on its commercial paper in the early 1970s, historically, the credit risk of commercial paper has been relatively low. Risk depends on the creditworthiness of the issuing corporation, and the risk of good-quality commercial paper is low.
- Owing to the short maturities, investors do not need to tie up their funds for long periods.

## The Disadvantages of Commercial Paper

- It is difficult for investors to get their money before maturity, since there is not a secondary market for commercial paper.
- Interest on commercial paper is taxed at the federal, state, and local levels, whereas interest on Treasury bills is taxed only at the federal level.
- You need a minimum of at least $5000 to $10,000 to be able to buy commercial paper directly.

## Caveats

Since the yields on commercial paper have traditionally been only slightly higher than those of Treasury bills, an investor may want to give extra consideration to the disadvantages of commercial paper (not as liquid and triple taxable) before choosing it over Treasury bills.

## BANKERS' ACCEPTANCES

Bankers' acceptances are the least understood of all the short-term money market investments, yet they are good investments for individual investors.

### What Are Bankers' Acceptances?

Bankers' acceptances are negotiable time drafts commonly issued for import-export transactions. For example, a seller (exporter) sells goods to a buyer (importer) in another country and would like to get paid when the goods are shipped. On the other hand, the buyer would like to pay for the goods in three months, when he receives them. To alleviate the seller's fears, the buyer (importer) applies to the bank for a bankers' acceptance, which is a promise from the buyer to pay the amount in a short period of time, usually between 30 and 180 days. The bank then accepts this promise by obligating itself to pay the seller (exporter).

The bank can either hold the acceptance until it matures, or it can sell the acceptance directly to investors or through dealers to investors. The investor buys the acceptance at a discount and holds it until maturity, when it is presented to the bank at face value (the difference between the amount received and the amount paid to the bank is interest to the investor). Banks generally charge small fees which go toward covering their costs.

The predominant investors in bankers' acceptances are central banks of foreign countries, Federal Reserve Banks, and other banks. Due to the large amounts that bankers' acceptances are written for, small investors have not been active participants.

### How to Invest in Bankers' Acceptances

As a start, an individual investor may approach his or her bank. If the bank does not offer acceptances, the investor should then try other banks, particularly the larger commercial banks and dealers who deal in bankers' acceptances. The amounts that can be invested in bankers' acceptances vary, but they typically range from $25,000 to $1,000,000 (Martin et al., 1991, p. 558). Bankers will group bankers' acceptances into packages at these higher denominations.

Individual investors also may hold bankers' acceptances indirectly through investments in money market mutual funds.

## The Advantages of Bankers' Acceptances

- Bankers' acceptances are high-quality, low-risk investments, since they are bank-guaranteed.
- Rates of return are generally higher than those of Treasury bills of similar maturities.
- If investors do not want to wait until their bankers' acceptances mature, they can sell them in an over-the-counter market. However, investors may have trouble selling one or two low-denomination bankers' acceptances.

## The Disadvantages of Bankers' Acceptances

- Investors have to look for banks or dealers carrying bankers' acceptances. Banks do not advertise that they have bankers' acceptances readily available for investors to invest in.
- The amounts to be invested in bankers' acceptances may be high for individual investors ($25,000 to $1,000,000).
- If short-term interest rates are volatile and start to fall, bankers' acceptances, being short-term, do not offer the investor the opportunity to "lock into" higher interest rates for a long period of time.

## Caveat

Investors should check that the rates of return offered by the banks on bankers' acceptances are competitive with prevailing rates on bankers' acceptances, which can be found in *The Wall Street Journal* and *Barron's*.

# OTHER SHORT-TERM FIXED-INCOME SECURITIES

## Repurchase Agreements

A *repurchase agreement* is a legal contract in which one party sells securities to another party and simultaneously executes an agreement to buy them back at a contracted price and at an agreed upon time in the future. Most of the securities used are U.S. government securities. The length of the holding period is tailored to the needs of the parties in the transaction, but most repurchase agreements are transacted for only a few days.

The interest rate is defined as the difference between the selling and the repurchase price of the repo. This difference (interest) is taxed at the Federal, state, and local levels of government. There are no regularly published repo rates because they are determined through direct negotiations between the buyers and sellers. However, the rates of repurchase agreements are closely related to Treasury bill and federal funds rates. Repo rates may be lower than the federal funds rate because of the security provided by the securities in the repurchase agreement. This does not mean that repurchase agreements are devoid of risk. In 1982, a securities company called Drysdale Securities defaulted on close to $4 billion of repurchase agreements. Since a repo is a loan with security, investors still need to pay attention to:

- The ability of the borrower to be able to repay the loan.
- Not paying more than the securities are worth, because if the seller defaults, they will lose money.

The question that comes to mind is why an investor or institution would want to buy a repurchase agreement instead of buying the securities.

- The first advantage is that the maturity of the repo can be tailored to the length of time that the short-term money is needed.
- A repo removes the risk of loss due to market fluctuations of the underlying securities in the transaction. Sellers could, of course, sell their securities when they needed the

cash, but there is a drawback to this. If the price of the securities falls below the original purchase price, there is a capital loss. The buyer of the repo avoids this risk, and is protected from the market fluctuations of the securities.

The major participants in repurchase agreements are securities dealers, corporations, and financial institutions. Unfortunately, due to the large size of the transactions, this does not include many individual investors. Repos are generally executed in amounts over $1 million or more.

## Certificates of Deposit

Certificates of deposit (CDs) offer investors with limited resources a convenient form of investing their short-term funds. Certificates of deposit can be bought through banks and thrift institutions for small amounts and specified periods. For example, an investor might decide to invest $500 in a six-month CD that pays interest of 4 percent per annum. The $500 is deposited in the bank, and the bank promises to pay the investor $510 at maturity in six months.

A certificate of deposit has many properties of a bond, but it is not a bond. It is an IOU in that there is a promise to pay back the interest and principal at maturity, but it is not a marketable instrument. In other words, if the holder needs the funds before maturity, there is no market of buyers for this security. The holder would have to go back to the issuing financial institution and pay the early-redemption penalty to cash in the CD.

There are money market CDs which do not have this limitation, but they require minimum amounts of $100,000. These money market CDs are negotiable, marketable receipts and can be traded prior to their maturities in a secondary market in New York City. The round lots for these trades are in millions of dollars, although lots smaller than $1 million may be traded. The prices will not be as good on the smaller-size lots. These money market, or "jumbo," CDs may be purchased through banks and thrift organizations.

Banks that are members of the FDIC (Federal Deposit Insurance Corporation, an independent agency of the U.S. government) provide insurance of $100,000 per ownership of accounts in a bank. Thus, many investors have gravitated to CDs as the investment vehicle of choice for their short-term funds.

The advantages of CDs are:

- The convenience and ease of investing.
- With FDIC membership, banks offer safety up to $100,000 of the ownership in an account.
- The investor can invest small amounts in a CD.
- At redemption, CDs can be paid out to the investor or automatically rolled over into another CD.

The disadvantages of CDs are:

- They are not marketable. Should investors need to cash them in before redemption, they pay a penalty.
- CD rates vary from bank to bank, and investors need to do some homework to find the banks with the most attractive rates.
- Rates on CDs may be lower than those offered by Treasury bills and money market mutual funds.
- Income from CDs is taxed at the federal, state, and in many cases, local levels of government.

## MONEY MARKET MUTUAL FUNDS OR THE INDIVIDUAL SECURITIES?

The question that is often asked is: Should I invest in money market mutual funds or in the individual securities—Treasury bills, CDs, bankers' acceptances, and commercial paper? Table 4-3 shows the advantages of the mutual funds versus the individual money market securities.

**TABLE 4-3**

Money Market Mutual Funds versus Separate Securities

|                                         | Mutual Fund | Individual Security      |
| --------------------------------------- | ----------- | ------------------------ |
| Ease of opening an account              | Yes         | Yes: CDs, Treasury bills |
| Liquidity and marketability             | Yes         | Yes: Treasury bills      |
| Loss of principal with early redemption | No          | Yes                      |
| Higher rate of return                   | No          | Yes                      |

Money market mutual funds have fixed share prices, which accounts for much of their advantage over the individual securities; they can be bought and sold without any tax consequences. This does not mean that the dividend income is not taxable. Income from money market funds is taxable, but there are no capital gains or losses from buying and selling shares in a money market mutual fund. This means that when cash is needed, investors can withdraw their funds by writing checks from their money market securities. There may be some capital gains or losses that may be passed on to the shareholders when the mutual fund sells securities before maturity, but these tend to be small. The individual securities are not as simple. Treasury bills are both liquid and marketable, but it would take at least three days to receive the proceeds from their sale in the secondary markets.

The other major advantage of money market mutual funds over the individual securities is that if money is needed earlier than planned, there is no loss in principal. With Treasury bills, which are the most liquid and marketable of the individual investments, there can be a loss or gain in principal due to fluctuations in market rates of interest. The other individual investments may offer more difficulties in liquidating. With CDs, there are early-withdrawal penalties.

The only disadvantage of money market mutual funds is that at times, the individual investments may earn higher rates of return. However, bear in mind that the purpose of these money market securities is to provide a parking place for emergency funds and short-term cash, not be the cornerstone of an investor's strategy. Hence, the old Wall Street saying: "Cash is trash."

The following chapters outline the benefits of the longer-term investment options for the bulk of investor's funds.

## REFERENCES

Faerber, Esmé: *Managing Your Investments, Savings and Credit,* McGraw-Hill, New York, 1992.

Kolb, Burton A., and Richard F. DeMong: *Principles of Financial Management,* Business Publications, Inc., Plano, TX, 1988.

**Martin, John D., J. William Petty, Arthur J. Keown, and David F. Scott, Jr.**: *Basic Financial Management*, 5th ed., Prentice Hall, Englewood Cliffs, NJ, 1991.

**Schultze, Ellen E.**: "Parking Places for Cash Can Be Costly," *The Wall Street Journal*, July 10, 1998, p. C1.

**Stigum, Marcia, and Frank Fabozzi**: *Dow Jones Guide to Bond and Money Market Investments*, Dow Jones-Irwin, Homewood, IL, 1987.

## CHAPTER 5

# Corporate Bonds and Corporate Bond Mutual Funds

## KEY CONCEPTS

- What are the features of corporate bonds?
- The types of corporate bonds
- What are the risks of corporate bonds?
- What are junk bonds?
- How to buy and sell corporate bonds
- What are the advantages of corporate bonds?
- What are the disadvantages of corporate bonds?
- Quasi-corporate debt preferred stock securities
- Corporate bond mutual funds
- How to choose a corporate bond mutual fund
- What are the risks of corporate bond mutual funds?
- How to buy corporate bond mutual funds
- What are the advantages of corporate bond mutual funds?
- What are the disadvantages of corporate bond mutual funds?
- Corporate bonds versus corporate bond mutual funds

In the past, investors have considered corporate bonds to be safe investments that provide a steady stream of income. In recent years, however, corporate bonds have become more volatile, and a growing category of corporate junk bonds deviates from the standard of safety referred to at the beginning of this paragraph.

The types of corporate bonds and the bond markets themselves have changed in recent years. However, investors still buy bonds because they offer greater yields than CDs and money market funds. But investors need to become more aware of bonds' features and risks in order to protect the safety of their principal.

## WHAT ARE THE FEATURES OF CORPORATE BONDS?

Bonds are debt instruments, and all bonds have similar features. A corporate bond is a loan made by a corporation in return for a specified amount of interest and the repayment of the face value of the bond at a specified maturity date. The interest (coupon) rate is generally fixed for the life of the bond (exceptions are variable-rate bonds), and the face (par) value of the bond is usually $1000. The maturity date is the date by which the bond must be paid off. So a corporate bond with a coupon of 7 percent and a maturity date of July 1, 2005, would pay interest of $70 per bond every year up to July 1, 2005, when the corporation would pay off the face value of the bond to the bondholder.

If a bond has 20 years to maturity at the date of issuance, it is said to have an *original maturity* of 20 years. After a year, that same bond will have a *current maturity*, or *term to maturity*, of 19 years.

### Forms of Bonds

Bonds are issued in one of three forms: registered, bearer, or book-entry form. *Registered* form is similar to owning stock certificates. Bonds are registered in the owner's name, and the interest payments are mailed to the owner. When the bond is sold, the transfer agent registers the bond in the name of the new owner.

In *bearer* (or coupon) form, possession signifies ownership. The bond does not have a registered owner, and the issuing company does not know where to mail the interest payments. Therefore, attached to bearer bonds are the coupons for the interest payments. At the due date of the interest payment, the bearer clips the coupon and sends it to the issuer's paying agent, who will send a check to the bondholder for the interest. The coupon can also be sent to the bondholder's bank, which will collect the interest for the bondholder.

It is easy to sell bearer bonds, since they do not need to be registered. However, they do present problems in terms of safekeeping. Because possession signifies ownership, bearer bonds are like money and need to be kept in a safe place.

Bonds may also be issued in *book-entry* form. Instead of a bond certificate, the bondholder receives a confirmation with a computer number that signifies ownership. Bondholders designate their bank or savings and loan accounts for the direct deposit of interest payments.

## Who Should Keep Your Bond Certificates?

Investors often debate whether to take possession of their bond certificates (in bearer or registered form) or leave them with their brokerage firms.

The advantages of leaving them in the custody of the brokerage firm are:

- They are protected against physical loss if that brokerage firm is covered by the SIPC (Securities Insurance Protection Corporation).
- In the event that your bonds are called, the brokerage firm is more likely to become aware of the call and redeem the bonds immediately.

The disadvantages of keeping them in the custody of the brokerage firm are:

- Should you decide to sell your bonds through another broker, you must have your existing brokerage firm transfer them to the new broker's firm. You have three days after the date of sale to deliver the securities before the brokerage firm assesses a late charge.
- Some brokerage firms are slow in remitting the interest payments. For example, a brokerage firm might receive interest payments at the beginning of the month and only remit them to their clients at the end of the month. This brokerage firm has the use of clients' money for 30 days.

- When bonds with a sinking fund provision are left in the brokerage firm's name, the brokerage firm chooses which customer's bonds will be redeemed early. A sinking fund is used by companies to redeem a certain number of bonds each year before maturity. The company will notify bondholders through the mail and in the newspapers of redemptions. This is particularly relevant for the small investor. With a sinking fund provision, you are better off holding your own bonds, which can be called directly, but it is not left to the brokerage firm to choose which client's bonds to redeem.

## THE TYPES OF CORPORATE BONDS

Corporate bonds can be classified into the following groups (Thau, 1992, p. 156):

- The utilities, which includes bonds issued by the telephone and electric companies. These securities tend to be viewed as safe, conservative investments.
- The transportation group, which consists of bonds issued by the railroads and airlines.
- The industrials, bonds issued by industrial companies.
- The financials, issued by finance companies, e.g., insurance companies and banks.

Within these groups, there are many types of bonds, such as mortgage bonds, debenture bonds, variable-interest bonds, convertible bonds, and zero-coupon bonds. These bonds are either secured or unsecured. For *secured bonds,* the issuer pledges an asset as collateral, and in the event of a default, the creditor can seize the asset (after proceeding to court). An example of a secured bond is a mortgage bond, which is frequently issued by utility companies. Investors should sleep well at night knowing that their bonds are backed by a power plant. But do investors have the expertise to operate the power plant in the event of a default by the utility company? Although pledging assets increases the safety of the principal of the bonds, in this case investors should hope that the utility company does not default on its interest and principal payments.

The transportation group issues bonds known as *equipment trust certificates*, which are secured by equipment such as airplanes and railroad cars. This equipment may be more marketable than power plants, but investors could still lose some of their principal in the event of a default. For example, when both Braniff Airlines and Freddie Laker's airline declared bankruptcy during the world-wide recession of 1981–1982, the market for used aircraft had declined significantly (Mayo, 1991, p. 382).

*Unsecured* bonds, or *debenture* bonds, are backed only by the issuer's creditworthiness (ability to pay annual interest and principal at maturity). Some companies issue *subordinated debenture bonds,* which are riskier in the event of insolvency, since subordinated debenture holders will be last in the line of lenders to be repaid. Seniority becomes important during bankruptcy because secured bonds and senior debt are first in line to be repaid. Riskier issues tend to offer higher coupon rates to entice investors.

Generally, investors should be concerned with the issuer's ability to service their debt (or creditworthiness), rather than with the security alone. In the event of bankruptcy, pledged property may not be marketable, and it may involve litigation, which can be time-consuming.

Corporations also issue *convertible bonds,* which are bonds that may be converted into the issuer's common stock. *Zero-coupon bonds* are issued at deep discounts, with interest paid at maturity.

## WHAT ARE THE RISKS OF CORPORATE BONDS?

The *risk of default* is more of a concern for investors in corporate bonds than for investors in other types of bonds, such as U.S. Treasuries and government agency bonds, where the risks of default are much less. U.S. Treasuries are considered to be free of default risk. This is why corporate bonds offer higher yields than Treasuries and government agency bonds. The greater the risk of default, the higher the coupon rate for that issue.

To evaluate the risk of default on individual corporate bond issues, most investors rely on the ratings of the issues given by the commercial rating companies, such as Standard & Poor's, Moody's, and Fitch. However, as pointed out in an earlier chapter, these ratings are not foolproof, and they are also subject to change. A company's financial position can deteriorate after being rated. For example, in 1998 the Allegheny Health System in Philadelphia defaulted on its bond issues shortly after their ratings were downgraded.

In addition to the commercial ratings, an investor can evaluate the bond issue on her or his own by looking at the bond's prospectus or the company's financial statements for:

- The amount of debt that the company has
- Where you stand in the claims line in the event of bankruptcy

There is another risk which affects bond prices of existing issues called *event risk*. This is the risk that large corporations will issue large amounts of debt to finance takeovers of other corporations (also known as *leveraged buyouts*). This causes the existing bond issues of the takeover corporations to plummet in price, because the corporation significantly increases its level of debt, resulting in downgraded ratings.

As a result, investors shun many corporate bond offerings. To entice investors to buy these new issues, corporate issuers introduce provisions which make takeovers more expensive. These are nicknamed "poison puts," which may allow bondholders to sell their bonds back to the issuer at par in the event of a takeover or in the event that the bond's ratings are downgraded.

Before buying a new corporate issue, check with your broker to see whether there is a "poison put" protection clause. The advantages of a put feature in the bond's indenture are often paid for through lower yields on the bonds. Regardless, a put feature is attractive because investors are protected against the risk of a rise in interest rates and inflation. When interest rates or inflation goes up, the price of the bond will fall, and holders of the bond can use the put option to sell the bond back to the issuer at par value before maturity.

All bonds except for floating-rate bonds are subject to *interest rate risk*. Citicorp was the first corporation to introduce floating-rate bonds in the 1970s. These were unique at the time in that the coupon rate fluctuated with the rate of Treasury bills, and after a two-year period (after issuance), the bondholders could redeem the bonds at par value. Therefore, unlike the prices of regular fixed-income bonds, floating-rate bonds will not fluctuate very much in price due to changes in interest rates. As pointed out in a previous chapter, bond prices fluctuate inversely with market rates of interest. The longer the maturity of the bond, the greater the price fluctuation in relation to changes in interest rates.

The impact of interest rate risk can be lessened by:

- Spreading out the maturities of the different bond issues in your portfolio to even out the impact of changing market rates of interest. For example, instead of investing only in bonds with 20-year maturities, you can ladder the maturities between 2, 5, 10, 15, and 20 years.
- Diversifying your bond portfolio by buying different types of bonds.
- Purchasing good-quality bonds.
- Lessening the length of the maturities.
- Buying bonds with a put feature, which allows bondholders to sell their bonds back to the issuer at face value when interest rates rise.

The downside is that bonds with these features have lower coupon rates and shorter maturities. However, in theory, the optimum strategy is to invest in short maturities when market rates of interest are increasing and then when they peak, to buy long-term bonds to lock into the high coupon rates. The obvious question is how do you know when market rates of interest are going to peak? Locking in at the exact peak of market interest rates is not as important as at least trying to follow the strategy.

Many corporate bonds have *call features*, which means that they are subject to *call risk*. The call feature allows the issuer to retire the bonds prior to maturity. When a bond is called, interest no longer accrues, which forces bondholders to retire their bonds. The call feature benefits the issuer rather than the bondholder. This is because issuers tend to call their bonds after a period of high interest rates. For example, if a corporation issued 11-percent coupon bonds when interest rates were high and then rates dropped to 7 percent, it would be advantageous for the issuer to refund the old bonds with new bonds at a lower coupon rate.

Early repayment is always disadvantageous for investors, as issuers will rarely refund bonds early if market rates of interest are going up. This is especially disadvantageous for investors who may have bought bonds when interest rates were at a peak.

Investors should pay particular attention to a bond issue's call and refunding provisions. There are three types of call provisions:

- *Noncallable bonds* offer investors the most protection, but there are many loopholes. Noncallable implies that the bonds will not be called before maturity. However, there are cases where noncallable bonds have been called, such as in the case of a fire or act of God, or when a healthy company stops making its interest payments on the bonds and the trustees call them in and the debt is paid off early. *Noncallable for life bonds* would be listed in the dealer's quote sheets as NCL.
- *Freely callable bonds* offer investors no protection, since issuers can call them anytime.
- *Deferred callable bonds* offer some protection because the bonds cannot be called until after a period of time, for example, 5, 10, or 15 years after issue. A bond that is noncallable until 2002 would be listed as NC02 on the dealer's quote sheet.

The call provision of the bond will specify the price above the face value that the issuer is willing to pay. This is referred to as the *call premium,* and it frequently equals the coupon rate of the bond. It is important to check the call provision of a bond issue before buying. For new issues, you may want to go one step further and insist on a final copy of the prospectus from the broker. Often, the preliminary prospectus is skimpy on early call details (Antilla, 1992). Even when buying noncallable or deferred callable bonds, seek written assurances from your broker as to their call status.

Besides the call provision, the refunding provision in the bond indenture can be important. There are nonrefundable bonds which can indeed be called and refunded. However, the refunding must be with "clean money," which is raised either from internal sources of funds or the selling of stock or assets. Nonrefundable bonds cannot be repaid from the proceeds of selling lower-coupon-rate debt. May Department Stores was named in a lawsuit for redeeming more than $160 million of high-interest bonds with a simultaneous offering of new bonds at a lower coupon rate. May used a technique known as a STAC, which is the simultaneous tender offer and cash call.

A STAC works in the following way: The company with outstanding bonds announces to its bondholders that they can voluntarily turn in their bonds at a premium price. The heavy hand is applied to those bondholders who do not voluntarily turn in their bonds. They are told that their bonds will be called for cash later at a lower price. In other words, the gist of a STAC is to turn in your bonds for a higher price, because if you don't, the company has enough cash to call them in.

Call and refunding provisions, then, are important to investors, particularly if the bonds are purchased at a premium price and/or market rates of interest are at or near their peak.

## WHAT ARE JUNK BONDS?

Junk bonds are not a special type of bond; they are regular high-risk, low-rated bonds. These corporate bonds have ratings of BBB (Standard & Poor's) or Baa (Moody's Investor Services, Inc.) or less, which includes a range of poor-quality debt close to default. Some of these bonds have no ratings.

In order to entice investors, coupon rates of junk bonds are higher than the coupon rates of investment-grade bonds. There are two major reasons for these higher coupon yields:

- The issuers of junk bonds may be young growth companies with weak balance sheets or financially troubled companies for whom junk bonds are one of the few alternatives left to raise capital.
- Many corporations have used junk bonds to finance the takeovers of other corporations.

This latter reason accounted for the major growth in the junk bond market during the decade of the 1980s. Michael Milken and Drexel Burnham and Lambert opened up the junk bond market and sold these bonds directly to the public. By establishing a network of potential investors, companies gained a low-cost fund-raising alternative to the traditional sources of borrowing from banks. However, with the economic slowdown in the late 1980s, the junk bond market was faced with an increasing rate of defaults.

This resulted in the collapse of the junk bond market, and mutual funds, institutional investors, and many small investors bailed out. The prices of junk bonds plummeted, and those investors who were left holding junk bonds found they had illiquid investments and an erosion of their investment capital. Junk bonds remained in the doldrums during 1990. Then, as bond prices went into steep decline, the junk bond market proved again to be an attractive speculation, and it rallied for about 18 months into 1992. With the low rates of interest in the late 1990s, junk bonds are in rally mode.

For investors who bought and sold junk bonds at the right time, the rewards were large. The risks are high, though, and that is why the yields of junk bonds are so attractive. Investors are giving up a degree of safety because junk bonds have greater price swings and have that overhanging specter of default. And junk bonds do indeed default, as evidenced by the increase in the junk bond default rate to 8 percent in 1990 (Thau, 1992, p. 165).

Various studies quote different rates of default, and there are studies done by some brokerage firms which tout the relative safety of high-yield junk bonds. In general, junk bonds will do well in a strong economy, because there is less risk of default. In a weak economy, the risk of default rises. Broad diversification of junk bond issues can lessen the risk of default.

Regardless of which study you choose to believe, you should carefully weigh the following risks against the "promised" higher returns (Faerber, 1992, p. 151):

- If interest rates go down, there is the risk that issuers of the high-yielding junk bonds will call them and refinance with lower-yielding securities.
- There is the risk that junk bond prices could plummet and investors could lose part of their initial investments.
- There is the risk that during sell-offs in the junk bond market, investors will find that there are no buyers for their bonds.

Investing in junk bonds is not for unsophisticated investors but for those who are able to analyze the financial statements of companies in order to differentiate the "quality" high-yield bonds from those that are descending along the path to bankruptcy.

Some advice for those who are not deterred by the risk of junk bonds:

- Buy only publicly listed bonds so you can follow the price quotes in the newspapers to guide your buying and selling. The junk bond market has gained a reputation that has not enhanced its credibility. As trading is unregulated and investors do not have access to accurate price information, prices quoted by dealers can vary significantly. For example, Equitable Bag Company was quoted by one dealer at bid and asked prices of 80 to 90 respectively, while a second dealer quoted an 85 bid and a 90 asked price on the same bonds (Mitchell, 1992). Individual investors are therefore at a disadvantage if they need to buy or sell quickly.
- Diversify your purchases to spread your risk. If you cannot afford to buy many different corporate junk bonds, invest in junk bond mutual funds to achieve diversification.
- Avoid buying bonds that are part of small issues (less than $75 million). They can be illiquid.
- Limit the amount you invest in junk bonds to a small percentage of your portfolio. That percentage should vary according to your investment objectives, risk, level of income, stage of life, and other personal characteristics.

## HOW TO BUY AND SELL CORPORATE BONDS

Corporate bonds can be bought and sold in the same manner as common stocks. They may be bought through brokerage firms with cash or on margin. Purchasing bonds on margin means the investor uses funds borrowed from the brokerage firm to purchase the bonds (or stocks). The amount that can be borrowed depends on the margin requirement (set by the Federal Reserve), which is the percentage requirement that must be put up by the investor in cash. The rest may be borrowed.

Using borrowed funds to buy bonds could lead to problems if the bonds do not return more than the interest cost on the borrowed funds. On the other hand, if the investment does well, the rate of return is greater since the investor has invested less money.

When you buy a new issue of bonds, you will pay no commission. It is absorbed by the issuing corporation. Before investing in a new issue, you should examine the company's prospectus to assess the overall risk.

From the balance sheet, you can determine the level of debt and the number of debt issues which are senior to this one. In the event of bankruptcy, the greater the number of senior issues to this one, the lower the priority of this bond investor's claims.

From the income statement, you can determine whether the company's level of earnings will provide adequate coverage of the interest payments on all the debt issues outstanding, including the issue to be financed. If there is a downturn in sales, you would want to see how much of an interest cover the company has before the earnings become insufficient to service its debt.

If the company is currently selling off assets to generate funds and the debt-to-total-assets ratio is high, warning flags should go up about this issue. This process of analyzing the financial statements is particularly important when considering the purchase of new lower-quality corporate issues. The financial statements of listed companies can be obtained on the Internet at the government Website *www.edgar-online.com*.

Existing corporate bond issues trade in the over-the-counter market, and a number of corporate issues are listed on the New York Stock Exchange and American Exchange. Trading of listed bonds does not take place in the same location on these exchanges as common stocks. Actively listed bonds on the NYSE (New York Stock Exchange) are traded in the "bond room," where members announce the bid and asked prices. These are either accepted by other members, or counteroffers are made. Thus, buying and selling is done through these members and not through specialists, as in the case of common stocks. Inactively listed bonds are traded through the computer system in the bond room. Members respond by entering their orders through the computer terminal.

The advantage of buying listed bonds is that their prices appear in the daily newspapers, which gives investors the opportunity to check up on actual trades. Bonds that trade over the counter are unlisted, and bond price quotes may vary considerably from dealer to dealer. This is especially true for lower-quality inactively traded bonds, for which the size of the spread between the bid and asked prices may be quite large. In fact, there is pressure to regulate the unruly trading in the junk bond market by instituting a price quotation system for the most actively traded junk bonds. This system would have to be approved by the SEC before being implemented. Until such time, small investors will continue to be put at a disadvantage by these abusive trading practices. When dealers have to report their prices, many of these inefficiencies will disappear. Thus, when buying unlisted bonds, it is almost imperative that investors shop around for the best quotes from different brokers.

It is always a good idea to ask for both the bid and asked price of the bond that you are interested in buying because the size of the spread tells you much about that bond issue.

- A large spread (4 percent or more) indicates that the bond more than likely is illiquid (cannot resell quickly), inactively traded, and possibly some other bad news, such as the potential for a downgrading in ratings (Thau, 1992, p. 13).
- A small spread indicates the opposite, active trading and little risk of resale.

When buying bonds, investors may pay more than the asked price due to the *accrued interest* on that bond. Bonds earn interest daily, but the corporation only pays out the interest once or twice a year. Therefore, if a bond is purchased between the dates that interest is paid, the buyer then owes the seller the accrued interest for the number of days that the seller owned the bond. The amount of accrued interest is added to the purchase price of the bond. The accrued interest will be stated separately on the confirmation statement sent from the brokerage firm when the bonds are bought or sold.

Bonds that are in default and are no longer paying interest are said to trade *flat*. These bonds do not trade with accrued interest. In the bond quotes in the financial pages of the newspapers, an F next to the bond signifies that it is trading flat.

Bondholders can sell their bonds in the secondary market before maturity or call. For listed bonds, investors can get an idea of the price from the newspapers. Bear in mind that newspapers only list one price for bonds, whereas bonds have a bid and asked price. In case you can never remember which price is which, you buy at the higher price (asked), and you sell at the lower price (bid). The difference, or spread, is how dealers and brokers make their money from the trade.

On-line bond trading has been slow to take off with individual investors and hasn't met with the same success as on-line stock trading. There are several reasons for this:

- A greater number of bonds than stocks trade over the counter, which means that individual investors may not be aware of the different issues available.
- Investors cannot check the prices of these bonds unless they call up the individual brokerage firms.
- Placing trades on-line does not ensure that investors are getting the best prices.

Several brokerage firms and on-line trading companies are planning to address some of these difficulties. The Discover Brokerage System of Morgan Stanley allows investors access to the bid and asked spread on any bond. Electronic bond trading may take off in the future, but even with electronic trading, investors should pay attention to finding the lowest costs for their transactions (Zuckerman, December 28, 1998, pp. C1, C15).

As mentioned earlier, bonds may be retired before their maturity dates. Many corporate bonds have *sinking fund* provisions in their indentures, which are used to help with the retirement of the bond issues. Instead of the entire bond issue being retired at maturity, a sinking fund allows the corporation to make periodic payments to retire parts of the bond issue before maturity.

With one type of sinking fund, the company randomly selects the bonds to be retired and then calls them for redemption. Once these bonds are called, they no longer earn interest. For bonds with this kind of sinking fund provision, you would not want to leave your bonds in street name (in the custody of the brokerage firm), unless you are a large investor with tremendous clout in that brokerage firm and therefore know that they will turn in other investors' bonds first.

In another type of sinking fund, a corporation makes payments to a trustee who invests the money. Then the entire amount accumulated goes toward retiring the bonds at maturity.

Corporations may also repurchase their bonds in the bond market and retire them. This occurs more frequently when the bonds are trading at a discount. Investors who sell their corporate bonds may not know it is the issuing corporation that is buying them back.

Corporations may also decide to repurchase their bonds by announcing their intention to bondholders and offering a certain price to buy them back. In this case, bondholders are not required to sell their bonds back to the corporation if they don't want to.

## WHAT ARE THE ADVANTAGES OF CORPORATE BONDS?

- Corporate bonds, as a group, have greater coupon yields than other types of bonds, namely, Treasuries and agency bonds. This, of course, varies according to the quality of the corporate bonds. Generally, good-quality corporate bonds can pay coupon rates of 1 to $1\frac{1}{2}$ percent more than those of Treasuries. The spread on junk bond coupons will be much greater.

- Corporate bonds give a higher total return relative to other fixed-income securities. Investors can increase their current rates of return by purchasing lower-quality bonds, but they face increased risk of default on interest and principal.

- Income and principal are relatively safe on high-quality corporate bonds.

- Investors can get capital gains from purchasing bonds when market interest rates are falling (bond prices and interest rates move in opposite directions). However, capital losses may be incurred if bonds are sold when market interest rates are rising. For investors willing to take higher risks, the junk bond market provides opportunities for larger capital gains and higher returns when nervousness about junk bond defaults drives all the junk bond prices down.

## WHAT ARE THE DISADVANTAGES OF CORPORATE BONDS?

- Corporate bond prices are adversely affected by rising inflation and rising interest rates. This affects all fixed-income securities and is a basic disadvantage of all bond investments.
- Interest from corporate bonds is taxable at all levels (federal, state, and local), whereas interest from Treasuries and certain agency bonds is exempt from state and local taxes.
- Corporate bonds are exposed to greater credit risk than Treasuries and government agency bonds as well as to event risk, which is nonexistent for Treasuries and agency bonds. The lower the quality of the corporate bond, the greater the credit risk.
- Investors who are selling corporate bonds may face illiquidity for several reasons:

  If the ratings of the issuer decline or there is bad news concerning the issuer's financial position. This is especially true in the junk bond market, where nervousness can send junk bond prices on a downward spiral.

  If investors only have a small number of bonds to sell.

  When market interest rates are rising, existing bond prices will be driven down further.

  When the spreads widen between the bid and ask prices, it may be more difficult to buy or sell specific amounts of bonds.
- Corporate bonds with call provisions can be called when investors least want their principal returned to them (after market rates have fallen).
- Spreads between bid and asked prices on corporate bonds are greater than those on Treasuries and government agency bonds.
- Spreads on unlisted junk bonds can be quite large.
- The junk bond market has been plagued by some abusive practices as well as sharp market moves in prices before important corporate news announcements, suggesting insider trading on advance knowledge.

## CAVEATS

Before buying corporate bonds, check the following:

- The credit ratings of the issue.
- The seniority of the issue.
- The call and refunding provisions. Investors can avoid losses of principal by not buying higher premium-priced bonds with higher coupon rates than market rates, which could be called at lower premium prices. In other words, check whether the premium price exceeds the call price.
- The sinking fund provision.
- Whether there is "poison put" protection against event risk.
- Whether the bonds are part of a small issue, less than $75 million. Avoid buying bonds of small issues.
- Whether the bonds are listed or trade over the counter.
- The maturity of the bond. The longer the maturity, the greater the risk. Every now and again, corporations issue bonds with 50-year and 100-year maturities. With a time period like this, a lot can happen to affect the company's ability to repay the issue. The Disney Corporation issued a 100-year bond which will mature for the next generation's, children, grandchildren, or great-grandchildren. With this time span, stocks would be a better investment.
- Risk-averse investors should buy good-quality corporate bond issues.
- Investing in corporate bonds requires large sums of money to achieve a diversified portfolio that lessens the risk of default.
- Investors should not invest a large portion of their investment funds in junk bonds.

Be sure first to compare the coupon yield of the corporate issue to the yields offered on similar maturity Treasuries and government agency bonds to see if the spread warrants the additional risk that corporate bonds are exposed to.

For investors who cannot tolerate higher risks, avoid junk bonds, which will only guarantee sleepless nights. For risk-averse investors, choose high-quality corporate issues.

## QUASI-CORPORATE DEBT PREFERRED STOCK SECURITIES

Wall Street has created some new hybrid securities which have features of debt and preferred stock. Each sponsor or investment bank has its own acronym for these securities: MIPS, TOPrS, QUIDS, and QUIPS, among others (Doherty, December 28, 1998, p. 20).

The common features of these securities are:

- A par value of $25 instead of the traditional $1000 par for a bond.
- Listing on the stock exchanges as opposed to the bond exchanges or OTC.
- Regular interest payment.
- Most have a maturity date. There are some issues that are perpetual like common stock.
- Many of these issues have call provisions.

Typically, these are easier to buy than regular bonds, since they are listed on the stock exchanges where prices are available, and with the lower par value, they do not require as large a capital outlay. Table 5-1 lists some of these securities. The first of the issues listed is Duke Capital's Trust Originated Preferred Securities (TOPrS), with a coupon of 7.35 percent and a maturity in the year 2038. The ratings on this issue by Moody's and Standard & Poor's, respectively, are Baa1 and A−. The closing price of this issue as of December 25, 1998, was $25³/₈, which is a slight premium to its par value. There is a call provision for this issue because the yield to call is 6.98 percent. If this issue is bought at $25³/₈ per share and held to maturity in the year 2038, the yield to maturity will be 7.25 percent.

The other issues, Shaw Communications' Canadian Originated Preferred Securities (COPrS) and Hartford Capital's Quarterly Income Preferred Securities (QUIPS), are read the same way.

There are some caveats that investors should be aware of:

- Be cautious when paying a premium for an issue with a call provision. If the issue is called, you will receive the par value, $25, which means that you will have lost some of your capital.
- These companies can suspend their dividends during times of financial hardship.

**TABLE 5-1**

Quasi-Corporate Debt Preferred Securities Issues

| Company | Issue | Rating | Price | Yield to Call | Yield to Maturity |
|---------|-------|--------|-------|---------------|-------------------|
| Duke Capital | 7.35% TOPrS due 2038 | Baa1/A– | $25^3/_8$ | 6.98% | 7.25% |
| Shaw Communications | 8.45% COPrS due 2046 | Ba2/BBB | $24^5/_{16}$ | 9.31% | 8.71% |
| Hartford Capital | 7.7% QUIPS due 2016 | A2/A– | $25^7/_8$ | 6.91% | 7.54% |

Source: *Barron's*, December 28, 1998, p. 20.

- Companies with balance sheets that are overleveraged sometimes use this type of security to raise funds. Consequently, you should look for issues with strong credit ratings.

## CORPORATE BOND MUTUAL FUNDS

Instead of investing directly in individual corporate bond issues, investors may choose to invest indirectly in these issues through corporate bond mutual funds. The mutual fund pools the money from investors and invests in different corporate bond issues. Investors receive shares in the fund proportionate to the amount of their investment. See Chapter 11 for a more complete discussion of the basics of mutual funds.

## HOW TO CHOOSE A CORPORATE BOND MUTUAL FUND

The types of corporate bonds chosen by the fund will be determined by its objectives. Corporate bonds may be categorized in terms of:

- *Quality.* The higher the credit quality of the fund, the lower the risk and the yields. The lower the credit quality of the fund, the higher the risk and potential returns.

■ *Maturity.*   This is the average length of time to maturity of the corporate bonds in the fund. These are generally classified as short-term, intermediate-term, and long-term. The longer the maturity, the greater the risk and the greater the potential returns (assuming a normal yield curve).

Table 5-2 shows the types of bond funds issued by mutual fund families using these two dimensions. Not every fund family offers all nine permutations of these corporate bond funds, but this is a good planning tool to use to determine which type of corporate bond fund or funds to invest in.

The lower your risk tolerance, the more you would move to the left side of the table, and depending on your time horizon, to the top, middle, or the bottom of the table. If you have a long time horizon, you would choose the middle or bottom rows (intermediate-term and long-term funds), which are also the most sensitive to changes in market rates of interest.

This grid is a good tool to identify the corporate bond mutual fund or funds that best conforms to both your time horizon and level of risk tolerance. If you cannot determine which types of funds are suitable, it is not advisable to invest in all nine different corporate bond funds by default. This would be overkill. Nor is it advisable to have all your eggs in one basket, so to speak. You do want some diversification in your bond portfolio.

## TABLE 5-2

Types of Corporate Bond Mutual Funds

| Maturity | | High | Medium<br>Quality | Low |
|---|---|---|---|---|
| | Short-<br>term | High-quality<br>short-term<br>fund | Medium-quality<br>short-term<br>fund | Low-quality<br>short-term<br>fund |
| | Int.-<br>term | High-quality<br>intermediate-term<br>fund | Medium-quality<br>intermediate-term<br>fund | Low-quality<br>intermediate-term<br>fund |
| | Long-<br>term | High-quality<br>long-term<br>fund | Medium-quality<br>long-term<br>fund | Low-quality<br>long-term<br>fund |

High-quality bonds have a low risk of default. Low-quality bonds and junk bonds have a high risk of default.

Short-term bond funds have an average maturity of 1 to 3 years for their bonds.

Intermediate-term bond funds have an average maturity of 7 to 10 years for their bonds.

Long-term bond funds have an average maturity of 15 to 25 years for their bonds.

## WHAT ARE THE RISKS OF CORPORATE BOND MUTUAL FUNDS?

In addition to the risks that pertain to the mutual funds, corporate bond funds are exposed to many of the same risks as the corporate bonds that are their underlying assets.

The *risk of default* is a greater risk for corporate bonds than for other types of bonds. However, with corporate bond mutual funds, the risk of loss from the default of an individual corporate bond issue is lessened. The diversification achieved by bond mutual funds diminishes the impact of the loss from unexpected defaults. This is because the percentage share of each individual bond issue may be a small part of the total value of the bond fund.

The *risk of loss of principal* invested is always present with bond mutual funds. Unlike money market funds, in which the net asset values (the share prices) are held constant, the share prices of bond mutual funds fluctuate. This is because the bonds held by the funds fluctuate in value daily, responding to changes in interest rates, credit quality, and length of time to maturity. If the share price of the bond mutual fund falls below the purchase price of the shares at the time of sale, the investor will experience a loss of principal invested.

*Interest rate risk* will impact the share price of bond funds differently depending on the composition of the bonds in the funds. For example, the share prices of two different long-term bond funds will react differently to the same increase in market rates of interest. If the one bond mutual fund has an average maturity of 15 years and the other 25 years, the latter fund will be exposed to a greater fall in share price when market rates of interest rise. Similarly, the quality of the bonds will affect the volatility of the share price. A high ratio of low-quality bonds (i.e., junk bonds, or bonds below investment-grade) will be much more volatile than a fund composed of higher-quality bonds. This is why it is important to read the prospectus of each mutual fund before investing. The stated objective of the fund will determine the latitude the mutual fund manager has in choosing investments. For example, if the stated objective of the mutual fund is to invest 65 percent in investment-grade corporate bonds, the investor then knows that the other 35 percent should be examined for credit quality. The mutual fund manager can then increase the overall yield of the fund by investing that 35 percent of the fund in higher-yielding lower-quality bonds.

## HOW TO BUY CORPORATE BOND MUTUAL FUNDS

Corporate bond mutual funds can be purchased directly through the mutual fund families or indirectly through brokers, financial planners, and banks. The key difference between buying mutual funds directly and indirectly is that in the latter case, you will be paying a load, or commission. When you buy indirectly through a broker or financial planner, you pay a commission for the advice. Table 4-1 in the previous chapter shows the effect of a load on the funds invested. These load funds have to work a lot harder to recoup the charges and equal the results of no-load funds, in which all the invested funds are put to work.

Why then do investors buy these load funds? The first reason seems to be that many investors feel insecure about choosing a fund on their own. Buying through a broker seems to give them the peace of mind that someone else has made the appropriate choice of mutual funds for them. Yet when you compare the mutual funds offered by the brokerage houses, such as Merrill Lynch and Smith Barney, with those offered by the Vanguard family of funds, the overriding difference boils down to cost. The brokerage house mutual funds charge loads and the operating costs of these funds are much higher than the no-load Vanguard funds, which have the lowest operating costs in the mutual fund industry. These operating costs are paid for by none other than you, the investor!

Second, many brokers tout that load funds outperform no-load funds. This is a stretch with bond mutual funds. After the loads are deducted, it is very hard for a load corporate bond fund to catch up to the no-load fund, let alone outperform it. This is because bonds are not like stocks, where the skill in picking stocks can be a factor. If investment-grade bonds return 8 percent, the only way a mutual fund manager can boost the returns of his investment-grade corporate bond fund is to invest in higher-risk lower-quality bonds. As pointed out in the previous section, buying a corporate bond fund for the higher yield can also result in a greater loss of capital should interest rates rise.

No-load corporate bond mutual funds may be purchased directly through the mutual fund family. The financial magazines and newspapers publish the quarterly results of the different bond funds. By analyzing the long-run performances of these funds, you can narrow your list of prospective funds to choose from. Call the toll-free numbers of these funds to obtain their prospectuses. Chapter 11 goes through the criteria you should examine before you invest.

When you have decided on a bond mutual fund, you need to fill out the application form, which can be sent through the mail, or you can sign up with the fund over the Internet. Many fund families are on the Internet, and you can get their information on-line.

Investors should also determine whether a fund has a *back-end load*. This is a charge deducted from your proceeds when you sell your shares in a fund. Many funds may include this back-end fee and advertise that there is no front-end load when shares are bought. Look for this fee in the prospectus of the fund. A no-load fund could have this back-end fee, which is as insidious as a front-end load. If a fund has a back-end fee, look for another fund to invest in.

By doing your own research, you can increase your overall return by making your own choice of corporate bond mutual funds to invest in.

## WHAT ARE THE ADVANTAGES OF CORPO-RATE BOND MUTUAL FUNDS?

- Corporate bond mutual funds offer small investors the opportunity to own a fraction of a diversified corporate bond portfolio. By investing the minimum amounts allowed by corporate bond mutual funds, investors own a proportionate share of an excellent cross section of corporate bonds, whereas buying individual corporate bond issues would require an investment of at least $100,000 for a diversified portfolio.
- Corporate bond mutual funds are professionally managed. This is particularly advantageous for investors who do not

have the time or inclination to research and evaluate individual corporate bond issues.

- Mutual funds offer a range of different corporate bond funds with different characteristics. Investors can choose those corporate bond funds that are consistent with their time horizons and levels of risk tolerance.
- The shares of corporate bond mutual funds are easier to sell than individual bond issues.
- Corporate bond mutual fund yields may be higher than those of other types of bond funds. This is especially so for high-yield junk bond funds, which if purchased when interest rates are falling, offer the opportunity of greater capital gains than lower-yielding funds.
- When there are small increases in market rates of interest, the share prices of high-yielding corporate bond mutual funds may not fall by as much as the share prices of lower-yielding corporate bond funds. However, the higher-yielding funds also may have greater risk of default, which could cause the share prices of these junk bond funds to fall more than better-quality funds.

See Chapter 11 for the advantages of all mutual funds, which, of course, apply to corporate bond mutual funds.

## WHAT ARE THE DISADVANTAGES OF COR-PORATE BOND MUTUAL FUNDS?

- With corporate bond mutual funds, there is always the risk of capital loss from having to sell shares at a lower price than the purchase price, even with a long time horizon. This is because *corporate bond mutual funds never mature.* When the individual bonds in the fund mature, they are replaced with new issues.
- Corporate bond mutual funds pay dividends that are taxed at all levels of government, whereas municipal bond and Treasury bond mutual funds offer some tax breaks.

See Chapter 11 for the disadvantages of all mutual bond funds, which also apply to corporate bond mutual funds.

## CAVEATS

- Load bond funds rarely outperform no-load bond funds. To increase total returns over long periods of time, stick with no-load corporate bond funds.
- In periods of rising inflation and rising interest rates, the share prices of corporate bond mutual funds will fall, resulting in capital losses for shareholders. In this economic climate, high-yielding corporate junk bond funds may not give shareholders immunity from sliding share prices due to the increased default risk from the lower-quality bond issues in those funds.
- Choose corporate bond funds from mutual fund families that have a wide range of different funds. This allows you greater flexibility to transfer from one fund type to another.

## CORPORATE BONDS VERSUS CORPORATE BOND MUTUAL FUNDS

Both corporate bonds and corporate bond mutual funds offer investors the opportunities to increase their yields over other bond investments. The best time to buy corporate bonds or corporate bond mutual funds is when market interest rates are falling and inflation is low. For investors who cannot tolerate high risk, junk bond issues and junk bond funds should be avoided. These risk-averse investors should look for high-quality issues and funds.

The advantages of investing in corporate bond mutual funds over individual issues are:

- You do not need a large sum of money to invest in a mutual fund. Whatever the stated minimum amounts of the funds are, that's all you need.
- With mutual funds, investors buy into a diversified portfolio of bonds, which would take significant amounts of money to achieve when buying corporate issues individually.
- Mutual funds have professional managers, who have both expertise and quick access to information about the individual bond issues and bond markets.

■ It is not as risky to invest in corporate junk bond mutual
  funds than individual junk bond issues. The diversification
  achieved by mutual funds minimizes the impact from any
  unexpected defaults.

The advantages of individual bond issues over corporate bond
mutual funds are:

■ Investors in individual corporate bonds avoid the fees
  charged by mutual funds, which reduce the returns of
  mutual funds. Mutual funds charge shareholders with
  operating fees, such as 12b-1 fees and other fees, which are
  over and above any loads charged. All mutual funds have
  these operating fees. Look for those funds that have low
  operating fees, such as the Vanguard family of funds,
  which currently are among the lowest-cost funds in the
  industry. Investors in individual corporate issues have the
  potential to earn higher total returns than mutual funds,
  depending on the composition of their bond investments.

■ Individual bonds have maturity dates. By laddering your
  portfolio of individual corporate bonds, you can time the
  maturities of the bonds to your needs for the cash, always
  getting back the full amount of your principal invested and
  avoiding interest rate risk. Corporate bond mutual funds
  never mature. So even if you have a long time horizon,
  when you need the money, the share price of the mutual
  fund may have fallen below your original purchase price.

■ For tax planning purposes, owning individual bonds offers
  investors more control over their capital gains and losses
  than owning mutual funds. Mutual funds do not pay taxes
  on the gains and losses from the sale of corporate bonds
  before maturity. These gains and losses are passed on to the
  shareholders at the end of the year, which can ruin any
  careful tax planning. Bear in mind that both interest income
  from individual corporate bonds and the dividend income
  from corporate bond mutual funds are taxable at all levels
  of government.

Table 5-3 summarizes the advantages of investing in corporate
bond mutual funds versus individual corporate bond issues.

**TABLE 5-3**

Advantages of Individual Corporate Bonds versus
Corporate Mutual Funds

|                              | Individual Bonds | Mutual Funds |
|------------------------------|:----------------:|:------------:|
| Small amount to invest       |                  | ✓            |
| Junk bonds                   |                  | ✓            |
| Risk of loss from default    |                  | ✓            |
| Risk of loss of principal    | ✓                |              |
| Possibility of higher returns| ✓                |              |
| Tax planning                 | ✓                |              |

# REFERENCES

**Antilla, Susan:** "Nonrefundable Bonds Can Indeed Be Refunded," *The New York Times,* November 21, 1992.

**Doherty, Jacqueline:** "Bite-Sized Bonds," *Barron's,* December 28, 1998, p. 20.

**Faerber, Esmé:** *Managing Your Investments, Savings and Credit,* McGraw-Hill, New York, 1992.

**Faerber, Esmé:** *All About Stocks,* McGraw-Hill, New York, 1995.

**Mayo, Herbert B.:** *Investments,* Dryden Press, Orlando, FL, 1991.

**Thau, Annette:** *The Bond Book,* McGraw-Hill, New York, 1992.

**Zuckerman, Gregory:** "Online Push Barely Budges Bond Trading," *The Wall Street Journal,* December 28, 1998, pp. C1, C15.

## CHAPTER 6

# Treasury Securities and Treasury Security Mutual Funds

## KEY CONCEPTS

- U.S. Treasury notes and bonds
- Treasury inflation-indexed securities
- U.S. savings bonds
- Inflation-indexed savings bonds
- Treasury bond mutual funds

The U.S. federal government issues a wide variety of debt instruments, primarily to fund the ever-increasing budget deficit. The budget deficit is the result of the government spending more than the revenues it collects from taxes. The government raises money to fund its expenditures by issuing securities in the money and capital markets. There are no limitations on the government's ability to pay its interest obligations, and so the government has few restrictions on its ability to create money. This is a major reason why U.S. Treasury securities are considered to be safe from default. The U.S. Treasury is very unlikely to default on its interest payments and principal repayments because not only can the government create money, it can also print money and tax the public.

The U.S. government is the largest single borrower in the U.S. long-term bond market, and there are many different investors who are snapping up the U.S. Treasury debt offerings.

---

The section on U.S. savings bonds has been previously published by Esmé Faerber in *Managing Your Investments, Savings, and Credit,* McGraw-Hill, New York, 1992, p. 85.

These include individual residents, institutional investors (banks, mutual funds, insurance companies, pension funds), and corporations in the U.S., and also foreign buyers. Foreigners have increased their holdings of U.S. Treasury securities. These foreign buyers come from both the private and public sectors abroad. For example, the central banks of the industrialized nations bought up U.S. Treasuries to stem the fall in the value of foreign currencies against the dollar. Of course, the speculation in the credit markets is whether these foreigners will continue to fund the U.S. deficit through such activities in the future.

Treasury offerings consist of U.S. Treasury bills, U.S. Treasury notes, and U.S. Treasury bonds. United States savings bonds are also issued by the government to fund the deficit. Treasury bills are non-interest-bearing, discount securities with an original maturity of one year or less. They are discussed in Chapter 4. Treasury notes are intermediate securities with maturities ranging from two to ten years, and Treasury bonds are long-term bonds that have maturities over ten years. Both Treasury notes and bonds are marketable securities, whereas U.S. savings bonds are nonmarketable government debt. U.S. savings bonds are small denomination securities with various maturities designed to encourage savings by small investors. Savings bonds are discussed after Treasury notes and bonds in this chapter.

## U.S. TREASURY NOTES AND BONDS

Treasury notes and bonds are coupon securities and differ from Treasury bills. Coupon securities pay interest every six months, whereas Treasury bills are discount securities on which periodic interest payments are not made. Instead, with Treasury bills the interest is received at maturity, and it is the difference between the face value received and the purchase price.

### U.S. Treasury Notes

U.S. Treasury notes are issued with original maturities ranging from two to ten years. Table 6-1 lists the basic information for new Treasury notes and bonds.

**TABLE 6-1**

Treasury Notes and Bonds

| Term | Minimum | Multiples | Announcement | Auction Date | Issue Date |
|------|---------|-----------|--------------|--------------|------------|
| 2-year note | $5000 | $1000 | Middle of each month | One week later | Last day of the month |
| 3-year note | $5000 | $1000 | First Wed. in the quarter | One week later | 2/15, 5/15, 8/15, 11/15 |
| 5-year note | $1000 | $1000 | Middle of each month | One week later | Last day of the month |
| 10-year note | $1000 | $1000 | First Wed. in the quarter | One week later | 2/15, 5/15, 8/15, 11/15 |
| 30-year bond | $1000 | $1000 | First Wed. in the quarter | One week later | 2/15, 5/15, 8/15, 11/15 |

Treasury notes are not callable, and interest payments are made semiannually (beginning six months from the date of issue).

## U.S. Treasury Bonds

Treasury bonds have original maturities of more than 10 years. Currently, 30-year Treasury bonds are offered for sale every three months, on the 15th of February, May, August, and November. These 30-year Treasury bonds can be bought with a minimum purchase of $1000 and in multiples of $1000 thereafter.

Many outstanding Treasury bond issues are callable, generally within five years of maturity. Since 1985, however, the Treasury has not issued any callable bonds.

In the newspapers, callable Treasury bonds can be identified by two dates in the maturity column, as shown in the following example:

| Rate | Maturity Mo/Yr | Bid | Asked Chg | Asked Yld |
|------|----------------|-----|-----------|-----------|
| 7 | May 93–98 | 100.29 | 101.05... | 3.65 |

This 7-percent coupon Treasury bond matured in May 1998, but it could have been called beginning in 1993. The yield to maturity was 3.65 percent and was based on the call date and not the maturity date. This is why the yield to maturity (asked yield) was so much less than the coupon rate, plus the fact that the bond was trading at a premium.

In the past, there have been many outstanding Treasury bonds which were very different from the rest of the Treasuries. Although these have all matured, it is useful to describe them in case they are reintroduced. They were called *flower bonds*, and they had the following coupons and maturities:

| Coupon | Maturity |
| --- | --- |
| $4^1/_8$ | May 15, 1989–1994 |
| 3 | February 15, 1995 |
| $3^1/_2$ | November 15, 1998 |

Flower bonds were issued by the Treasury in the 1950s and early 1960s. All have subsequently matured and are no longer issued. They were used to settle federal estate taxes. For example, if an individual decedent owned $150,000 par (face) value flower bonds and the decedent's estate owed $150,000 in federal taxes, these bonds were accepted by the Internal Revenue Service at par values (even though they were worth less at market value). Due to their low coupon rates, these bonds sold at a discount. For instance, the 3-percent, February 15, 1995, bonds had an asked price of $99.10 ($99^{10}/_{52}$), or $993.125, per bond on January 6, 1993. Thus, if these were used to settle the $150,000 federal estate tax liability in the example above, the Internal Revenue Service would have accepted 150 of these bonds, even though the market value was only $148,968.75. However, if flower bonds were sold at a premium at the time of the holder's death, the gain was taxed as a capital gain.

In the early 1980s, several brokerage firms packaged U.S. Treasuries in the form of zero-coupon Treasury packages, such as Salomon Brothers' Certificates of Accrual on Treasury Securities (CATS) and Merrill Lynch's Treasury Investment Growth Receipts (TIGRs). In 1984, the Treasury Department announced its own program of packaging zero-coupon Treasuries, known as STRIPS (Separate Trading of Registered Interest and Principal of

Securities). See Chapter 10 on zero-coupon bonds for a detailed description of these securities.

## What Are the Risks of Treasuries?

Since Treasuries are direct obligations of the federal government, there is no *credit risk* and no *risk of default*. This is why Treasury securities have lower coupon yields than agency and corporate bonds.

Treasuries issued since 1985 are free from both *event risk* and *call risk* (if you avoid buying outstanding Treasury bonds, which are subject to call). Treasury securities are subject to *inflation rate risk*. (See the next section on the new inflation-indexed Treasury securities, which protect against the risk of inflation.)

As with all fixed-income securities, Treasuries are subject to *interest rate risk*. Bond prices react inversely to changes in market rates of interest, but prices are also tied to the length of time to maturity. Thus, long-term (30-year) Treasury bond prices will see the greatest volatility due to changes in market rates of interest. The shorter the maturities, the lower the price volatility in relation to changes in interest rates.

## How to Buy and Sell Treasury Notes and Bonds

Investors may purchase new issues or outstanding Treasury issues that trade on the secondary market.

### New Issues

New issues of Treasury notes and bonds may be purchased at auction or through brokerage firms and commercial banks. Buying through banks and brokerage firms involves paying commissions, which will vary depending on the face value of the securities purchased and the markup charged for the purchase. For example, on a purchase of $10,000 in Treasury bonds, the commission would typically be in the range of $50.

To avoid having to pay commissions, investors may purchase new issues directly, as they are being auctioned by the Federal Reserve Bank.

Auctions of new issues take place on a regular schedule (Table 6-1). You can also call the Federal Reserve Bank in your area (see Figure 4-1) to put you on their mailing list for new note and bond issues. There is also a 24-hour Reserve Bank information number about forthcoming auctions. The financial newspapers also list the schedules of forthcoming auctions.

When buying directly, you will first need to open an account with the Federal Reserve. By completing a new account request form (Figure 4-2), you can establish a Treasury Direct account where your Treasury securities are held in book form. Treasury certificates are no longer issued. After submitting this form to the Federal Reserve Bank or branch in your area, you will receive confirmation of your account and your own account number pertaining to the information in your account. This account number is used for all your purchases of Treasury securities (bills, notes, bonds, and inflation-indexed securities) and is maintained free of charge up to $100,000. For security amounts over this, there is a $25 fee per year.

You are now ready to fill out a tender form to buy Treasury notes or bonds at auction from the Federal Reserve Bank (see Figure 4-3). This is the same form used for Treasury bills and the new inflation-indexed Treasury securities.

Besides filling in your personal information on the tender form, you will need to supply information about your bank account so that payments by the Treasury can be made by direct deposit to your account. The routing number is a nine-digit number that identifies the financial institution where you bank. It can be found on the bottom corner of your check before your account number.

On the form, you have a choice of buying Treasuries using a competitive or noncompetitive bid.

More sophisticated investors use the *competitive bid,* in which they submit a yield bid for the issue to two decimal places (e.g., 4.06 percent). Investors can get an idea of the probable range of the yield to submit by watching the preauction trading of that issue. Dealers begin trading these securities a few days before the auction on a "when-issued basis," and the when-issued yield is often reported in *The Wall Street Journal* and *The New York Times* financial section.

Investors submit their sealed, written bids, and the Treasury accepts the bids with the lowest yields until the supply is sold. Thus, within the range of accepted bids, the accepted bidders who bid lowest are penalized with a lesser return than the accepted higher bidders. Understandably, this is known as the "winner's curse." However, investors who bid too aggressively run the risk of losing out in that auction by not having their bids accepted.

In an attempt to lower its borrowing costs, the Treasury Department experimented with a new method of selling the 2- and 5-year Treasury notes during the period from September 1992 through August 1993. This experiment was called the *single-price,* or "Dutch," auction and worked in the following way:

- Like the regular auction, investors submitted their sealed bids.
- The Treasury started accepting bids from the lowest yield on up to the yield where the supply of notes was used up.
- All the winning bidders received the highest accepted bids for the auction.

For example, if the Treasury announced a $9 billion 2-year note sale and the range of accepted bids was between 4.72 percent and 4.74 percent, all the bidders received 4.74 percent. This method eliminated the winner's curse.

You might wonder how this method would have helped the Treasury reduce borrowing costs, since it ended up paying the highest accepted yields at these "Dutch" auctions. The premise for this type of auction method was that by eliminating the winner's curse, more bidders would participate and would offer lower yields (higher prices).

For the four single-price auctions for 2-year and 5-year Treasury notes held between September 22–23 and December 22–23, 1992, the results were mixed. From the Treasury's point of view, the 2-year notes were more successful than the 5-year notes in that for the 2-year note, dealers paid higher prices (lower yields). This saved some money for the Treasury. But on the 5-year notes, the Treasury lost money. The Treasury has now adopted this single-price, or Dutch, auction method for all 2-year and 5-year notes.

Investors who do not want to run the risk of having their bids rejected or who do not know what to bid can submit *noncompetitive bids.* With noncompetitive bids, investors are able to buy Treasury notes and bonds at the average accepted bid in the auction. All noncompetitive tenders up to $1,000,000 per bidder are accepted.

Tender forms to submit bids may be sent by mail or taken in person to the Federal Reserve Bank or a branch before the close of the auction. Competitive bids must be received by the time designated in the offering circular. Noncompetitive bids that are mailed must be postmarked by no later than midnight the day before the auction and received on or before the issue date of the securities.

Payment must accompany the tender form, and the amount of the check should be for the face value of the securities. If the auction price is less than the face value, you will receive a check for the difference. If the auction price of the note or bond is higher than the face value, you will receive an amount due notice for the difference.

On acceptance of your bid, you will receive a confirmation receipt from the Federal Reserve. The treasury pays interest on notes and bonds every six months.

About 45 days before maturity of the notes or bonds, a reinvestment option notification is mailed to all note or bondholders giving them the option of reinvesting in a new issue. If you decline the reinvestment option, the redemption payment is made directly into your bank account on the maturity date.

The U.S. Treasury Department has made Treasury notes and bonds available to investors who would like to purchase them online through the Treasury Direct program.

Should investors decide to sell their Treasury notes or bonds before maturity, there is an active secondary market. If you bought directly from the Federal Reserve, before selling, you fill out a transfer request form (PD 5179), which transfers your account from the Treasury Direct book-entry system to the commercial book-entry system. Then you can sell your Treasury notes and bonds. The commercial book-entry system records Treasuries bought through financial institutions and government-security dealers. You need to use a bank or broker to sell Treasuries in the secondary market.

Information, updates on auctions, and news on all Treasury securities can be obtained at *www.publicdebt.treas.gov.*

Existing Issues

Investors can buy and sell existing issues through banks or brokers. There are many issues and a wide range of maturities trading at discounts or premiums, depending on their coupon rates and length of time to maturity. Like corporate bonds, Treasury notes and bonds are quoted in the financial sections of newspapers under the heading Treasury Issues. Ask your banker or broker for a dealer's quote sheet to see what existing issues are available.

The secondary market for Treasuries is an over-the-counter market, where dealers quote bid and asked prices. Due to the liquidity of many of the issues, the spreads on Treasuries are the smallest of all the fixed-income securities (rarely larger than $\frac{1}{8}$ of a point). It is an active market, with huge quantities of Treasuries being traded.

## What Are the Advantages of Treasury Notes and Bonds?

- Virtually no credit or default risk exists, since they are direct obligations of the federal government.
- A wide range of maturities is available.
- Interest is exempt from state and local taxes.
- Thanks to an active secondary market, they are extremely liquid and marketable.
- Transaction costs and fees can be avoided by buying directly from the Federal Reserve Bank and its branches.
- Markups on trading Treasuries are the lowest of all the fixed-income securities.
- Some issues (5- and 10-year notes and 30-year bonds) have lower purchase minimums of $1000, making them affordable for small investors. Treasury notes with 2- and 3-year maturities have $5000 minimum purchase amounts.

## What Are the Disadvantages of Treasury Notes and Bonds?

- Yields on Treasuries are lower than agency and corporate bonds of comparable maturities.

- They do not protect against rising inflation. Losses in purchasing power and investment capital will occur if the rate of inflation exceeds the coupon rate.
- For the longer-maturity Treasury bonds, there is interest rate risk. If interest rates go up after long-term bonds are bought, the market price of these bonds will go down. Investors could lose a significant part of their investment if they are forced to sell under these conditions before maturity.

Interest rates have become quite volatile since 1979. Investors who have locked into current coupons of 5 to 6 percent for 30-year maturities may see coupons go up considerably in the future for equivalent maturities, resulting in declining bond prices.

### Caveats

Avoid longer maturities unless you are confident that both inflation and market rates of interest are headed downwards in the future.

## TREASURY INFLATION-INDEXED SECURITIES

As part of its new program to provide inflation-indexed securities, the Treasury has unveiled three inflation-indexed bonds, which began trading in January 1997, and the new inflation-indexed savings bonds, which began trading September 1998. Inflation-indexed savings bonds are discussed later in this chapter.

Treasury inflation-indexed bonds offer protection against rising inflation, but because inflation is at historic lows, around 2 percent as of this writing, these bonds have not generated all that much enthusiasm. According to an article in *The Wall Street Journal*, only $58 billion of 5-year, 10-year, and 30-year inflation-indexed bonds were auctioned in the 18-month period from January 1997 to mid-1998 (Simon, July 13, 1998, C1).

These inflation-indexed Treasury securities pay a regular coupon rate plus an amount that is indexed for inflation. For example, assume an investor purchases a bond with a rate of $3\frac{1}{2}$ percent at $1000. If inflation averages 2 percent for the year, the price of the bond is adjusted for this inflation to $1020. The coupon rate of $3\frac{1}{2}$ percent is paid on the adjusted value of the bond ($3\frac{1}{2}\% \times \$1020$). The opposite is true if inflation falls. The price of the bond is adjusted downward, and the interest payments are calculated against the lower bond price. See Table 6-2 for more information on inflation-indexed securities.

Currently, the 10-year Treasury note is yielding 5.6 percent, and the 10-year inflation-indexed bond is yielding 3.8 percent. This means that for the inflation-indexed bond to do better than the regular Treasury note, inflation would have to increase by more than 1.8 percent (5.6% − 3.8%) over the next 10 years (Simon, July 13, 1998, pp. C1, C18).

The downside to these inflation-indexed Treasuries is that holders must pay federal income taxes on the interest plus the inflation adjustment, even though this inflation adjustment is only paid out when the bond matures. In other words, there is a negative cash flow on this "phantom" adjustment income, which makes these investments more suitable as part of tax-deferred accounts. Interest is exempt from state and local taxes.

## TABLE 6-2

### Treasury Inflation-Indexed Securities

- The interest rate, which is set at auction, remains fixed throughout the term of the security.
- The principal amount of the security is adjusted for inflation, but the inflation-adjusted principal is paid only at maturity.
- Semiannual interest payments are based on the inflation-adjusted principal at the time the interest is paid.
- The auction process uses the single-priced (Dutch) auction method for these securities.
- The securities are eligible for "stripping" into principal and interest components in the Treasury's Separate Trading of Registered Interest and Principal of Securities (STRIPS) Program. See Chapter 10 for a more complete discussion on stripped securities.
- At maturity the securities are redeemed at the greater of their inflation-adjusted principal or par amount at original issue.

Source: www.publicdebt.treas.gov.

## What Are the Risks of Inflation-Indexed Treasury Securities?

Like regular Treasury notes and bonds, there is neither *credit risk* nor the *risk of default* with inflation-indexed bonds.

These securities, like all other fixed-income securities, are subject to *interest rate risk*. Yields on these securities are much lower than regular Treasury issues, and if inflation remains low, any changes in interest rates will make the prices of these securities more volatile. This is especially so for the longer-maturity issues.

Although these securities protect against *inflation risk*, there is a downside if inflation does not rise during the holding period. Total returns on these securities will be much lower than all other fixed-income securities.

## How to Buy Inflation-Indexed Treasury Securities

Investors may purchase new inflation-indexed issues directly or outstanding issues that trade on the secondary market.

### New Issues

These securities can be bought directly at auction through the Federal Reserve Bank system as part of the Treasury Direct program. Table 6-3 lists the denominations and auction information. These securities are bought through the Federal Reserve Bank system in the same way described in the previous section of this chapter for regular Treasury notes and bonds.

### Existing Issues

Like regular Treasury notes and bonds, existing inflation-indexed securities can be bought and sold through brokers, who charge commissions for their services. There is a secondary market for these issues, and quotes for the individual issues can be found in the Treasury note and bond sections of the newspapers. Because of the newness of this type of security, there are not that many issues to choose from on the secondary markets.

## TABLE 6-3

Treasury Inflation-Indexed Securities

| Term | Minimum | Multiples | Auction | Issue Date |
|---|---|---|---|---|
| 5-year | $1000 | $1000 | Quarterly | One week later |
| 10-year | $1000 | $1000 | Jan., Apr., July, Oct. | One week later |
| 30-year | $1000 | $1000 | Quarterly | One week later |

## What Are the Advantages of Inflation-Indexed Treasury Securities?

- Low purchase minimums of $1000 make these securities affordable for small investors.
- No credit or default risk makes them safe investments for those who have trouble sleeping at night if the economy goes into recession.
- Interest payments are exempt from state and local taxes.
- These securities are liquid and marketable due to the active secondary market.
- Investors can avoid any transaction costs by buying the securities directly from the Federal Reserve Banks.
- These securities provide protection against rising inflation.

## What Are the Disadvantages of Inflation-Indexed Treasury Securities?

- Inflation-indexed securities are subject to interest rate risk, which has more of an effect on the longer-maturity issues due to the low coupon yields of these securities. When interest rates rise, the prices of these securities will fall.
- If inflation remains low, returns on these securities will be lower than regular Treasury notes and bonds of similar maturities.
- Paying federal taxes on the inflation adjustment, which is only received at maturity, creates a negative cash flow.

## Caveats

Unless inflation rises during the holding period, these securities will yield lower returns than regular Treasury securities.

# U.S. SAVINGS BONDS

U.S. savings bonds are nonmarketable securities issued and backed in full by the U.S. government. In the 1960s and 1970s, when inflation was high, investing in U.S. savings bonds was a patriotic decision rather than a good investment. Rates of return on savings bonds were low and did not equal the returns of other comparable investments. Thus, in order to compete with other investments, the U.S. Treasury increased the rates of interest on U.S. savings bonds. With market rates of interest currently on the low end of the spectrum, U.S. savings bonds look quite attractive with their guaranteed floor yield of 4 percent per annum over a five-year period.

## EE Savings Bonds

In 1980, the Treasury issued EE and HH savings bonds. EE series bonds are issued at a discount: a face value $50 EE bond costs $25, and similarly, a $200 EE bond costs $100. There are eight denominations for EE bonds, $50, $75, $100, $200, $500, $1000, $5000, and $10,000. The $50 and $75 savings bonds are not available through payroll savings plans.

The interest is paid at maturity or when the bond is cashed in. EE bonds are accrual securities. The interest is added every six months to the original amount of the price paid for the EE bond, which establishes the redemption value. In other words, the savings bond increases in value when the interest accrues.

EE bonds bought on or after May 1, 1997, will receive interest based on 5-year Treasury security yields right from the start. The new rate on the EE bonds will be 90 percent of the average yields on the 5-year Treasury securities for the preceding six months. EE bonds will increase in value every month instead of every six months, as was the case in the past. Interest is compounded semiannually.

However, there is a three-month interest penalty which will apply if these bonds are cashed in before five years. For example, if, after holding EE bonds for 18 months, the holder cashes them in, interest paid will only be for 15 months.

EE savings bonds can earn interest for 30 years. There is a floor price for these bonds (a floor yield) of 4 percent. If market rates of interest fall so low that the savings bond does not reach its face value by 17 years, the Treasury will make a one-time adjustment to increase the bond's value to the face value at that time. The value of the savings bond can increase to greater than its face value depending on interest rates and how long you hold them.

The yields for older savings bonds vary, and information on these bonds can be obtained at *www.publicdebt.treas.com,* or directly from the Federal Reserve Banks (see Figure 4-1).

Interest earned on EE bonds can be deferred from federal income taxes until the bonds mature or are redeemed. Interest is exempt from state and local taxes. EE bonds can be used for tax planning purposes and have the following tax advantages:

- By deferring the interest income annually until the bonds are cashed in, you can lower your federal taxable income in the years that you hold the bonds. You can also postpone the tax on the interest income for a further period by swapping the EE bonds at maturity for HH bonds. However, the interest received semiannually on the HH bonds is taxable at the federal level each year.

- EE bonds can be purchased for children under 14 years of age to avoid the children's income being taxed at their parent's marginal tax rates. At the time of this writing, children under 14 years of age pay no tax on investment income under a threshold level of income set by Congress. Investment income above a certain amount is taxed at the parent's marginal tax rates. After 14 years of age, investment income is taxed at the child's marginal rate. By deferring the interest income until the child turns 14 years of age, you can lower the child's tax liability. However, changes are always being made to the tax code, so check with your accountant to see if this treatment is still in effect.

- Currently, interest on savings bonds used to finance educational expenses is tax exempt at the federal level for married couples within adjusted gross income limits. This exemption is phased out proportionally over a certain level of adjusted gross income. Again, since changes are constantly being made to the tax code, check with your accountant as to possible changes and the adjusted gross income limits (also see Table 6-4).

## HH Savings Bonds

HH series bonds are only available through an exchange of E, H, or EE series savings bonds. (E and H series savings bonds have been replaced by EE and HH, respectively.) HH bonds differ from EE bonds in the following ways:

- HH bonds are issued at par value (or face value) in larger denominations.
- Interest is received every six months and is subject to federal tax each year. However, when you exchange your

### TABLE 6-4

Educational Benefits of Savings Bonds

The Educational Bond Program allows interest to be completely or partially excluded from federal taxes when the bond owner pays qualified higher education expenses at an eligible institution.

The bond owner may qualify for the exclusion for the educational expenses of a spouse or dependents. These bonds must have been purchased after 1990, and the funds must be used for tuition, not for room and board.

To qualify, the bond owner:

- Must be at least 24 years old by the first day of the month in which the bonds were bought.
- If the value of the bonds redeemed exceeds the amount of the eligible expenses paid, only a proportional amount of interest income may be excluded.
- A full exclusion is available only if the taxpayer's adjusted gross income (which must also include the interest earned on the redeemed savings bonds) is under certain limits for the year the bonds are redeemed. For 1998, the income limit is $52,250 of modified adjusted gross income or less for single taxpayers, and the exclusion is eliminated for adjusted gross incomes of $67,250 and above. For married taxpayers filing jointly, the tax exclusion begins to be reduced with $78,350 of modified adjusted gross income and is eliminated for adjusted gross incomes of $108,250 and up.

Source: www.publicdebt.treas.gov.

EE bonds for HH bonds, you can continue to defer paying federal taxes on the accumulated interest earned on the EE bonds.

- Holders receive only the face value at maturity, since interest is paid out every six months.
- Series HH bonds pay interest at fixed rates (now 4 percent) that can change 10 years after issue.

The denominations for HH savings bonds are: $500, $1000, $5000, and $10,000.

## How to Buy U.S. Savings Bonds

EE savings bonds can be bought (and redeemed) directly through the Bureau of Public Debt, at banks, savings and loan associations, and even through employers as payroll deductions.

Large-denomination bonds are handled through any of the Federal Reserve Banks. The denominations of EE bonds range from $50 to $10,000. The maximum investment in EE bonds is $30,000 per person per year.

HH bonds can be acquired through an exchange of E, H, or EE bonds through the Bureau of Public Debt or any of the Federal Reserve Banks or branches. The denominations for HH bonds range from $500 to $10,000.

There are no fees, handling charges, or commissions when you buy or sell U.S. savings bonds.

## What Are the Advantages of U.S. Savings Bonds?

- U.S. savings bonds are safe investments because interest and principal are guaranteed by the U.S. government.
- There are no fees, handling charges, or commissions when buying and selling.
- EE bonds provide a buildup of capital; HH bonds provide a steady source of income (every six months).
- The interest earned on U.S. savings bonds is exempt from state and local taxes.

- Interest earned on EE bonds is deferred from federal income taxes until the bonds are redeemed.
- U.S. savings bonds are not subject to interest rate risk.
- Investors are assured a minimum rate of return on their EE bonds held for five years, even if market rates of interest fall to lower levels, and if interest rates go up, investors can share in the higher yields.
- For bondholders who qualify, interest received on the redemption of savings bonds may be excluded from federal taxes when applied to qualified higher education expenses for a spouse or dependents.

## What Are the Disadvantages of U.S. Savings Bonds?

- Savings bonds must be held for five years in order to get the full interest rate. If held for less than five years, you receive the lower rates of interest due to the three-month penalty.
- They do not protect against rising rates of inflation. See the next section for a discussion on the new inflation-indexed savings bond.
- The Treasury does not allow them to be used as collateral, and neither can they be transferred as gifts. However, they may be transferred through an estate.
- Investors are limited to $30,000 face amount Series EE bonds per person per calendar year.
- Other securities pay higher rates of interest.

## Caveats

- Compare the returns of other "safe" investments, such as Treasury bills and Treasury notes; you may be able to increase your rate of return.
- Interest is always credited from the first day of the month, so when buying U.S. savings bonds, buy them at the end of the month to increase your overall rate of return.

# INFLATION-INDEXED SAVINGS BONDS (I-BONDS)

The U.S. Treasury Department unveiled a series of new savings bonds that are inflation-indexed for the benefit of small investors. These inflation-indexed savings bonds have returns that are pegged to the rate of inflation. Holders receive a fixed rate of interest for the life of the bond, plus an amount indexed for inflation, which is tied to the CPI-U (Consumer Price Inflation Index for Urban Workers).

These new savings bonds are offered in eight different denominations (see Table 6-5), with the lowest denomination at $50 in order to appeal to small investors. Unlike the EE savings bonds, which sell at a discount to their face values, these inflation-indexed savings bonds sell at their face values. A $50 inflation-indexed bond sells for $50 and matures in 30 years.

Interest payments for these inflation-indexed bonds come in two parts. First, there is a permanent fixed rate that is lower than the conventional savings bond. The second part is a variable rate which is reset every six months (in May and December), according to changes in the CPI-U, a measure of inflation. These interest payments are received at maturity or when the bond is cashed in. Holders of the bonds do not have to pay taxes on their gains until they cash in their bonds. In other words, both the interest payments and the taxes on the gains are deferred until the holders cash them in.

## TABLE 6-5

Denominations of Inflation-Indexed Savings Bonds

| | |
|---|---|
| $50 | Has the face of Helen Keller, the blind author, on the bond. |
| $75 | Hector Garcia, activist, on the bond. |
| $100 | Martin Luther King, Jr., American civil rights leader. |
| $200 | Chief Joseph of the Nez Perce Native Americans. |
| $500 | George Marshall, World War II general. |
| $1000 | Albert Einstein, German-Jewish physicist. |
| $5000 | Marion Anderson, the African-American vocalist. |
| $10,000 | Spark Matsunaga, Japanese-American senator. |

Inflation-indexed bonds will not be redeemed until six months after they are sold. Similarly, if holders redeem their bonds, having held them for less than five years, there is a three-month interest penalty.

Like EE savings bonds, inflation-indexed savings bonds offer small investors the safety and stability of bank savings accounts, plus inflation protection, should inflation increase.

## How to Buy Inflation-Indexed Savings Bonds

These can be bought and redeemed directly through the Bureau of Public Debt, banks, or savings and loan associations, and as with EE savings bonds, through employers as payroll deductions. Investors are limited in their purchases to up to $30,000 of these savings bonds in any one year.

There are no fees, handling charges, or commissions when you buy or sell inflation-indexed savings bonds.

## The Advantages of Inflation-Indexed Savings Bonds

- Returns on the inflation-indexed savings bonds are pegged to inflation, which gives holders protection against rising inflation.
- There are no fees, handling charges, or commissions to buy and sell these securities.
- Inflation-indexed savings bonds are safe investments because the interest and principal are guaranteed by the U.S. government.
- Inflation-indexed savings bonds provide a buildup of capital in that the interest is deferred from taxes and paid out when the bond is cashed.
- Inflation-indexed savings bonds can be purchased in amounts as little as $50.

## The Disadvantages of Inflation-Indexed Savings Bonds

- If inflation remains low, holders will earn lower rates than they would on conventional savings bonds.

- Inflation-indexed savings bonds must be held for five years to avoid the penalty of three months of interest for selling early.
- Sellers of inflation-indexed savings bonds have to wait six months after selling to receive their cash.
- Inflation-indexed savings bonds stop paying interest after 30 years.

### Caveats

- If inflation remains at its historic lows, inflation-indexed savings bonds will offer lower returns than regular EE savings bonds.
- Inflation-indexed savings bonds do not provide a good parking place for cash or for funds which are needed in less than five years. This is because of the penalty (three months of interest) if the bonds are sold within five years and the fact that the bonds will only be redeemed six months after they are sold.

## TREASURY BOND MUTUAL FUNDS

Investors can also invest in Treasury securities through Treasury mutual funds. The mutual fund investment company pools funds from investors and invests in different Treasury securities. Investors receive a number of shares proportional to the amounts invested in the fund. For a more complete discussion of the basics of mutual funds, see Chapter 11.

### How to Choose a Treasury Mutual Fund

Although the name *Treasury bond mutual fund* implies that the investment holdings should consist entirely of Treasury securities, this may or may not be the case. Many of these funds hold other types of securities besides Treasury issues, such as U.S. agency bonds, corporate bonds, foreign bonds, zero-coupon bonds, CMOs (collateralized mortgage obligations), and derivative issues tied to Treasury securities to boost the funds' returns. Looking at the name of the fund alone will not tell you very much about the fund's holdings.

Besides regular Treasury mutual funds, there are three mutual funds which invest in the new inflation-indexed Treasury securities: American Century Benham Inflation-Adjusted Treasury Fund, 59 Wall Street Inflation-Indexed Securities Fund, and Pimco Real Return Bond Fund (Simon, July 3, 1998, p. C1).

In this category of funds, in order to determine what you are investing in, you need to examine the prospectus of each fund that interests you.

The *objectives* of the fund will specify the types of securities, the quality, and the maturity range of the issues. Generally, if a fund uses the name Treasury in its title, it must hold at least 65 percent of its investments in Treasury securities. However, from a risk standpoint, what the fund holds in the other 35 percent is, or should be, just as important to the investor. Zero-coupon bonds, for example, can provide a wild roller-coaster ride when market rates of interest fluctuate. This is not what an investor wants to see when the title of the fund implies conservative holdings.

- Examine the holdings of the fund before investing. This might require a telephone call to the mutual fund investment company to ask specific questions about the holdings. For example, it is difficult to distinguish whether a bond is a regular bond or a CMO from its name.
- Ask about the risks of the fund. Treasuries have no credit risks, but other types of securities are subject to credit and default risks.
- Look at the average maturities of the holdings. In general, the longer the maturities, the greater the price fluctuations when interest rates change.
- Examine the fees charged by the funds, which can vary significantly. For bond funds of all types, it is always a good idea to go with the low-cost fund families.
- Don't choose a fund of this type based on the highest yield alone without looking at the other factors mentioned. In order to boost the returns over those yielded by Treasury securities, the fund could do any or all of the following:
  Invest in other types of securities, which increases the credit risk and the risk of default.

Actively trade their holdings, which provides greater capital gains and/or losses.

Increase the maturities of their holdings.

Hedge its positions, which can be costly if circumstances change in an unanticipated direction.

Use derivative securities to boost returns, but which also increases risk.

Temporarily reduce fees.

## What Are the Risks of Treasury Mutual Funds?

When Treasury securities are bought individually, there are no *credit risks* or *default risks*. However, this is not the case with a Treasury or government mutual fund that holds riskier non-Treasury securities as part of the other 35 percent of its holdings. Thus, there is an increase in the credit risk and risk of default for mutual funds. That is not to say that these risks are large. They are reduced by the diversification achieved by mutual funds. The risk of loss to an individual fund shareholder due to the default of an issue in the fund's holdings will not have as great an impact as it would have had that investor held the issue in an individual portfolio (unless the investor has an abnormally large diversified holding of bond issues).

*Interest rate risk* impacts the share price of Treasury security mutual funds. The fluctuations depend on the composition of the holdings and the maturity. In the early 1990s, some government mutual funds which held large mixes of derivative securities suffered much greater losses in share price when interest rates turned in an unanticipated direction than government funds with a higher percentage of their holdings in Treasury securities.

## How to Buy Treasury Mutual Funds

Treasury mutual funds may be purchased directly through the mutual fund families or indirectly through brokers, financial planners, and banks. If purchased indirectly, a commission or fee is charged for the service (in the form of loads, which can be quite large).

Avoid load funds if you possibly can, because the charge is a percentage of every dollar invested. This means that these funds have to work much harder to equal the results of a no-load fund. Treasury bond yields for each auction do not vary much, which means that ideally, all Treasury bond mutual funds should earn similar returns. This makes it more difficult for the load fund to equal the results of the no-load fund. This explains why many funds also invest in riskier securities. A second factor is the fee that is charged for operating and administering the fund. Examine the prospectus of each of the funds that you are interested in for the different fees charged. For bond funds, it is a good idea to choose low-cost funds over high-cost ones. For equity funds, there is always the argument that the manager's stock-picking abilities are worth the additional charges. However, this has not been shown to bear out for bond funds.

Many mutual fund families have Websites where you can download the prospectus and registration forms. Alternatively, there are the (800) toll-free telephone numbers of the mutual funds to obtain the information to open an account.

## What Are the Advantages of Treasury Bond Mutual Funds?

- Treasury mutual funds offer investors the convenience of being able to invest funds at their discretion instead of having to wait for a particular auction date for individual Treasury securities.
- It is easier to sell shares in Treasury mutual funds than to sell individual Treasury securities before they mature.

See Chapter 11 for the advantages of all mutual funds, which also apply to Treasury mutual funds.

## What Are the Disadvantages of Treasury Bond Mutual Funds?

- With Treasury bond mutual funds, there is always the risk of capital loss from having to sell shares at a lower price than the purchase price, even with a long time horizon.

This is because Treasury bond mutual funds never mature. When individual Treasury security issues mature in the fund, they are replaced with new issues.

- Returns from holding individual Treasury securities may be higher than those of mutual funds that hold a large percentage of Treasury securities (as opposed to hybrid funds). This is mainly due to the annual fees and expenses charged by mutual funds.

- To boost the returns of Treasury bond mutual funds, many Treasury funds buy other types of bonds with greater risk.

- Mutual fund shareholders have no control over the distribution of the capital gains of a fund. This is particularly so for mutual funds that actively trade their holdings to boost their overall returns.

### Caveats

- The risks of Treasury mutual funds may be higher than the risks of owning individual Treasury securities.

- Treasury mutual funds that hold other types of individual bond securities are subject to some state and local taxes on the interest earned.

## CONCLUSION

Treasury securities are the safest and also the lowest-yielding fixed-income securities. If inflation remains at its current low level, regular Treasury notes and bonds will provide higher returns than the new Treasury inflation-indexed securities. However, if inflation rises, the new Treasury inflation-indexed securities will provide higher returns, pegged to the increase in inflation.

Regular and inflation-indexed savings bonds are for the most conservative investors. Inflation-indexed savings bonds provide for additional returns if inflation rises. Yields on savings bonds are less than those provided by regular Treasury notes and bonds, which means that they will not provide very much growth to a portfolio of investments. Instead, savings bonds may be viewed as good alternatives to bank accounts, but bear in mind the penalties for early withdrawals.

Investors should consider the yield differential between Treasuries and other types of bonds before investing. If the yield differential is not significant, Treasuries may be the better investment. However, when the yield differential is significant, it's advisable to consider other bond alternatives to Treasuries.

## Should You Choose Individual Treasury Securities or Treasury Mutual Funds?

For the bond investor, mutual funds provide many advantages, which are listed in the chapters for specific types of bonds and the chapter on mutual funds. However, for small investors, owning Treasury securities individually is one of the few fixed-income-security options which has decided advantages over Treasury mutual funds.

Buying Treasury securities directly through the Federal Reserve Banks is not only easy but also free of fees. For investors who plan to hold their bonds to the maturity dates, their actual returns will not be reduced by the commissions, annual fees, and operating expenses that would be assessed by mutual funds. Similarly, at maturity, the full principal is recovered. This may not be the case for mutual funds if the share price has fallen below the purchase price at the time the shareholder withdraws some money. The downside to owning individual Treasury securities purchased directly through the Federal Reserve Banks comes if the investor needs to sell the securities before maturity. Investors would first need to transfer the securities to a bank or brokerage house, which could mean some delays in receiving their money.

However, if investors buy and sell Treasury securities through brokers, they will pay commissions the way they would for any other type of bond. To obviate the need for having to sell Treasury securities before they mature, investors can ladder their portfolios so that they have bonds maturing at different stages.

Individual Treasury securities have no credit risk or risk of default, but due to the hybrid nature of their holdings, some Treasury mutual funds have greater risks. The usual advantage of diversification achieved by mutual funds does not really apply in this case because of the safety from default of individual Treasury securities.

Investors do not need large amounts of money to invest in individual Treasury securities, as compared with other types of bonds which have to be purchased in round lots. This makes it easy for small investors to invest in individual Treasury securities.

Summing up, investors who are willing to purchase Treasury securities directly through the Federal Reserve Banks and hold them through maturity are better off taking that route. Their returns will be higher than those of Treasury mutual funds with 100-percent Treasury holdings. So there is a compelling case for choosing individual Treasury securities over Treasury mutual funds. For those investors who have no desire to invest in individual Treasury securities at auction, Treasury mutual funds are an acceptable alternative.

# REFERENCES

Faerber, Esmé: *Managing Your Investments, Savings, and Credit*, McGraw-Hill, New York, 1992.

Simon, Ruth: "New `Inflation' Savings Bonds Draw Backers," *The Wall Street Journal*, July 13, 1998, pp. C1 and C18.

## CHAPTER 7

# Government Agency Bonds and Agency Mutual Funds

## KEY CONCEPTS

- Mortgage pass-through securities
- The types of mortgage pass-throughs
- Government National Mortgage Association pass-through securities
- Federal Home Loan Mortgage Corporation pass-through securities
- Federal National Mortgage Association securities
- Collateralized mortgage obligations
- Government agency securities
- Government agency and pass-through mutual funds

Government agency bonds appeal to investors who are interested in high-quality bonds. Agency bonds are issued by the major federally sponsored agencies, such as the Federal Home Loan Mortgage Corporation (FHLMC), Federal National Mortgage Association (FNMA), Federal Home Loan Bank (FHLB) System, Farm Credit Banks, the Student Loan Marketing Association (SLMA), and many others. The first three of these agencies, FHLMC, FNMA, and FHLB, provide funds to the mortgage and housing sectors of the economy. The Farm Credit Banks provide funds for the agricultural sector, and the SLMA provides funds for loans for higher education.

These agencies were created by acts of Congress to form a network of federally sponsored agencies that would provide credit for specific sectors of the economy. The agencies are privately owned financial intermediaries that issue securities in the market to raise funds, which are then lent through intermediaries to borrowers in these sectors of the economy. Since they come under Congressional authority and scrutiny, their offerings are exempt from registration with the Securities and Exchange Commission (SEC), unlike corporate bonds, which require registration with the SEC.

The debt of federally sponsored agencies is not backed by the credit of the U.S. government, as are Treasury securities. Instead, there is a moral backing, an implied assumption that in the event of a default, the government would cover the obligations of these agencies. This accounts for the excellent credit risk of these agencies' securities. The risk of default is only slightly greater than that of Treasury issues, and this partly explains why the yields of agency securities are slightly greater than Treasuries of similar maturities. The other major reason for the yield spread is that Treasury issues are more liquid and more marketable.

Besides the five major agencies mentioned, there are many other federally sponsored agencies which offer many issues with slightly higher yields and similar credit risks.

Some of these are the Small Business Administration (SBA), which offers participation certificates; the Department of Housing and Urban Development (HUD), which issues U.S. Government Guaranteed Notes; obligations from the Financing Corporation; and secured notes from the Private Export Funding Corporation (Jonson and Silver, 1989).

An important sector of the government agency securities market is mortgage-backed, or pass-through securities. Since the creation of the Government National Mortgage Association (GNMA) by the National Housing Act in 1970, the pass-through securities market has grown to be a very large sector of the agency market. The government succeeded in increasing the investment base in the mortgage market by attracting institutional investors. Since then, several government-sponsored agencies and private institutions have entered this market. Besides the Government National Mortgage Association, the other major mortgage-related agencies are the Federal National Mortgage Association (FNMA), the

Federal Home Loan Mortgage Corporation (FHLMC), and the Federal Home Loan Bank System.

Since the securities offered by the different federally sponsored agencies vary considerably, the mortgage-related agencies are discussed first, followed by some of the other major agency offerings.

## MORTGAGE PASS-THROUGH SECURITIES

Mortgage pass-through securities are much more complex than regular fixed-income securities. They arise out of mortgage transactions. Most people who buy houses don't have the resources to pay cash. They borrow the funds from financial institutions such as banks and mortgage companies who issue mortgages. The borrowers promise to pay back the amounts loaned in monthly payments through the life of the mortgage loans. Most banks and mortgage companies do not hold these mortgages to maturity. Instead, they sell them to other institutions (government and private), who package these mortgages into pass-through securities and then sell them to investors.

Mortgage pass-through securities are shares in pools or collections of similar mortgages. The mortgage holders pool their mortgages and sell shares in the pools to investors. The investors then receive the interest and principal repayments on a monthly basis (less a modest fee of normally about one-half a percentage point)—hence the name *pass-through*. Mortgage pools vary. Some consist of several thousand mortgages; others have just a few. These pools are issued at a minimum of $1,000,000.

Pass-through securities can be better understood by examining how mortgages work. For illustrative purposes, assume that one mortgage pool is $1,000,000 and that it consists of a single conventional 30-year mortgage of $1,000,000 at 9 percent. The monthly payment that the mortgagor will make to the mortgage holder is $8046.23. This payment consists of interest and a portion which goes towards the reduction of the principal balance. Table 7-1 shows the amortization schedule for the first 12 months of this mortgage. For the first payment, the amount of interest is $7500, and $546.23 goes towards reducing the principal balance from $1,00,000 to $999,453.77. The interest rate is 9 percent per year, and the interest rate per month is 9 percent divided by 12, which is 0.0075. The interest expense is calculated by multiplying the monthly rate by the mortgage balance. Hence, the interest for the first payment is 0.0075 multiplied by $1,000,000, or $7500.

These monthly payments are designed to reduce the mortgage balance to zero at the end of the mortgage term (30 years, or 360 payments). As you can see from the first 12 payments, the amount of the interest expense declines each month, which means that each month, more of the monthly payment will go toward reducing the outstanding loan (mortgage) balance. In other words, the fixed amount of the payment is the same, but the proportion of interest received declines and the proportion of the principal repayments increases.

In this case, the investor in this pass-through security will receive the pass-through interest and principal. The amount that is received will have the servicing fees and any other charges by the servicing institution deducted.

The investor cannot always count on the monthly amount being the same, since mortgagors have the option to prepay their mortgages. This could be the entire amount of the mortgage or a

**TABLE 7-1**

Amortization Schedule for a 30-year, 9% Mortgage of $1,000,000

| Month/Year | Payment | Interest (9%) | Principal | Loan Balance |
|---|---|---|---|---|
| | | | | $1,000,000.00 |
| 1/1999 | $8046.23 | $7500.00 | $546.23 | 999,453.77 |
| 2/1999 | 8046.23 | 7495.90 | 550.32 | 998,903.45 |
| 3/1999 | 8046.23 | 7491.78 | 554.45 | 998,349.00 |
| 4/1999 | 8046.23 | 7487.62 | 558.61 | 997,790.39 |
| 5/1999 | 8046.23 | 7483.43 | 562.80 | 997,227.59 |
| 6/1999 | 8046.23 | 7479.21 | 567.02 | 996,660.57 |
| 7/1999 | 8046.23 | 7474.95 | 571.27 | 996,089.30 |
| 8/1999 | 8046.23 | 7470.67 | 575.56 | 995,513.75 |
| 9/1999 | 8046.23 | 7466.35 | 579.87 | 994,933.87 |
| 10/1999 | 8046.23 | 7462.00 | 584.22 | 994,349.65 |
| 11/1999 | 8046.23 | 7457.62 | 588.60 | 993,761.05 |
| 12/1999 | 8046.23 | 7453.21 | 593.02 | 993,168.03 |

part of it. For example, if the mortgagee prepaid an additional $1000 a month in the example above, the mortgage pass-through security holder would receive this additional payment, which is, in essence, a return of that holder's principal, or investment capital.

For many reasons, mortgagees prepay the entire amount of their mortgages before their maturity dates. This happens when homeowners sell their homes, when they refinance their mortgages as interest rates go down, in the case of the death of the homeowner, or if fire or another casualty destroys the property and the insurance proceeds are used to pay off the mortgage.

Consequently, in a mortgage pool, if many mortgagees prepay their mortgages, there will be uncertainty regarding the amount of cash flow to investors and the length of time to maturity of the pool.

There is also uncertainty as to the timing of the cash flows. For example, assume that mortgage payments are due by the first day of the month. If the mortgagees are late sending in their payments and there are delays in processing these payments, then the payments to investors are delayed. The time delay also varies depending on the type of pass-through.

Besides the level-payment conventional mortgage described above, which is the most common for pass-through securities, there are other types of mortgages which are used for pass-through securities.

The *adjustable rate mortgage* (ARM) has a floating rate of interest which varies according to a particular index. For instance, if the adjustable rate mortgage is tied to the rate of short-term Treasury notes, the rate will be adjusted up or down with the movement of the rate on the Treasury note every six months, one year, or whatever period the mortgagor chooses at the outset of the mortgage.

Most ARMs have periodic caps on interest rates. They can only increase or decrease by a certain number of percentage points within a period of time, and there usually are also lifetime caps on interest rates. They can only increase or decrease by a certain number of percentage points over the life of the mortgage.

The cash flows of ARMs are even more difficult to predict, which means that the amounts received by investors in pass-through securities will fluctuate. There will also be prepayment risk with ARMS.

*Graduated payment mortgages* (GPMs) have also been used for pools of pass-through securities. With a GPM, the level monthly payments in the early years of a mortgage, say, the first five years, are less than the level payments in the later years of the mortgage. The interest rate is fixed, like a conventional mortgage, but the monthly payments in the initial years may not be enough to cover the interest expense each month. This is *negative amortization*, which means that the shortfall in interest expense gets added back into the mortgage balance. Instead of decreasing, the mortgage balance increases, and so do the monthly payments. Thus, by the end of the mortgage term, the mortgagee will have repaid a greater amount of principal than was originally borrowed at the inception of the mortgage.

All types of mortgages are subject to prepayment risk, which affects the amount of the cash flows for investors in pass-through securities. However, there is a level of comfort for these investors in that historically, during times when mortgage rates have fallen to 7 percent, there are still some homeowners who hang on to their 10-percent mortgages.

Besides the prepayment risk, mortgage pass-through securities present a challenge for investors in terms of valuation. Since mortgages are self-amortizing (the principal gets paid back in monthly amounts throughout the mortgage term), they cannot be valued like other fixed-income securities, such as Treasury bonds, where the entire principal is returned at maturity.

## THE TYPES OF MORTGAGE PASS-THROUGHS

There are various types of mortgage pass-through securities, each with its own features. Despite the differences, investors in all mortgage pass-through securities are concerned with the following:

- The safety of the issue
- The liquidity and marketability of the issue
- The overall rate of return of the issue
- The expected maturity of the issue

The majority of pass-through securities have been issued by three government agencies, namely the Government National Mortgage Association, the Federal National Mortgage Association, and the Federal Home Loan Mortgage Corporation. There has also been a marked growth in the number of mortgage pass-through securities issued by private issuers since the mid-1980s.

The main characteristics of each of these major issuers of pass-through securities are discussed in the remainder of this section.

## GOVERNMENT NATIONAL MORTGAGE ASSOCIATION (GNMA) PASS-THROUGH SECURITIES

The Government National Mortgage Association, also known as *Ginnie Mae*, is a wholly owned agency of the Housing and Urban Development Department (HUD). Hence, the timely interest and principal payments of Ginnie Mae pass-through securities are guaranteed by the full faith and credit of the U.S. government. This means zero credit risk, which is very appealing to investors.

The agency does not issue pass-through securities but insures them. These securities are issued by mortgage bankers and thrift institutions, who bundle mortgages into pools of at least $1 million. These mortgage bankers apply to the Government National Mortgage Association for backing, and if accepted, they get a pool number. Shares of these pools are sold to investors, mainly banks, pension funds, and insurance companies. The minimum investment purchase amount is $25,000, which explains why the majority of investors in these pools are institutions. Once all the shares of the GNMA pool are sold, the GNMA securities are traded on the securities markets.

GNMA will accept only VA (Veterans Administration) and FHA (Federal Housing Administration) mortgages, which are assumable mortgages. This feature makes prepayment less variable than on mortgages which are not assumable.

There are a variety of Ginnie Mae pools. The major pools are GNMA I and GNMA II. The former includes fixed-rate 20- to 30-year mortgages totaling a minimum face value of $1 million, all with the same interest rates.

GNMA II pools:

1. Are larger than GNMA I pools
2. Have mortgages with a variety of interest rates and maturities (Thau, 1992)

There are also GNMA midgets (mortgages with a 15-year term), GNMA GPMs (graduated-payment mortgages), GNMA ARMs (adjustable rate mortgages), GNMA mobile homes, GNMA buydowns, and GNMA FHA projects. The different types of mortgages, maturities, interest rates, and pool sizes make the analysis more difficult for each type of pool. In general, the larger the pool size, the more liquid and the smaller the impact of prepayments. The shorter the term of the mortgages, the shorter the average life and half-life of the pool.

The *average life* is defined as the weighted-average time that each dollar of principal is outstanding. This is a measure of the investment life of the mortgage-backed securities in the pool. The average life depends on the prepayment rate. The greater the prepayments in the pool, the shorter the average life; and the shorter the weighted-average life, the lower the volatility in price of the GNMA. GNMAs and other mortgage securities are traded on their assumed average life, as opposed to their maturity dates, like other bonds.

The *half-life* is defined as the time taken to return half the principal in the pool. The average life and half-life are useful measures for comparison purposes because you can use these, and not the length of time to maturity, to compare GNMAs with other fixed-income investments. For example, if you wanted to compare the yield on a GNMA with a five-year half-life and a maturity of 12 years with a Treasury note, you would look at Treasury notes with five-year maturities.

GNMA investments are much more complex than the other fixed-income investments. Not only is there uncertainty as to the length of time to maturity for the investment but also uncertainty as to the amount and timing of the cash flows. GNMA provides statistics as to the prepayment histories for each GNMA pool, but these are not cast in stone and may vary. Hence, these estimated payments are constantly being revised.

As you might expect, the yield on GNMAs is also difficult to determine accurately. If you are not sure what the cash flow will be, you can't determine the precise yield. However, various calculation methods have been developed based on different assumptions of prepayment speed (fast, average, and slow). In an offering sheet, you will see a number of yields quoted, depending on the FHA estimated experience of prepayment speed. The slowest speed offers the highest yield. Thus, from a safety point of view, when buying GNMAs, assume that you will earn the lowest of the predicted yields.

When comparing the estimated yields on GNMAs with yields on other fixed-income securities, keep in mind the following factors:

- Reinvestment risk is greater for GNMAs than other fixed-income securities because interest and the return of principal payments are made monthly for pass-through securities, as opposed to semiannually or annually for regular bonds. For example, if there is a significant downturn in market rates of interest, the returned interest and principal will be reinvested at lower rates, and the total return will be lower for the GNMA investment than the quoted yield to maturity, which assumes reinvestment at the quoted yield.

- Exact rates of return cannot be determined due to the uncertainty of reinvestment risk.

- If the monthly interest and principal payments are spent instead of reinvested, the total rate of return will be even lower.

- The principal repayments should not be included in the cash flow yield, since these are a return of the investor's initial investment.

Like all other fixed-income securities, GNMAs and all pass-through securities are sensitive to changes in market rates of interest. When market rates of interest go up, bond prices decline. However, when market rates of interest come down, many homeowners will prepay their mortgages and refinance them at lower rates. This is a damper on GNMA prices, so generally speaking, they will not go up by as much as regular bond prices when market rates come down. Not only will investors receive their principal earlier, they will also be faced with reinvesting the proceeds in investments with lower yields.

## How to Buy GNMAs

GNMAs can be purchased directly from the issuer through dealers or brokers. Minimum purchase amounts are $25,000. However, investors can buy GNMA mutual funds or unit investment trusts by investing as little as $1000 to $2500 (the minimum amount spec-ified by the GNMA mutual fund or investment trust). Mutual funds and investment trusts are discussed in detail in a later sec-tion in this chapter and in later chapters.

Existing GNMA issues can be bought and sold in the sec-ondary market. GNMAs are both marketable and liquid owing to the large volume of issues traded. When buying from a broker or bank, you should be aware of the following:

- Prices quoted in the newspapers or offering sheets are for large buyers (institutions). Small investors will be quoted larger spreads between bid and asked prices.
- Yields quoted are based on prepayment assumptions. If only one yield is quoted, ask your broker for the different prepayment assumptions and the corresponding yields. Use the most conservative yield, because even then, it may not be realized.
- The remaining term of the mortgage pool, or length of time to maturity, is not as important as the weighted-average life, because the former assumes no prepayments. In the secondary market it is assumed that a 30-year GNMA will be repaid on average in 12 years.
- Price is important. If the GNMA is trading at a premium, you may be more likely to suffer a capital loss. If interest rates decline, mortgagors may prepay their mortgages in the pool faster than estimated. Hence, you may not recover the premium paid over the face value, and you will also have to reinvest the money at lower interest rates. Buying at a discount offers the opportunity of capital gains, but the coupon yield for the GNMA is lower in that case than currently offered coupons.

### What Are the Advantages of GNMAs?

- Large sophisticated investors can use the futures market to hedge their portfolios against adverse swings in interest rates.
- GNMAs offer investors cash flows on a monthly basis, as opposed to semiannually or annually, like other fixed-income investments.

- GNMAs have no credit risk because interest and principal payments are guaranteed by the U.S. government.
- GNMAs are marketable due to the large size of the GNMA market. They are also liquid in that the bid and asked spreads tend to be similar to those for Treasury securities (about $\frac{1}{8}$ of a point) and less than most corporate securities.
- Thirty-year GNMAs are not as volatile as 30-year Treasuries because part of the principal on the GNMA is repaid on a monthly basis.
- Yields on GNMAs tend to be higher than those on Treasuries but lower than those offered by corporate bonds.

## What Are the Disadvantages of GNMAs?

- It is difficult to determine the amount of the monthly cash flows due to the prepayments of mortgages in the pools.
- It is difficult to determine the exact yield for GNMAs due to the uncertainties of the cash flows.
- Reinvestment risk is greater for GNMAs than for Treasuries and corporate bonds, particularly when market rates of interest decline.
- Interest is fully taxable at the federal, state, and local levels, whereas Treasuries and certain agency issues are exempt from state and local taxes.
- They are subject to interest rate risk. Prices of GNMAs move in the opposite direction to changes in interest rates.

## Caveats

- To reduce the prepayment risk, investors should avoid buying GNMAs from small mortgage pools. By buying into large mortgage pools, investors can spread out the prepayment risk. For this reason, small investors might consider GNMA mutual funds, where diversification can be achieved through the size of the mutual fund's investments in these securities. By investing in one or a few pools, investors with relatively small amounts cannot achieve the diversification that mutual funds can.

- With GNMAs, investors receive a return of principal and interest monthly. Investors should not spend their entire monthly checks but rather should invest a portion of their proceeds to keep their investment capital intact.
- When GNMAs are trading at a premium price, their coupon yields are greater than current coupon rates for new GNMAs. Investors should be cautious in buying at a premium because prepayment volatility is greatest for GNMAs whose coupons exceed current mortgage rates by 3 percent (Hayre and Mohebbi, 1989, p. 283). A faster rate of prepayments can lead to a capital loss.

## FEDERAL HOME LOAN MORTGAGE CORPORATION (FHLMC) PASS-THROUGH SECURITIES

The Federal Home Loan Mortgage Corporation, also known as *Freddie Mac*, is the second largest issuer of pass-through securities. Freddie Mac is an agency of the U.S. government, and its shares are owned by the 12 Federal Reserve Banks.

The participation certificates offered by Freddie Mac are similar in many ways to GNMAs. The major differences are:

- Participation certificate pools contain conventional mortgages (most are single-family loans with 30-year terms), which are underwritten and purchased by Freddie Mac. Pools tend to be larger than those of GNMAs.
- Freddie Mac guarantees the timely payment of interest and ultimately the repayment of principal (within a year). Being an agency, this is a weaker guarantee than the "full faith and credit" provision by the government for GNMAs. Some participation certificates only guarantee the timely payment of interest.
- Participation certificates are not as marketable as GNMAs because fewer of them are traded in the secondary markets than GNMAs. To improve the marketability of its participation certificates, Freddie Mac will buy them back directly from holders.

- Yields on participation certificates are slightly higher than those on GNMAs because of the slight discrepancy in safety and the slightly lesser degree of marketability. This does not mean that participation certificates are not safe or that they are not marketable. Compared with GNMAs, their credit risk is slight (far less than a corporate issue), and they are marketable (and liquid), but because GNMAs have a greater presence in the marketplace, participation certificates are not as marketable or liquid.

Besides participation certificates, the Federal Home Loan Mortgage Corporation also has a mortgage pass-through called the *guaranteed mortgage certificate* (GMC). The GMC was designed for institutional investors with minimum amounts of $100,000 (as opposed to $25,000 for GNMAs and participation certificates), and they make semiannual payments of interest and principal. Freddie Mac guarantees the interest payments and the full payment of principal on these.

## FEDERAL NATIONAL MORTGAGE ASSOCIATION (FNMA) SECURITIES

The Federal National Mortgage Association, also known as *Fannie Mae*, or FNMA, is a quasi-private organization whose common stock is traded on the New York Stock Exchange. Fannie Mae was established by Congress in 1938 but was rechartered by Congress in 1968 as a private corporation with a mandate to assist in the development of a secondary market for conventional mortgages.

Some of the features of Fannie Mae pass-throughs are:

- FNMA guarantees timely interest and principal payments, a weaker guarantee than that given for GNMA pass-through securities.
- FNMA pools tend to be larger than GNMA pools.
- FNMAs are not as marketable as GNMAs, and yields on FNMAs tend to be higher than those offered on GNMAs.

A study comparing the prepayment rates on 30-year FNMA, FHLMC, and GNMA fixed-rate mortgage-backed securities showed that FNMA and Freddie Mac pools prepay at a faster rate than GNMA pools at equivalent interest rates (Scott, 1989). To off-set the prepayment and cash flow uncertainties, collateralized mortgage obligations were developed.

## COLLATERALIZED MORTGAGE OBLIGATIONS

The first collateralized mortgage obligation (CMO) was issued in 1983. The main innovation of the CMO is that it provides investors with a steady stream of income for a predictable term. A CMO is a debt security based on a pool of mortgages (like GNMAs) in which the mortgagees make their interest and principal payments on a monthly basis. However, the return of principal payments is segmented and paid sequentially to a number of different portions of the pool's investors.

CMO pools are divided into from 3 to 17 tranches (or slices), and investors buy bonds with varying maturities in these tranches. For example, the classic CMO has four tranches. The first three (Class A, Class B, and Class C) pay interest at the stated coupon rate to the bondholders of each tranche. The fourth tranche (often referred to as a Class Z, or a Z-bond class) resembles a zero-coupon bond, where interest is accrued. The last tranche is always the Z tranche.

The cash flows received are used first to pay the interest on the first three classes of bonds and then to retire the bonds in the first tranche. All prepayments go to the first tranche, A. Then when all the bonds are retired, the prepayments continue to tranche B. This process continues until class B bonds are paid off, and then C bonds follow. Z bonds receive no payments (interest or principal) until all the other tranches are paid off. The subsequent cash flows are used to pay off the accrued interest, and then the return of principal to retire the Z bonds.

Z bonds are much more complex than the A, B, or C bonds in CMOs for a number of reasons. First, the length to maturity cannot be accurately predicted for Z bonds, whereas regular A, B, and C tranches have stated maturities. Second, Z bonds are long-term bonds and thus face greater risks than shorter-term securities. Hence, Z bonds can be quite volatile, and you should understand the risks before buying Z tranche bonds in a CMO. Credit risks vary depending on the backing of the CMO pool. If CMO pools are backed by GNMA or FNMA, then the credit risk is minimal. The risks rise for private issuers who are not as creditworthy.

## The Advantages of CMOs

- For earlier tranches, there is greater certainty as to cash flows (quarterly or semiannually).
- For the earlier tranches, there are shorter, predictable maturities. Consequently, there is less exposure to interest rate risk.
- The later tranches have less prepayment risk, since they cannot receive any principal payments until the earlier tranches have been paid off.
- CMO pools are much larger than GNMA pools.
- Depending on the backing of the mortgages, CMOs can have very little to no credit risk. Some pools are backed by GNMA, FNMA, or FHLMC, which have no credit risk. There are also privately backed pools with pool insurance, which carry greater credit risk.
- Depending on the brokerage firms selling CMOs, minimum amounts for investing can be as low as $10,000.
- Yields on Z tranche bonds are higher than those of GNMAs, but the risks are also much greater for Z tranche bonds.

## The Disadvantages of CMOs

- CMOs are less liquid and may be less marketable than GNMAs, FNMAs, and Freddie Macs.
- Z tranche bonds can be quite volatile when market rates of interest change.
- Yields on the earlier tranches tend to be lower than those on GNMAs.
- Z tranche bonds are more complicated from a tax standpoint. Interest is taxed as accrued, even though the

investor does not receive the actual interest payments in the early years (only when the Z tranche pays out).

## Caveats

Before investing in CMOs, investors should:

- Understand the characteristics of each tranche, the relationships between the tranches, and the prepayment structure.
- Understand who has guaranteed or insured the mortgages in the pools.
- Ascertain from the brokerage firm selling the CMOs whether they make a market in the securities. If not, the CMOs may be difficult to sell.

# GOVERNMENT AGENCY SECURITIES

Agencies of the government issue traditional securities in addition to mortgage pass-through securities.

## Federal Home Loan Bank (FHLB) System

The Federal Home Loan Bank System plays a similar role to the savings and loan associations as the Federal Reserve Banks do to commercial banks. The FHLB System consists of 12 regional banks and has a central board in Washington. These 12 banks are owned by the private savings and loans that are members of the system. Despite this ownership, the FHLB System is responsible to Congress for regulating the savings and loans as well as lending to them.

The FHLB borrows in the open market by issuing consolidated bonds and shorter-term discount notes. Consolidated bonds have maturities of one year or more (up to 20 years). Many of the new issues may be purchased in minimum amounts of $10,000, and additional amounts in multiples of $5000. Interest is paid semiannually, and these bonds are not callable.

The FHLB's consolidated discount notes are short-term securities with maturities ranging from 30 to 360 days. They are sold in minimum denominations of $100,000.

The credit quality of FHLB securities is high because the U.S. government is unlikely to allow one of its agencies to default on its obligations. Interest income on both the consolidated bonds and discount notes is taxable at the federal level, but it is exempt at the state and local levels.

## Farm Credit Agencies

The Farm Credit Administration oversees the Federal Farm Credit System, in which the country is divided into 12 farm credit districts, each with its own Federal Land Bank, a Bank for Cooperatives, and a Federal Intermediate Credit Bank. These banks issue securities through a fiscal agent in New York City to raise funds so that they can lend to agricultural borrowers in their districts.

The Farm Credit agencies issue three types of securities through their banks:

- Short-term discount notes, which are auctioned daily. Maturities range from 5 to 270 days. The minimum denomination is $50,000.
- Short-term bonds, which are auctioned monthly, have maturities of three to nine months, and come in minimum denominations of $50,000.
- Long-term bonds, which have maturities of one to ten years and minimum denominations of $1000.

Interest income from these is taxed at the federal level but exempt at the state and local levels. Credit risk is negligible due to the de facto backing from the U.S. government. This was evidenced during the middle and late 1980s, when Congress passed legislation to aid the Farm Credit System, which had experienced financial difficulties.

## Other U.S. Government Agencies

### Resolution Funding Corporation

The Resolution Funding Corporation issues bonds to provide funding to bail out failed thrift institutions. The interest payments on the bonds are guaranteed by the U.S. Treasury, and the principal is secured by U.S. Treasury bonds. This makes these securities very safe for investors in terms of credit and default risk.

### Student Loan Marketing Association
The Student Loan Marketing Association, also known as Sallie Mae, was created to provide liquidity to financial institutions that lend to students by purchasing the loans. Bonds are then issued and sold to investors.

### Tennessee Valley Authority
This agency issues securities to provide liquidity to develop the Tennessee Valley and regional areas. The bonds of this agency are not guaranteed by the U.S. government, since the interest and principal are payable only by the Tennessee Valley Authority.

## Conclusion

There are many different government agencies that issue securities, which may vary considerably. However, they do have many common features, such as:

- New issues of agency securities are sold through a syndicate of dealers. These dealers also buy and sell these securities in the secondary markets.
- Agencies with large issues have marketable and fairly liquid securities.
- Agency securities are exempt from registration with the SEC.
- Some agency issues have tax advantages in that interest income is exempt from state and local taxes.
- Agency securities have either de facto or de jure backing from the federal government, making them safer than corporate bonds.

## GOVERNMENT AGENCY AND PASS-THROUGH MUTUAL FUNDS

There may be a blurring of the securities held by government agency mutual funds and federal government mutual funds. If a fund has "government agency" in its title, it must hold 65 percent of the fund's security holdings in government agency securities. The other 35 percent can consist of any other securities— Treasuries, foreign government bonds, corporate bonds, zero-coupon bonds, and convertible bonds.

Since not all agency bonds are guaranteed or backed by the U.S. government, and these other types of bonds, besides Treasuries, vary in credit risk, investors should examine the holdings of these types of mutual funds before investing. Credit risk and the risk of default can vary considerably, depending on the holdings of the mutual fund.

The same may be said of the holdings of GNMA and other pass-through mutual funds, which hold a variety of mortgage pass-through securities of varying degrees of credit quality. In a GNMA fund, the majority of the holdings are GNMAs, but the other 35 percent might consist of riskier securities, such as CMOs and derivative securities.

There are also ARM (adjustable rate mortgage) funds, which purchase mortgage securities with adjustable rates. Although many of these mortgages may be guaranteed by federal agencies, the credit risk will vary on these funds for the same reasons as cited above. These funds may hold risky CMOs and derivative securities in addition to their holdings of ARM securities.

## What Are the Risks of Government Agency and Pass-Through Mutual Funds?

Government agency and pass-through mortgage securities provide higher yields than Treasuries because they are subject to greater risk. The same holds true of mutual funds with these holdings. Besides credit risk and the risk of default, which both rise as mutual funds increase their holdings of CMOs, derivative securities, corporate bonds, zero-coupon bonds, and bonds of the less creditworthy agencies, there are other risks.

Government agency and pass-through mortgage mutual funds are subject to *interest rate risk*. Generally, when market rates of interest fall, the prices of existing fixed-income securities rise. However, as mentioned earlier in this chapter, there is a ceiling on the rise in price of pass-through securities. This is because many homeowners are likely to refinance their older, higher-interest mortgages for lower-interest mortgages. Thus, with falling rates of interest, the prices of pass-through securities do not rise as much as other fixed-income securities. The flip side of the coin is that when interest rates rise, homeowners will not refinance their mortgages. This means that holders of pass-through securities receive lower yields than other securities because the pass-through pools will have longer lives and holders will not receive their principal back to reinvest at higher rates. With rapid swings in interest rates, pass-through securities do not perform as well as other fixed-income securities. This means that pass-through security mutual funds do not perform well with rapid swings in interest rates. Adjustable rate mortgage (ARM) funds theoretically should perform better when there are rapid swings in interest rates, but this was not the case in 1994, when ARM funds returned lower yields than money market funds.

Pass-through mortgage securities are complex; payments are unpredictable and yields are only estimates at best. This makes it more difficult to analyze the risks of pass-through mortgage securities, and in particular, pass-through security mutual funds. For these reasons, with pass-through security mutual funds, there is always the *risk of loss of principal* due to the volatility of mutual fund share prices.

## How to Buy Government Agency and Pass-Through Security Mutual Funds

Government agency and pass-through security mutual funds may be bought directly through the mutual fund families or indirectly through brokers, financial planners, and banks. To save on sales commissions, you are better off investing directly with the mutual fund family in no-load funds, especially in light of the share price volatility of pass-through security mutual funds. In addition, look for low-expense-ratio funds. This can make quite a difference to overall returns. High-expense-ratio funds have to earn greater returns than low-expense-ratio funds just to equal the same total returns.

Many financial magazines and newspapers publish quarterly, yearly, and longer-term operating results of the different agency and pass-through mortgage mutual funds. From such a list, investors can narrow the list of potential funds by examining the following in the prospectus:

- The objectives of the fund, which determine the latitude the fund manager has to purchase riskier securities for the fund.

- The types of securities held in the fund.
- Whether the fund charges a load (front-end and/or back-end).
- The expense ratios of the fund.

A prospectus and application form can be obtained off the Internet from the mutual fund company or by calling the toll-free number in order to open up the mutual fund.

### What Are the Advantages of Government Agency and Pass-Through Mutual Funds?

- Although mortgage pass-through and government agency mutual funds may hold riskier securities in their portfolios to boost their yields, they still offer mutual fund shareholders a more diversified portfolio than investing in individual agency or pass-through securities. The greater diversification achieved by mutual funds can lessen the impact of credit and default risk.
- The minimum purchase amount for individual pass-through securities, such as GNMAs and FNMAs, is $25,000, which makes pass-through security mutual funds, with their lower minimums of around $1000, more accessible for investors who have less to invest.
- When interest rates move within a narrow range, government agency and pass-through security mutual funds offer the potential for greater returns than Treasury mutual funds.

In addition, see the advantages of mutual funds mentioned in Chapter 11, which also apply to government agency and pass-through security mutual funds.

### What Are the Disadvantages of Government Agency and Pass-Through Mutual Funds?

- Wide swings in market rates of interest will make the prices of pass-through security mutual funds quite volatile, causing potential losses in principal should mutual fund shareholders have to sell when their shares are at lower prices than their purchase prices.

- Due to the unpredictability and unevenness of the cash flows of mortgage pass-throughs, yields on pass-through security mutual funds may not be comparable with those of government agency, Treasury, and corporate bond mutual funds.

## Caveat

Not all agency securities are exempt from state and local taxes, which may mean that a portion of the dividends received from these mutual funds may be subject to state and local taxes.

## Should You Choose Individual Government Agency and Pass-Through Securities or Mutual Funds?

Table 7-2 summarizes the advantages of individual securities versus mutual funds for this category of bonds.

Buying individual government agency and pass-through securities is a complex undertaking for the lay investor, but mutual funds make it easier for small investors to participate in this group of fixed-income securities. Similarly, government agency and pass-through mutual funds offer investors professional management,

**TABLE 7-2**

Advantages of Individual Agency and Pass-Through Securities versus Mutual Funds

|                               | Individual | Mutual Funds |
| ----------------------------- | :--------: | :----------: |
| Small amount to invest        |            |      ✓       |
| Risky CMOs                    |            |      ✓       |
| Risk of loss from default     |            |      ✓       |
| Risk of loss of principal     |     ✓      |              |
| Possibility of higher returns |     ✓      |              |
| Tax planning                  |     ✓      |              |
| Ease of buying and selling    |            |      ✓       |

diversification, smaller investment minimums, and the ease of owning a share in these otherwise complex securities.

Should investors want to invest in the riskier CMOs, mutual funds offer the advantage of a diversified portfolio of holdings, which can lessen the risk of loss due to defaults of individual securities.

There is always the risk of loss of principal with mutual funds, but buying individual securities and holding them to maturity ensures that holders will not lose any principal.

Investing in individual pass-through securities and government agency bonds over mutual funds allows investors the freedom to choose their portfolios of securities and their risks, along with being able to eliminate the fees that they would pay for mutual funds. Thus, overall returns may be higher by investing in securities of this type individually.

# R E F E R E N C E S

Hayre, Lakhbir S., and Cyrus Mohebbi: "Mortgage Pass-Through Securities," in Frank J. Fabozzi (ed.), *Advances and Innovations in the Bond and Mortgage Markets*, McGraw-Hill, New York, 1989.

Jonson, Judith, and Andrew Silver: "NADCO, NASBIC, HUD, PEFCO, and FICO: High-Quality Investment Opportunities Worth Investigating," in Frank J. Fabozzi (ed.), *Advances and Innovations in the Bond and Mortgage Markets*, McGraw-Hill, New York, 1989.

Scott, F. Richard: "Relative Prepayment Rates on 30-Year FNMA, FHLMC, and GNMA Fixed-Rate Mortgage-Backed Securities," in Frank J. Fabozzi (ed.), *Advances and Innovations in the Bond and Mortgage Markets*, McGraw-Hill, New York, 1989.

Thau, Annette: *The Bond Book*, McGraw-Hill, New York, 1992.

## CHAPTER 8

# Municipal Bonds and Municipal Bond Mutual Funds

## KEY CONCEPTS

- What is different about municipal bonds?
- Are municipal bonds suitable for you?
- Types of municipal bonds
- What are the risks of municipal bonds?
- How to buy and sell municipal bonds
- What are the advantages of municipal bonds?
- What are the disadvantages of municipal bonds?
- Municipal bond mutual funds
- What are the risks of municipal bond mutual funds?
- How to invest in municipal bond mutual funds
- What are the advantages of municipal bond mutual funds?
- What are the disadvantages of municipal bond mutual funds?

Municipal bonds are debt securities issued by state and local governments, their agencies, and enterprises with a public purpose. There are over 50,000 state and local entities that issue municipal bonds, making the municipal bond market both large and remarkable. The agencies of local governments include authorities for housing, toll roads, transportation facilities, school districts, and the like. Some examples of enterprises with a public purpose are hospitals and universities.

Ownership of municipal securities is diverse. An individual household can hold municipal bonds indirectly, through mutual funds, unit trusts, banks, insurance companies, or pension funds, or directly.

## WHAT IS DIFFERENT ABOUT MUNICIPAL BONDS?

For investors, the most important feature of municipal bonds is that the interest income is exempt from federal income taxes. Generally, interest income is also exempt from state and local taxes if investors live in the state and county issuing the municipal bonds. In such a case, the issue would be triple tax-exempt. For example, if you live in a high-tax state, you may want to buy bonds issued by your state or local government, which can improve your yield by a percentage point or so. This federal tax exemption benefits not only individuals who buy municipal bonds but also the states and localities issuing them, since they can pay lower coupon yields than regular taxable bonds.

Most of the municipal bonds issued are tax-exempt at the federal level, but there are some that are not. With the Tax Reform Act of 1986, Congress deemed municipal issues with nonessential purposes to be taxable at the federal level. However, they remain exempt from state and local taxes. Nonessential purposes would include bonds raising funds for sports stadiums, parking facilities, conventions, industrial parks, and pollution control facilities.

Another tax wrinkle from the Tax Reform Act of 1986 involves industrial development bonds issued after 1986. Industrial development bonds are those in which 10 percent or more of the proceeds raised by the sale of the bonds are used by private firms. For example, a state may issue industrial development bonds to finance a building which it then leases to a private corporation.

Interest income received from industrial development bonds is treated as a preference item and may be subject to the alternative minimum tax (AMT) that some individuals pay. The alternative minimum tax is an additional tax that individuals in high income tax brackets with large deductions may have to pay. The AMT is designed to ensure that individuals in high income tax brackets who may not be subject to regular federal income taxes (due to large deductions) will be required to pay some federal taxes.

Thus, interest income on industrial development bonds that is exempt from federal income taxes may trigger the alternative minimum tax. This would not concern investors who are not subject to the alternative minimum tax. In fact, industrial development bonds may be attractive to investors, since they tend to have slightly higher yields than tax-exempt bonds that are not subject to the alternative minimum tax.

Investors in high tax brackets can circumvent the alternative minimum tax by buying tax-exempt bonds issued before August 7, 1986, in the secondary market. This is the good news. The bad news is that the supply of these bonds is limited because institutional investors such as mutual funds may already have purchased them. Thus, industrial development bonds may not be that attractive to investors who are subject to the alternative minimum tax.

There is always an exception to the rule. This time it is 501(c) bonds, which are not subject to the alternative minimum tax. These are bonds issued by private nonprofit hospitals and universities.

Under certain circumstances, interest income on regular municipal bonds may be taxable for some retirees. Interest from municipal bonds currently is added to the retiree's adjusted gross income, together with half of his or her Social Security payments. If the total exceeds a certain dollar amount, then a portion becomes taxable. However, the Internal Revenue Tax Code changes on a yearly basis, and if in doubt as to the tax status of your municipal bonds, ask your accountant.

Despite the fact that private activity bonds are not tax-exempt (at the federal level) and industrial development bonds issued after August 7, 1986, may trigger the alternative minimum tax, the vast majority of municipal bonds issued by state and local governments and their authorities are tax-exempt at the federal level. It is this freedom from federal—and possibly state and local—taxes that makes municipal bonds so appealing to investors in the higher tax brackets.

## ARE MUNICIPAL BONDS SUITABLE FOR YOU?

Most investors look to lower their tax bills, but as you can see, municipal bonds may not be the right investment for everyone. Buying tax-exempt issues purely to lower tax liability may mean that some investors in some cases may earn as much as they could have on an after-tax basis if they had bought taxable bonds. This may be true for investors in low tax brackets, who might earn more from taxable bonds, even after paying the taxes.

In order to compare municipal bonds with taxable bonds, you need to convert the tax-exempt yield of a municipal to the equivalent of a taxable bond. See Table 8-1 for some examples of what taxable bonds would have to yield in order to equal the yields of municipal bonds.

The *equivalent yield* of a taxable bond at the investor's tax bracket is the yield an investor would have to earn on a taxable bond to equal the yield on a municipal bond. For example, an investor in the 15-percent tax bracket purchasing a taxable bond with a yield of 7.65 percent could earn the same from a $6^{1}/_{2}$-percent tax-exempt municipal bond. Put another way, the investor in the 15-percent tax bracket would purchase a municipal bond yielding $6^{1}/_{2}$ percent only if taxable bonds of similar maturities were yielding less than 7.65 percent. If this investor could earn more than 7.65 percent on taxable bonds, municipal bonds would not be considered. However, for investors in higher tax brackets, the taxable equivalent yield will be much greater. In the 36-percent tax bracket, the taxable equivalent yield on a $6^{1}/_{2}$-percent municipal bond is 10.16 percent. Thus, as tax brackets (rates) increase, the taxable equivalent yields increase and municipal bonds become more

## TABLE 8-1

Comparison of Taxable Bond Yields to Those of Municipals at Different Tax Brackets

| Federal Income Tax Bracket | Municipal Bond Yield | | | |
|---|---|---|---|---|
| | 5% | 5½% | 6% | 6½% |
| | Equivalent Taxable Bond Yield | | | |
| 15% | 5.80% | 6.47% | 7.06% | 7.65% |
| 28% | 6.94% | 7.64% | 8.33% | 9.03% |
| 31% | 7.24% | 7.97% | 8.70% | 9.42% |
| 36% | 7.81% | 8.59% | 9.38% | 10.16% |
| 39.6% | 8.28% | 9.11% | 9.93% | 10.76% |

attractive. For a taxpayer in the highest marginal tax bracket of 39.6 percent, a 5-percent muni-coupon is the equivalent of an 8.28-percent taxable bond coupon.

This presents earnings opportunities for investors in the highest tax brackets, especially when comparing these yields with 10-year Treasury bonds, which are currently yielding under 5 percent. With the decline in market rates of interest over the past years, and with the current currency crises of Asian, Latin American countries, and Russia, there has been a flight to the quality of Treasury bonds. This has driven prices of Treasury bonds up. Similarly, there has been an erosion of prices in the corporate bond market, where investors have been concerned with credit quality and the possible decline in profit margins (Pesek, September 7, 1998, p. 24).

With the current declines in the stock markets around the world, due largely to the meltdowns in both Asia and Latin America, the high yields of municipal bonds, because of their tax-exempt status, make them very appealing to high-income taxpayers. Bear in mind too, though, that the ongoing political talk of changing to a flat tax system and reminders of the 1994 default of Orange County on its bonds have deterred many investors from investing in municipal bonds.

Before buying tax-free municipal bonds, you should decide whether the yield at your tax bracket is high enough to warrant the purchase.

Brokerage firms publish tables of taxable equivalent yields like the one in Table 8-1, but it is a simple calculation to convert municipal bond yields to taxable yield equivalents. The formula is:

$$\text{Taxable equivalent yield} = \frac{\text{tax-free yield}}{1 - \text{tax rate}}$$

A 6-percent coupon municipal bond bought by an investor in the 28-percent marginal tax bracket will have a before-tax return of 8.33 percent:

$$\text{Taxable equivalent yield} = \frac{6\%}{1 - 0.28}$$

$$= 8.33\%$$

Some states have higher rates of taxation than other states, and this raises another question: Should you buy an in-state or out-of-state bond?

Most states give favorable tax treatment to in-state municipals by exempting the income from state taxes. This also applies at the local tax level if the issue is a local issue. This exemption from state and local taxes increases the taxable equivalent yield when comparing an in-state municipal bond with a taxable bond. To answer the question of whether to buy an in-state or out-of-state bond requires another simple calculation.

Suppose that you are considering an out-of-state municipal bond with a yield of $6^{1}/_{2}$ percent and an in-state bond with a yield of $5^{3}/_{4}$ percent, and the state and local taxes combined are 6 percent.

$$
\begin{aligned}
\text{After-tax out-of-state yield} &= (1 - \text{tax rate}) \times \text{out-of-state yield} \\
&= (1 - 0.06) \times 0.065 \\
&= 6.11\%
\end{aligned}
$$

The after-tax yield on the out-of-state bond is 6.11 percent, which is higher than the in-state bond yield, so the out-of-state bond is more attractive in this case. High-tax states like New York and California have such a high demand for their in-state issues that their yields are often lower than out-of-state municipal bond issues. For comparative purposes, bear in mind that Treasury issues and certain government agency issues are also exempt from state and local taxes. These, however, are not exempt from federal taxes.

Investors who are subject to the alternative minimum tax should consult their tax advisors or accountants to determine their equivalent yields.

Tax laws change continually, and investors should keep abreast of these changes and how they affect their investments. Municipal bonds are probably the last great tax shelter left in the code. However, they do not benefit all investors. Generally, investors in the higher tax brackets benefit the most from municipal bonds, but those in lower tax brackets may not find them particularly advantageous to own.

## TYPES OF MUNICIPAL BONDS

State and local governments and their agencies issue a variety of debt instruments. These are classified either by the length of time to maturity or by the way in which the debt is supported. In the former case, the debt would be classified as short-term or long-term, depending on the time to maturity. In the latter, the debt issue is secured either by the taxing power of the issuer, in which case it is a *general obligation bond,* or by the revenues generated by the project, which is called a *revenue bond.*

*General obligation bonds* are issued by states, counties, cities, towns, schools, and special districts. These are usually secured by the taxing power of the issuer. In other words, the interest paid to bondholders comes from taxes and the ability of the issuer to raise more taxes. Theoretically, issuers may have unlimited taxing authority, but in reality, it may not be that easy to enact their "unlimited" taxing powers. This is evidenced by New York City's default on its general obligation notes in 1975. New York City was later compelled by the courts to pay up on their defaulted issue. Many cities have subsequently seen their bond issues downgraded in ratings. This raises questions as to the so-called ironclad security of general obligation bonds. It is apparent that not all general obligation bonds are equal. Their safety in terms of credit and default risk depends on the economic and financial strengths of the issuers.

Changes in the federal bankruptcy laws in 1979 made it easier for municipal bond issuers to seek protection from bondholders by filing for bankruptcy, and this aroused investors' concerns even more. Just because the issue is a general obligation bond backed by the taxing power of the issuer does not mean that there are no credit risks.

There are some obligation bonds which are not secured by the unlimited taxing power of the issuer. There are limits on their taxing sources and these are known as *limited-tax general obligation bonds.* There are also certain obligation bonds which, besides their own characteristics, have certain features of revenue bonds. These are referred to as *double-barreled* securities.

*Revenue bonds* are issued by enterprises such as hospitals, universities, airports, toll roads, and public utilities. The revenues generated by these enterprises or from their projects are used to pay the interest on the debt.

For example, airport revenue bonds may generate revenues from traffic usage at the airport or from the use of airport facilities, such as leasing a terminal building. In the first instance, bondholders should determine whether there is a growing demand for both passenger and airline traffic usage of the airport. In the second, they should examine whether the lease revenues will be sufficient to service the debt.

Proceeds from highway revenue bonds can be used to build toll roads or bridges or to make improvements to the highway infrastructure. Bondholders would have a claim to tolls collected on the roads and bridges, but what about the improvements to the highways? Improving a highway does not generate revenue. Revenue bonds that are not self-supporting will have revenues earmarked to secure the debt. In this case, it could be gasoline taxes, license fees, or automobile registration fees.

So, the security or safety of revenue bonds depends on how essential the services are that the enterprise provides, the flow of revenues, whether these are increasing or decreasing, and whether there are any other claims to the revenues before those of the bondholders. The relative strength of the issuer of the revenue bonds to generate revenues and the ease with which the issuer can cover the interest payments will determine the rating of the revenue bonds.

Besides general obligation and revenue bonds, state and local governments issue short-term municipal notes, which have maturities for periods up to three years. *Anticipation notes* are issued to even out irregular cash flows of the treasuries of the state and local governments. Among the anticipation notes are *tax anticipation notes* (TANs), which are issued in anticipation of taxes to be collected; *bond anticipation notes* (BANs), in anticipation of the proceeds from the sale of long-term bonds; *revenue anticipation notes* (RANs), which are issued in anticipation of revenues coming in; and *tax and revenue anticipation notes* (TRANs), which are a combination of taxes and revenues coming in.

There are also municipal bonds which have special features. *Zero-coupon municipal bonds* are like regular zero-coupon bonds in that they are sold at a deep discount to their face values. Interest is paid at maturity, when the investor receives the face value of the bond. The zero-coupon municipal bond offers tax advantages over regular zero-coupon bonds. The interest that accrues is not subject to federal income taxes. For regular zero-coupon bonds, interest accrues each year and is subject to federal income taxes, even though the interest is not received until the bond is sold or matures. These bonds are discussed in more detail in Chapter 10.

*Put or option tender municipal bonds* are those with which bond-holders have the option of returning the bond to the bond trustee before maturity at face value. Typically, this type of bond is backed either by the revenues of the issuer or by a letter of credit from a bank. The put feature is the opposite of a call feature in the bond provision.

Wall Street bankers, always looking for new types of securities, have dreamed up a new municipal security, a *municipal bond derivative with detachable call-option rights*. In November 1992, the Municipal Electric Authority of Georgia sold securities of this type. The attraction of these to issuers is that the detachable call-option rights can be sold separately from the underlying bond issue (and may also trade separately from the underlying bond), and they have the potential of bringing in additional dollars to the issuers.

These were originally developed by the Paine Webber Group to remove some of the downside effects that call provisions have on municipal bonds. Most tax-exempt securities are issued with call provisions. In periods of falling interest rates, municipal bond issuers are apt to call in their bonds. Thus, municipal bonds tend to appreciate much less than Treasuries and corporate bonds during bond market rallies. This has a direct effect on the performance of municipal bond mutual funds.

Managers of these municipal bond mutual funds can solve this problem by buying the detachable call rights from the issuer. The issuer, therefore, gives up the right to call the bonds in return for an additional sum of money. These securities give investors the opportunity to hedge against their bonds being called as well as the ability to speculate on the direction of market rates of interest (Mitchell, 1993).

For risk-averse investors who want a safe investment with some tax advantages, there are *prerefunded municipal bonds*. These are backed by U.S. Treasury bonds. Prerefunded bonds were issued when interest rates were higher and came into existence when municipalities issued new, lower-coupon bonds. The proceeds of these were used to buy U.S. Treasury securities. The Treasuries are used as security for the first issue of bonds (prefunded), which will be called at the first call date.

Prefunded municipals have AAA ratings and usually pay slightly higher premium coupons. The disadvantages are that they generally sell at premium prices, and they have relatively short maturities, since they will be called within a few years.

Merrill Lynch & Co. has very recently begun to market a speculative, complex municipal bond to individual investors. It is called an *inverse floater*, or TEEMS, which stands for tax-exempt enhanced municipal security. This security is very new and has been used over the past few years primarily by mutual funds to boost their returns.

Inverse floaters are derivative securities, which reflect the changes in price of the underlying bonds sold with them. It seems from the paucity of information available on these inverse floaters that the bond issue which is underwritten is divided into two parts. One part contains bonds, which pay holders coupon rates that fluctuate with money market rates, and the second part of the issue gets the rest of the interest. The second part contains the inverse floaters. When short-term rates fall, holders of the bonds from the first part will get less interest, which leaves more money for the inverse floaters. Similarly, prices of the inverse floaters will increase more than regular municipal bonds when short-term rates of interest fall. Thus, holders of inverse floaters benefit in two ways when interest rates go down: they get more interest, and the prices of the bonds appreciate more than other bonds.

When short-term rates of interest move up, the price of the inverse floaters will drop more than that of plain vanilla bonds, since inverse floaters will get less of the money available for interest payments. When long-term rates increase, this will depress the price of the inverse floater even more.

Merrill Lynch offered $15 million of inverse floaters to individual investors in the third week of March 1993 as part of an offering by the Puerto Rico Telephone Authority (Vogel, 1993). Along with the offering came a brochure filled with warnings about the risks and complexities of this security. The target market for inverse floaters is affluent clients who are not sensitive to instruments that provide variable income and are volatile in price.

These securities have performed well for mutual funds during the past few years as market rates of interest have been falling. It is not evident what the downside risk will be when market rates of interest level off and begin to go up. Samuel B. Corliss, Jr., a managing director of municipal derivatives at Merrill Lynch, is quoted as saying that yields on these inverse floaters will not drop to zero if short-term rates go up rapidly (Vogel, 1993). This raises the question of who will bear the risk of loss? Another question is who will maintain a market for these securities when interest rates rise? Or will investors find that they are stuck with an investment that no one wants to buy when the stakes are down?

Until more is known about inverse floaters, individual investors should not be in too much of a hurry to invest in them, bearing in mind that there are no free lunches on Wall Street. New, complex, speculative derivative securities should be left for institutional investors who can withstand greater variability in prices without their investments being wiped out, and who have more options open to them to deal with the risks involved.

## WHAT ARE THE RISKS OF MUNICIPAL BONDS?

In the past, municipal bonds were always perceived to be very safe investments and tended to rank second only to Treasury securities. This changed during the decade of the 1970s, when New York City defaulted on some of its obligations. This shattered the perception that since the issuers could always raise revenues by increasing taxes, there could be no defaults on government obligation bonds.

A default by a city, town, or municipality is very different from a default by a corporation. In the latter case, bondholders will go to court and the assets will be seized and sold off to pay the creditors. With cities it is very different. In New York's case, bondholders could not easily and practically have sold the New York subway system or parts of it on the market.

So what is the small investor to do regarding the safety of municipal bond issues? A glib, easy answer is: avoid issues which are financially shaky.

To follow that advice, query all those investors who invested in the municipal bonds issued by New York City and Cleveland before their respective defaults. They would probably say that they were investing wisely. Both cities had A ratings. In 1973, New York City obligation bonds were upgraded by ratings services to investment-grade quality. In 1975, New York City defaulted on these bonds. New York City claimed that it did not default but had a "moratorium."

Another major default which shook the municipal bond market was that of the Washington Public Power System (WPPSS, also referred to as WHOOPS). WPPSS sold $2.25 billion of tax-exempt bonds to build two nuclear power plants. Construction on the plants was halted midway when the power company was unable to raise rates to cover the construction costs, and this resulted in a default on the bonds.

Although the number of defaults on municipal issues has been small, these highly publicized examples have made investors very conscious of the risk of default. Following these steps may reduce the risk of default:

- *Ratings.* Investors should consider the ratings of the bond offering. Moody's and Standard & Poor's rate these offerings based on a substantial amount of financial information. As municipal bonds do not have to be registered with the Securities and Exchange Commission, there is very little information available for investors about the issuer's financial status. States and municipalities may not publish their annual financial statements. Therefore, limit your purchases to AAA or AA ratings to minimize the risk of default.

- *Insurance.* Check whether the issue is insured. Bond insurance can increase the ratings of an issue. When a bond is insured, it is given a triple-A rating even if it had a lower rating before insurance. A bond issue that has a rating of AAA or AA without insurance is a stronger offering than an insured bond with the same rating. Insurance corporations such as Municipal Bond Insurance Association (MBIA) and Financial Guaranty Insurance Co. (FGIC) sell insurance whereby they will guarantee the interest payments and the return of principal. The quality of the insurance company will also affect the ratings of the issue. For example, in 1988, when Standard & Poor's downgraded the debt of Verex Assurance, which insured housing authority bonds, the market prices of the housing authority bonds declined. The insurance is only as good as the insurer, and issues with insurance generally have lower yields than uninsured bonds.

- *Credit enhancements.* Instead of insurance, some issuers have letters of credit from banks and insurance companies. These do not guarantee interest payments by the banks or insurance companies. Instead, they offer the issuer a line of credit. If the issuer does not have enough cash to cover the interest payments, the bank or insurance company will lend the issuer the money. This is a lower degree of protection than insurance, and investors should check the ratings of the bank or insurance company providing the line of credit.

- *Official statement.* Obtain a copy of the official statement or offering circular, which is like the prospectus for a corporate security. In it, review:

  The legal opinion. If there is any doubt as to the tax exemption, avoid the issue.

  How the issue will be repaid. This ought to be fairly clear.

  The qualifications, such as "no assurance can be given." If phrases are used that make you nervous, find another issue to invest in.

- *Diversification.* Purchase bonds of different issuers. This spreads the risk associated with any one particular issuer.

A word of caution: Ratings are not cast in stone, and they can change over time, as evidenced by WPPSS. Standard & Poor's gave WPPSS projects four and five ratings of A+ in 1980, which by 1984 deteriorated to a D rating. Therefore, do not base your decision on ratings alone.

*Interest rate risk* may be greater than the risk of default if you choose quality tax-exempt issues. This is not unique to municipal bonds; it applies to all fixed-income securities. Value Line Investment Service estimates that a 20-year municipal bond trading at par will decline 8.6 percent in price for a 1-percent increase in the market rate of interest and will have a 9.9 percent increase in price for a 1-percentage-point drop in interest rates (Dunnan, 1990). The longer the term to maturity, the greater the price volatility due to fluctuations in interest rates.

Although investors will receive greater yields from long-term (30-year) than shorter-term municipals, they should bear in mind the increased volatility and the fact that yield spreads between maturities tend to be wider for municipals than they are for bonds in the taxable bond market.

Investors can lessen interest rate risk without giving up yield by buying AA rated 15-year municipal bonds instead of AAA rated 30-year municipals. As of this writing, yields on shorter-term maturities a notch lower in rating are the same as for a longer-maturity municipal bond a notch higher. Rates change, and the success of this practice would also depend on the yield spread at the time of purchase.

The *risk of a municipal bond being called* is a common risk. Most municipal bonds have call or refunding provisions, which allow issuers to call the bonds in when interest rates have decreased significantly. This explains the high level of redemptions of municipal bonds currently, this and the fall in interest rates. Bondholders will receive the face value of the bond (and in some cases more, depending on the terms set out in the indenture), but they will have to reinvest their money at a lower rate of return.

Investors should read the call provisions of their bonds before purchase to see if there are any unusual features. Housing revenue bonds, for example, may not stipulate a call date, meaning that they could be called anytime after issue. Be careful if you are paying a premium on these bonds, because if they are called, you may not recoup your premium.

Ask your broker for the yield to call as well as the yield to maturity, because if your bond is called, the yield to call becomes your actual return, not the yield to maturity. If the yield to call is less than the coupon rate, you know that the bond is trading at a premium price.

Remember that there are no free lunches on Wall Street (or if there are, they are very few in number). The higher the coupon rate of the bond, the more costly it is for the issuer, and hence the greater the likelihood of that bond issue being called when interest rates fall.

Municipal securities are not as actively traded as government bonds, which means that the spreads between the bid and asked prices tend to be relatively wide. This is true even for the most actively traded issues. This makes municipal bonds less liquid than Treasury issues and agency bonds.

The larger issues of general obligation bonds and the well-known authorities tend to be marketable, but the smaller, thinly traded issues may not be marketable. In fact, for some small issues, there may be no market outside the issuing locality.

Investors should be aware that if they invest in the longer-term maturity municipal issues, illiquidity and lower marketability may expose them to higher selling costs. The best strategy is to buy and hold municipal bonds through maturity (or call).

Then there is the *risk of paying excessive markups on the pricing of individual municipal bonds.* Under current pricing practices, investors do not know if they are being charged excessive markups by their brokerage firms when they buy individual municipal bonds. That's because these bonds are traded in the over-the-counter markets, where the prices are not publicized (not quoted in the newspapers as they are for stocks). Investors call up their brokers and ask for a price quote. The broker can quote any price. Moreover, it is difficult to shop around at another brokerage firm unless you have an account at the firm. A brokerage firm might not quote you its prices for the same bond issues unless you have an account.

For example, a brokerage firm might buy a particular bond issue at $90 per bond and sell it to investors for $99 per bond. This is a $9 markup, or 9.89 percent. This is in lieu of commissions, since the brokerage firm owns the bonds and faces the risk of the bonds falling in price. Another brokerage firm may have bought the same issue of bonds at $89 and may offer it to investors at $93 per bond. Lack of pricing information is a big disadvantage; investors never know if they are paying excessive markups on the individual municipal bonds that they purchase and sell. That's a major reason to buy bonds and hold them to maturity rather than use them as trading vehicles for capital gains, because this lack of pricing also affects the sale of the bonds. The SEC is hoping to rectify this problem of the lack of pricing information in the corporate bond and municipal bond markets.

# HOW TO BUY AND SELL MUNICIPAL BONDS

Investors can buy municipal bonds at issue or on the secondary market. The major financial newspapers, *Barron's*, *The Wall Street Journal*, and *The New York Times*, list the forthcoming sales of new municipals for the week. *The Bond Buyer*, which is a trade publication for municipal bonds, also gives information on forthcoming sales, as well as the results of the previous week's sales of municipal bonds.

In some cases, state and local governments market their issues by placing them in the market privately, usually directly to institutional buyers. Mostly, they are placed through investment bankers, who offer them for sale to the investment community (the public). The investment banker forms a syndicate of brokerage firms to sell the new issue. If there is an issue that interests you, you can put in your order through your brokerage firm. If your brokerage firm is part of the syndicate, there will be no sales commission on the purchase. The other advantage of buying at issue is that the bonds are priced at a uniform price (the syndicate offering price) until all the orders for the syndicate have been filled. Only then can the bonds trade at market prices.

Buying municipals on the secondary market is slightly more difficult because the financial newspapers only print the prices of a small list of some of the popular revenue bonds. Prices of government obligation bonds are not quoted in the newspapers. To learn what bonds are available in the secondary market, you may want to obtain a copy of the *Blue List*, which is published daily by Standard & Poor's. It lists the bonds that dealers currently own in their portfolios and wish to sell. The listing for each bond includes such information as:

- The number of bonds for sale in each issue
- The name of the issuer
- The coupon rate and maturity date
- The price (this does not include the bid and asked spread)
- The name of the dealer selling the bonds

The *Blue List* is the best source of information, but it is also very costly for most individual investors to subscribe to.

Consequently, you should ask your broker to let you see a copy. Do not be surprised to find that by the time you see the *Blue List*, some of the bond issues are already sold. Because the bid and asked spreads are not quoted, there may also be some deviation from the prices quoted in the *Blue List.*

There are many initiatives under way to provide municipal bond pricing to individual investors. J.J. Kenny, an affiliate of Standard & Poor's, operates a toll-free telephone number (1-800-BOND INFO) where investors can obtain prices of up to 25 bonds which have not traded.

There are also Internet sites where daily information on municipal bonds can be obtained. One such Website is *www.bond-markets.com,* which has many municipal bond links. Another Website is *www.investinginbonds.com.* This one lists municipal bond prices, yields, and the credit ratings of the bonds traded.

The municipal bond secondary market is supported by many municipal bond dealers throughout the country. Brokers serve as intermediaries between dealers and institutional and individual investors in municipal bond issues. Many brokerage firms will maintain markets in their local and regional issues.

Pricing of municipal bond issues can vary significantly from dealer to dealer, so when buying (or selling), you should get several quotes from different brokerage firms. The bottom line is to shop around, because paying high commissions and wide spreads lowers your overall return.

Another factor that increases the markups is whether you buy in round or odd lots. When buying or selling, orders of less than $25,000 are considered to be odd lots. Spreads between the bid and asked prices quoted by dealers for these odd lots tend to be wider because dealers find it harder to sell small numbers of municipal bonds. Since such higher costs erode returns, investors might prefer to buy and hold these issues to maturity. Before buying, investors should evaluate the overall risks and returns.

Municipal bonds on the secondary market trade at a discount or a premium, depending on a number of factors: quality, coupon yield, issuer, and length of time to maturity, among others.

When buying municipal bonds at a discount or premium, you should be aware of the likelihood of incurring capital gains when the bonds are sold or called. For example, if you buy 50 municipal bonds with a face value of $50,000 at a discount of $45,000 in 1998, and another 50 municipal bonds with a face value of $50,000 at a premium of $55,000 in 1999, and both issues mature in 2000, $5000 will be subject to capital gains tax in 2000. Puzzled? Well, most people are.

According to the Internal Revenue Tax Code (section 171), for tax-exempt bonds there is no allowable deduction for the amortization of the premium. In other words, the $5000 gain cannot be offset against the $5000 loss because the loss is not recognized (which means that the loss cannot be deducted). The premium is amortized down over the life of the bond to maturity or until call. As a result, municipal bondholders could be doubly penalized: they could buy high-coupon bonds at a premium and then find that they can be called at a lower price (than the premium purchase price paid). So,

1. The loss is not deductible against other capital gains.
2. The bonds may be called sooner than anticipated, not giving the bondholder the chance to recoup the costs of having paid a premium price for a high-coupon security.

This nondeductibility of the amortization is unique to tax-exempt bonds, and investors should be aware that they may face a tax liability on gains from buying bonds at a discount and through the process of amortization of a premium. To illustrate the latter process, consider an example in which an investor buys a tax-exempt bond at a premium of $1100 and in five years sells the bond for $1100. As a result of having to amortize, or write down, the premium over time, the adjusted basis of the tax-exempt bond will be less than $1100, and there will be a taxable gain between the adjusted basis and the selling price.

Municipalities often issue *serial bonds*, which are groups of bonds with different maturities within the issue. Bear in mind that with a serial issue, investors can choose the maturity they desire when the issue is originally sold in the market.

## WHAT ARE THE ADVANTAGES OF MUNICIPAL BONDS?

- Interest on most municipal bond issues is exempt from federal income tax, and it may be exempt from state and local taxes if the bonds are issued in that state and locality.

This benefits high-income investors in the higher tax brackets.

- They provide regular interest payments for income-dependent investors.

## WHAT ARE THE DISADVANTAGES OF MUNICIPAL BONDS?

- Municipal bonds are less liquid and less marketable than government securities. Investors may have difficulty in selling some of the smaller, less actively traded issues in the secondary market.
- Many high-coupon municipals have call provisions. Be aware of the call provision, especially when buying a tax-exempt bond trading at a premium. You could lose part of your investment if the issue is called at a lower price than the purchase price.
- When bonds are called, investors are exposed to the reinvestment risk of having to reinvest their money into lower-yielding securities.
- Default risk is of increasing concern owing to a number of defaults in the past and the increasing number of financially troubled cities.
- Municipal bond prices fluctuate with the changes in interest rates. The longer the maturity of the issue, the greater the price volatility.
- Dealer spreads can be quite wide and can vary considerably among dealers, resulting in excessive markups for investors.

## CAVEATS

- Before investing, taxpayers in lower marginal tax brackets should compare the yields of taxable bonds with those of municipal bonds.
- Municipal bonds are not entirely risk-free. Buy municipals with the highest quality ratings and stay away from small, unrated issues and speculative revenue bonds.

- When buying a new issue, check the offering circular for the legal opinion and the ratings for the issue.
- Be aware of tax nuances, of the possibility of incurring capital gains on the redemption of municipals bought at a discount or premium price.
- Interest on IDBs (industrial development bonds) issued after August 7, 1986, is treated as a preference item, which could trigger the alternative minimum tax for high-income investors.
- Interest on private activity bonds for nonessential purposes is not tax-exempt from federal income taxes.
- Investors should not buy municipal bonds for their IRAs, Keoghs, or tax-deferred pension accounts. They are already tax-deferred.

## MUNICIPAL BOND MUTUAL FUNDS

Instead of investing in individual municipal bonds, investors can choose municipal bond mutual funds. The two major types of municipal bond mutual funds are general tax-exempt funds and single-state tax-exempt funds. In addition, there are other choices pertaining to the length of maturities and high-yield versus high-grade.

*General municipal bond funds* invest in the fixed-income securities issued by states and localities throughout the U.S. *Single-state municipal bond funds* invest primarily in the obligations issued by a single state and the localities in that state, such as the Pennsylvania tax-exempt mutual fund or the New York tax-exempt mutual fund. The primary advantage of single-state municipal bond mutual funds is that for residents of that state, the interest income generated by that fund is exempt not only from federal taxes but also state and possibly local taxes. This is particularly advantageous if you live in a high-tax state like New York, Massachusetts, or California. Investing in general municipal bond mutual funds means that investors are required to pay state and possibly local taxes on the interest income of the fund generated by the obligations of the states outside of their state of residence. Keep in mind that capital gains generated by the fund are taxed at the federal and state levels.

The decision of whether to invest in a general tax-exempt mutual fund or a single-state tax-exempt fund would be determined by your after-tax returns. If you are in a low-tax state, it might not be necessary to invest in a single-state fund.

A well-*diversified* fund is exposed to fewer risks of loss from default and credit than a concentrated fund. Although historically, there have not been many defaults by states and municipalities, there is always the specter of another Orange County. In 1995, Orange County declared bankruptcy and defaulted on some of its short-term taxable and tax-exempt obligations. In this case, the mutual fund families bailed out many of their affected funds so that the shareholders did not have to bear the losses. Investors can follow the ratings of their tax-exempt mutual funds, which will expose the credit risks of the fund. Standard & Poor's rates municipal bond mutual funds.

Another feature which differentiates municipal bond funds is *insurance.* Some of these funds are insured. How this works is that the mutual fund pays an insurance company to insure the principal and interest payments of at least 65 percent of the bonds in the portfolio. The insurance gives the mutual fund portfolio manager more leeway to increase the proportion of riskier, high-yield bonds held in the fund. This, then, becomes a tradeoff between the higher costs of the insurance premiums and the higher yields from the riskier bonds. Paying for insurance reduces the overall return to shareholders.

The *quality* of the holdings of the mutual fund is another consideration. A municipal bond fund with investment-grade holdings will have lower yields than one with lower-than-investment-grade bond holdings. However, the share prices of the lower-quality funds may be more volatile than those of higher-quality funds when there are changes in market rates of interest. In general, the higher the credit quality of the fund, the lower the risks and the returns. The lower the credit quality, the higher the risk and the potential returns.

Municipal bond funds vary as to the average length of *maturity* of their bond holdings. They may be classified as short-term, intermediate-term, or long-term. The longer the maturity of the fund, the greater the potential returns (assuming a normal yield curve) and risks. Not all funds in these classifications will have exactly the same maturities.

# WHAT ARE THE RISKS OF MUNICIPAL BOND MUTUAL FUNDS?

In addition to the risks affecting mutual funds, municipal bond mutual funds are exposed to many of the same risks as their under-lying assets, municipal bonds.

Municipal bond mutual funds would be affected if a *flat tax* or *simplified tax system* were imposed. Such a tax system would elimi-nate many of the current deductions and would include all income as taxable, including municipal bond interest income. With the lowering of the top tax rates, municipal bonds would become less desirable for taxpayers in higher tax brackets. This could result in a sell-off of municipal bonds, which could have a downward effect on the prices of municipal bond mutual funds.

*Interest rate risk* impacts the share price of bond funds differ-ently, depending on the composition and length of maturity of the bonds in the funds. Share prices of municipal bond funds with longer average maturities are more volatile when market interest rates change than share prices of shorter average maturities. A composition of low-quality municipal bonds will be much more volatile in price than a composition of high-quality bonds when interest rates fluctuate. Insured municipal bond mutual funds that hold a large portion of low-quality bonds are not immune to this volatility in share price because of the insurance.

*Credit risk and the risk of default* are always possible with munic-ipal bonds. Municipal bonds in a mutual fund can be downgraded, which would result in a decline in the share price of the fund. Nor are insured mutual funds immune to credit risk. The municipal bond insurer could be downgraded, which would affect the share price of an insured fund. Diversification diminishes credit risk and the risk of unexpected defaults of single issues. This point illustrates the diversification benefits of general funds over single-state funds. California municipal bond funds that held the defaulted Orange County securities were much harder hit than general mutual funds, which likely held a smaller percentage of these obligations.

There is always the *risk of loss of principal* for mutual fund shareholders, since mutual funds do not have a maturity date on which the original principal is returned. To reduce the risk of loss of principal, investors should choose average maturities that match their time requirements for the funds invested.

# HOW TO INVEST IN MUNICIPAL BOND MUTUAL FUNDS

Municipal bond mutual funds may be bought directly through the mutual fund families or indirectly through brokers, financial planners, and banks. Buying indirectly results in investors paying sales commissions. By choosing the mutual fund family and the specific municipal bond fund, investors save on commissions, but in so doing, investors should make sure that they are selecting funds that do not have loads, either front-end or back-end. Second, investors should choose low-expense-ratio funds, which will increase their overall returns over time. The average expense ratio for municipal bond funds is 1.08 percent of assets, which reduces your annual yield on a 5-percent municipal bond by 20 percent (McGough, September 24, 1998, p. C25). The Vanguard family of funds offers several general and single-state municipal bond funds of varying qualities and maturities, all of which are low-expense-ratio funds.

In order to compare the overall returns of the different municipal bond mutual funds, investors should review quarterly, yearly, and longer-term results, which are published in the financial newspapers and business magazines on a quarterly basis. The next step is to request a prospectus from each of the potential fund families. This can be done by using their toll-free telephone numbers, which are published in the quarterly results in the financial newspapers and magazines or can be downloaded from the fund families' Websites on the Internet. Vanguard's, for example, is *www.vanguard.com.*

The prospectus should be examined for the following:

- The objectives of the fund, which determine the fund manager's latitude in purchasing riskier securities
- The types of bonds held in the fund
- The expenses charged by the fund
- Whether the fund charges a front-end load and/or a back-end load
- The total returns of the fund

It is important to examine the objectives and the holdings of a fund because this will determine the risks of the fund. If the fund manager has the latitude to invest in less-than-investment-grade securities, investors should not be surprised to find that the share price of this fund is much more sensitive to changes in interest rates and credit scares than funds with higher-quality bonds.

Before investing in a fund, an application form needs to be filled out and sent to the mutual fund company with a check for the initial investment amount. Investors can add to their fund's investments by sending checks with an investment stub showing the account number and the amount being invested. Similarly, withdrawals can be made as easily. Investors select the methods of withdrawal from the fund on their application form. They notify their fund either in writing or by phone as to the amount they wish to withdraw and the money is either sent by check through the mail, transferred electronically to their accounts, or transferred to another type of fund in the family of funds.

## WHAT ARE THE ADVANTAGES OF MUNICIPAL BOND MUTUAL FUNDS?

- Municipal bond mutual funds offer small investors the opportunity to own a fraction of a diversified municipal bond portfolio. By investing the minimum amounts allowed by the mutual fund, investors can own a share of a cross-section of municipal bonds, whereas buying individual municipal bond issues would require an investment of over $100,000 for a diversified portfolio.
- With the interest income exemption from federal taxes, municipal bond mutual funds offer investors in higher tax brackets the opportunity for higher after-tax returns than other types of bonds.
- Investors can lower their taxes by investing in a single-state municipal bond fund (same state where they reside), which means that the interest income is exempt from federal, state, and possibly local taxes.
- Shares in municipal bond mutual funds are easy to buy and sell.

See Chapter 11 for the advantages of all mutual funds, which also apply to municipal bond mutual funds.

## WHAT ARE THE DISADVANTAGES OF MUNICIPAL BOND MUTUAL FUNDS?

- With municipal bond mutual funds, there is always the risk of capital loss if investors are forced to sell shares at a lower price than the purchase price. This is because mutual funds do not mature.
- Some municipal bond mutual funds may hold a percentage of other bond securities, which are not exempt from federal taxes, which means that shareholders may incur some federal taxes on the interest income from those bonds.

See Chapter 11 for the disadvantages of all mutual funds. They also apply to municipal bond mutual funds.

## CAVEATS

- For high-income taxpayers, some municipal bond mutual funds could trigger the alternative minimum tax (AMT) due to their holdings of industrial development bonds which were issued after August 7, 1986. Before investing, check with the mutual fund as to whether it is subject to the alternative minimum tax.
- All capital gains incurred by the fund are taxable at all levels of government.
- Do not consider municipal bond funds for your tax-deferred accounts, since they are already tax-deferred.

### Should You Choose Individual Municipal Bonds or Municipal Bond Mutual Funds?

The advantages of investing in municipal bond mutual funds over individual issues are:

- You do not need a large sum of money to invest in a mutual fund. Whatever the stated minimum of the fund, that's all you need.
- With mutual funds, investors buy into a diversified portfolio of bonds which would take significant sums of money to achieve if buying municipal issues individually.

- Mutual funds have professional managers, who have both expertise and quick access to information about the individual bond issues and bond markets.
- It is not as risky to invest in high-yield municipal bond funds as high-yielding individual municipal issues. The diversification achieved by mutual funds over individual issues minimizes the impact from any unexpected defaults or downgrades in credit ratings.
- Buying and selling shares in a mutual fund is far easier than buying and selling individual municipal bond issues, particularly with the lack of published pricing information.

The advantages of individual municipal bond issues over mutual funds are:

- Investors in high marginal tax brackets can avoid buying industrial development bonds, which could trigger the alternative minimum tax. When buying mutual funds, investors do not have a choice in the composition of the fund's bond holdings.
- Investors in individual municipal bonds know both the timing and amount of interest income they will receive. With municipal bond funds, the timing of dividends paid out by the fund is known, but the amounts may vary from month to month.
- Investors in individual municipal bonds avoid the fees charged by mutual funds, which reduce overall returns. Mutual funds charge shareholders operating fees, such as 12b-1 fees and others, which are over and above any loads that are charged. All mutual funds have these operating fees, so it becomes important to look for low-operating-cost, low-expense-ratio funds. Thus, for the investor in individual municipal bonds, there is the potential to earn greater returns than those of mutual funds.
- Individual bonds have maturity dates and you know when you will receive the return of your principal. By laddering your portfolio of individual municipal bonds, you can time the maturities of the bonds to your needs for cash and always get back the full amount of your principal invested, thereby avoiding the effects of interest rate risk. Municipal bond funds never mature. Even if you have a long time

**TABLE 8-2**

Advantages of Individual Municipal Bonds versus
Municipal Bond Mutual Funds

|                                       | Individual Bonds | Mutual Funds |
|---------------------------------------|:----------------:|:------------:|
| Small amount of money to invest       |                  | ✓            |
| Diversification                       |                  | ✓            |
| Professional management               |                  | ✓            |
| Risks of low-quality issues           |                  | ✓            |
| Ease of buying and selling            |                  | ✓            |
| Alternative minimum tax               | ✓                |              |
| Certainty of interest                 | ✓                |              |
| Potential of earning greater returns  | ✓                |              |
| Loss of principal                     | ✓                |              |
| Tax planning                          | ✓                |              |

horizon with mutual funds, when you need the money, the
share price of the mutual fund may have fallen below the
original purchase price.

- Owning individual municipal bonds over mutual funds
  offers investors control over their capital gains and losses
  for tax planning purposes. Mutual funds do not pay taxes
  on the gains and losses from the sale of municipal bonds
  before maturity. These gains and losses are passed on to the
  shareholders at the end of the year, which can ruin any
  careful tax planning.

Table 8-2 summarizes the advantages of investing in individual
municipal bonds versus municipal bond mutual funds.

# REFERENCES

**Dunnan, Nancy:** *Guide to $Your Investments$*, Harper & Row, New York, 1990.

**McGough, Robert:** "Muni-Bond Funds Look Good to Some," *The Wall Street Journal*, September 24, 1998, p. C25.

**Mitchell, Constance:** "Latest Muni Derivative Gets U.S. Scrutiny," *The Wall Street Journal*, February 11, 1993, p. C1.

**Pesek, William:** "Tax Free and Cheap," *Barron's*, September 7, 1998, p. 24.

**Vogel, Thomas T., Jr.:** "Muni Floaters Are Marketed to Individuals," *The Wall Street Journal*, March 31, 1993, p. C1.

## CHAPTER 9

# Convertible Bonds and Convertible Bond Mutual Funds

## KEY CONCEPTS

- What are convertible securities?
- Features of convertible bonds
- How do convertibles work?
- The different types of convertible securities
- What are the risks of convertibles?
- How to buy and sell convertible securities
- What are the advantages of convertible securities?
- What are the disadvantages of convertible securities?
- Are convertible securities suitable for you?
- Convertible security mutual funds
- What are the risks of convertible security mutual funds?
- How to buy and sell convertible security mutual funds
- What are the advantages of convertible security mutual funds?
- What are the disadvantages of convertible security mutual funds?

Portions of this chapter have been previously published by Esmé Faerber in *Managing Your Investments, Savings, and Credit*, McGraw-Hill, New York, 1992.

Some years, convertible securities have outpaced all other investments. In 1992, convertible securities measured by Smith Barney's convertible index increased by 25 percent, which was more than six times the increase in the Dow Jones Industrial Average and the Standard & Poor's 500 Index (Bary, 1993).

You might think that investors were falling all over themselves to buy convertible securities, but you would be wrong. According to mutual fund managers, most investors either had never heard of convertible securities or did not know what they were. Confirming this fact, the convertible fund in the Vanguard Group of mutual funds had the highest return for 1992 (19 percent), but had assets of only $165 million (Bary, 1993).

## WHAT ARE CONVERTIBLE SECURITIES?

Convertibles are hybrid securities which come in two primary forms, convertible bonds and convertible preferred stock. These are bonds and preferred stock that can be exchanged for a specified number of common shares of the issuing corporation at the option of the convertible holder. In a few cases, convertible bonds have been exchanged for preferred stock or other bond issues. Then there are some other rare types of hybrid convertibles, including PIKs (payment in kind), hybrid convertibles, LYONs, commodity-backed bonds, and stock-indexed bonds. Each of these different types of securities has conversion options or relationships to other types of securities or assets. PIKs, for example, pay their holders more of the same units of the securities they hold. These are all discussed in more detail later in the chapter.

## FEATURES OF CONVERTIBLE BONDS

Convertible bonds are long-term debt instruments which have many of the features of regular bonds. They are usually issued with a face value of $1000 and have a maturity date (in the event that they are not converted). Interest may be paid semiannually or annually by the issuer.

Some issues have call provisions, which issuers often use to force the holders to convert their bonds. When convertible bondholders convert their bonds, the issuing firm no longer has to repay the bonds.

So why do companies issue convertible bonds when they could raise money by issuing regular debt or equity? By issuing convertible bonds, companies can tap into the credit markets more easily. Because of the conversion feature, companies can issue convertible bonds with lower coupon rates than they would have to pay on regular bonds. These bonds are usually subordinated to the issuing company's other outstanding debt issues.

Why would investors want to invest in lower-quality, lower-yielding debt? Again, it is the conversion feature that makes the difference. Investors are willing to accept lower coupon rates and lower quality in return for the possible appreciation if the stock price of the issuing company rises. In other words, investors are sacrificing current income for possible future capital gains. Convertible securities appeal to investors who are nervous about investing directly in the common stock of companies. This is because convertibles generally fall less than stocks in down markets, but they also rise less than the stock when markets are going up.

The fact that convertibles are subordinated debenture issues does not mean that only weaker, financially troubled companies issue them. Many financially weaker companies do issue convertibles because they can raise funds which may not have been available through either ordinary debt or equity issues. However, in many cases, financially strong companies have issued convertibles to lower their interest costs from issuing regular debt. Companies such as Xerox, Westinghouse (now CBS), Ashland Oil, Compaq Computer, Browning Ferris, and Ford Motor Company have all issued convertible securities.

In 1991, Ford Motor Company sold a large convertible issue when its stock price was $25. Ford's stock price reached a high of $50 during the 1992–1993 period, which was a 100 percent gain on the stock price. The convertible bonds appreciated by a smaller percentage (70 percent). Due to the conversion feature, convertible bonds appreciate when the stock price goes up but generally not as much as the common stock (as confirmed by the Ford Motor Company issue). When the stock price declines, the coupon rate on the convertible bond acts as a cushion against the downward pressure of the price of the convertible.

# HOW DO CONVERTIBLES WORK?

Convertible securities have their own terminology, and these terms are often confusing to investors. A good starting point to understanding them is to use an example. Suppose a corporation wanting to raise funds decides that because the market price of the stock is low, it does not want to issue more common stock. To raise enough cash, it would have to issue many more shares of common stock, which would dilute earnings for existing share-holders. A straight debt issue would also be too costly because the company would have to match the coupon rate of comparable existing corporate debt issues with similar risks and maturities.

Instead, the company decides on a convertible bond on which, because of the conversion feature, investors will accept a lower coupon rate. The company will need to consider the current market price of its common stock to determine the number of shares that each bondholder will receive on conversion. For instance, if the company's stock is currently trading at $18 per share, the company may decide on a conversion price of $25 to make the bonds more appealing to investors. The *conversion ratio*, which is the number of common shares received for each bond, is 40 (shares per bond = 1000/25). This is the face value of the bond divided by the conversion price. Figure 9-1 describes an example of a convertible bond issue by Seagate Technology.

The reader will see immediately that the convertible bond can be valued either in relation to the conversion value of the stock or as a straight bond. In reality, both of these factors are taken into account in the valuation of the convertible security.

## The Value of a Convertible Bond as Stock

The value of the convertible security as stock depends on the market price of the common stock. The value is the number of shares into which the bond is convertible multiplied by the market price of the stock. In the hypothetical example above, the convertible can be exchanged into 40 shares, which is multiplied by $18, the current market price of the stock, to give a value of $720.

The relationship between the value of the convertible bond as stock and the price of the common stock is illustrated in Table 9-1.

FIGURE 9-1

### Seagate Technology's Convertible Bond

In 1993, Seagate Technology issued a subordinated convertible bond with a coupon yield of 6.75 percent and a maturity date of 2012. This bond had both call and sinking fund provisions. The conversion ratio was 23.5 shares of common stock for each convertible bond. This means that particular Seagate bond was convertible at a conversion price of $42.50 (1000/23.5). In other words, Seagate bondholders could surrender each of their bonds, with a par value of $1000 per bond, for 23.5 shares of Seagate's common stock. However, in order to equal the $1000 par value of the bond, Seagate's common stock price would have to trade at $42.50 per share.

At the time of the issuance of the convertible bond, Seagate's common stock was trading in the low $20s per share. This meant that the stock price would have to appreciate more than 90 percent in order to make it worthwhile for bondholders to convert their bonds into common stock.

In the event of a stock split, the convertible bond's conversion ratio would be adjusted accordingly. For example, a two-for-one common stock split of Seagate's stock would adjust the conversion ratio to 47 shares (23.5 × 2), and the conversion price to $21.25 ($42.50/2) (Ross et al, 1999, p. 607).

From Table 9-1, we see that as the market price of the stock rises (column 2), the value of the convertible increases. The value of the convertible is obtained by multiplying the conversion ratio by the market price of the stock. When the price of the common stock is below a conversion price of $25, the value of the convertible is less than the face amount of the bond ($1000). When the stock price is above the conversion price of $25, the value of the convertible is greater than the face value of the bond. Thus, the conversion feature allows for the upside potential of capital gains through the appreciation of the stock price. Moreover, there is a floor price below which the price of the convertible will not fall, and that is the straight value of the bond.

For example, assume that in the above illustration, the market price of the common stock falls to $10 per share. The conversion value is $400, but the market price will not fall below the value of the bond because of the value of the coupon interest payments on the bond. Similarly, the market price of the convertible will not be less than the conversion value of the security. This is due in part to

**TABLE 9-1**

Relationship of Convertible Bond Value and Stock Price

| Conversion Ratio* | Market Price of Stock | Value of Convertible as Stock |
|---|---|---|
| 40 | $10 | $ 400 |
| 40 | 18 | 720 |
| 40 | 25 | 1000 |
| 40 | 30 | 1200 |
| 40 | 35 | 1400 |
| 40 | 40 | 1600 |

*The number of shares the convertible is exchanged into.

the activity of arbitrageurs, who buy and sell the same security in two different markets to take advantage of price differentials.

For instance, if the market value of the debt is $900 when the stock price is $24, arbitrageurs will exploit this price differential for their own profit. The conversion value is $960 (40 shares × $24 per share), and they will sell the stock short. To *sell short* is to borrow a security and sell it on the market. They will simultaneously buy the convertible bond for $900 and sell short 40 shares of the stock for $960. The conversion option is then exercised, and they tender the shares that they borrowed. The resulting profit is $60 per bond before taking into account the commissions for buying and selling the securities. In this way, arbitrageurs will bid up the price of the bonds until there is no longer a price differential. In reality, the price of convertible bonds is rarely the same as the conversion value into stock. Usually, the price of the convertible exceeds the conversion value due to the bond's value. In addition to the upside appreciation attributable to the conversion value, the value of the bond as debt provides a floor price for the convertible bond.

### The Value of the Convertible Bond as Debt

The value of the convertible as debt depends on the coupon rate, the risk of default on the interest payments, the length of time to maturity, the call provision, and market rates of interest. The investment value of the bond can be determined by discounting both the coupon payment that the convertible pays and the face value of the bond at maturity (assuming it is not converted) at the interest rate paid on similar debt. In other words, the value of the convertible bond is the *present value* of the cash flows of the coupon payments and the *face value* of the bond at maturity discounted at an interest rate which includes the risk for that security.

As with regular bonds, the value of the convertible bond as debt fluctuates with changes in market rates of interest. When interest rates increase, the price of the convertible bond declines. Conversely, when interest rates decline, the price of the convertible will go up. This is because the coupon rate on the convertible is fixed.

The value of the convertible as straight debt is important because it sets a floor price. When the stock price is trading below the conversion price, the straight bond value provides the floor value, and the convertible will not fall below this value. Of course, the convertible option is of no consequence at lower stock prices. When stock prices go up above the conversion price, the minimum price for the convertible bond becomes the conversion value as stock. This is where the bond is equity in disguise.

## The Value of the Convertible Bond as a Hybrid Security

Thus far we have seen that at low stock prices, the floor price of the convertible will be no lower than its value as a straight bond, and at sufficiently high stock prices, the price of the convertible will be the same as the conversion value into stock. In between these extremes in stock prices, the convertible security generally trades at a premium price over its value as equity and over its value as debt.

These relationships are examined in Table 9-2, using the example of a 6-percent 20-year convertible bond which has a conversion ratio of 40 shares. The market rate of interest used is 8 percent.

At low stock prices ($5 and $10 per share), the market price of the convertible bond is the same as its value as straight debt, and the premium over the stock price is large. At $25 per share, the conversion price, or the market price for the convertible, is $1100, which exceeds the value of the debt by $296.36 and the value as stock by

## TABLE 9-2

Premiums on Convertible Bonds

| Share Price | Conversion Ratio | Value as Stock | Value as Debt | Market Price of Convertible Bond* | Premium over Stock Price | Premium over Bond Price |
|---|---|---|---|---|---|---|
| $ 5 | 40 | $ 200 | $803.64 | $ 803.64 | $603.64 | $    0 |
| 10 | 40 | 400 | 803.64 | 803.64 | 403.64 | 0 |
| 18 | 40 | 720 | 803.64 | 850.00 | 130.00 | 46.36 |
| 25 | 40 | 1000 | 803.64 | 1100.00 | 100.00 | 296.36 |
| 35 | 40 | 1400 | 803.64 | 1420.00 | 20.00 | 616.36 |
| 40 | 40 | 1600 | 803.64 | 1600.00 | 0 | 796.36 |

*In reality, it is difficult to calculate the market price of the convertible security due to its hybrid nature and the many factors affecting the market price. Therefore, the market prices between the extremes in stock prices in this example are hypothetical and could fluctuate.

$100. At a significantly high stock price of $40 for this company, the market price of the convertible is the same as the value as stock, and the premium over the value as debt is very high ($796.36).

The example illustrates that as the stock price rises, the premium paid over its value as straight debt increases. This is due to the importance of the conversion feature on the convertible and the fact that the straight debt becomes less important as the stock price increases.

There is also the probability that the bond would be called when the stock price exceeded the conversion price, which would force conversion. For example, assume that the convertible bond was bought at $1420 and the company calls in the bonds when the stock price is at $35. Convertible bondholders will not turn in their bonds for $1000 per bond. Instead, they will convert their bonds into equity, receiving $1400 per bond (40 shares × $35), which results in a loss of $20 per bond for the bondholders. Thus, as the stock price rises and puts downward pressure on the premium over the stock price, the market price for the convertible converges with the stock value of the convertible.

Most convertible securities trade at a premium over either the stock value or the value as a straight bond. Investors should analyze the fundamentals of the company before buying. For example, Battle Mountain 6-percent convertible bonds were trading at a 141-percent premium over its equity value, whereas another mining company, Couer d'Alene 7-percent convertible bonds, were trading at a 31-percent premium over the equity value. In this case, the lower premium over the equity value offers greater appreciation potential than the convertible bond with the higher premium over its equity value.

## THE DIFFERENT TYPES OF CONVERTIBLE SECURITIES

*Convertible preferred stock* is similar to convertible bonds. The convertible preferred stockholder has the option to convert each share of preferred stock into a fixed number of shares of common stock of the issuing company. Generally, the conversion ratio for convertible preferred securities is small. For example, it may be one share of preferred for one share of common stock.

Convertible preferred stock issues have many characteristics similar to convertible bonds. However, with convertible preferred stock, dividends are paid only if the board of directors of the company declares them. They are not like interest payments on convertible bonds, where a default in the interest payments is liable to cause the bondholders to bring action against the company. Although the number of convertible preferred stock issues has increased in the last few years, they are not as popular as convertible bonds.

Small companies in need of cash have issued some risky *convertible preferred securities with floating conversion ratios,* also known as *death spirals,* or *toxic convertibles.* Many of the companies that have issued these securities have seen their stock prices fall due to dilution and an increase in short-selling. When preferred stockholders convert their securities to common stock, there is a larger number of shares outstanding, which results in lower earnings per share. This puts downward pressure on the price of the common stock. Short-sellers also exacerbate the situation. Short-sellers sometimes jump in when these securities are issued, since they are viewed as a type of financing of last resort for companies. Short-sellers bet that the stock price will go down. They sell "borrowed" stock, and then buy the stock back at a later stage when the stock price goes down. This puts further downward pressure on the stock price (Lucchetti and Scism, September 28, 1998, pp. C1, C7).

Another type of combination security is *hybrid convertibles.* These are convertible debentures of one company that are convertible into the common stock of another company. Companies that have accumulated a substantial number of shares of another company can issue hybrid convertibles as a source of funds. For example, Mesa Petroleum had accumulated shares of General American, and it issued hybrid convertibles that were convertible into the shares of General American.

Buying hybrid convertibles means that not only should the debt of the issuing company be attractive to you, you should also like the equity of the convertible company. A nuance with hybrid convertibles is that it is a taxable exchange because the securities involve not one, but two companies.

There are many different *zero-coupon convertible bonds,* one of which is Merrill Lynch's LYON, or liquid yield option note. Zero-coupon bonds are sold at a deep discount from their face value and do not pay yearly cash interest. Instead, the interest accrues, and at maturity the bond is redeemed for its face value. However, these also have call provisions, which makes their valuation more complex.

Zero-coupon convertible bonds tend to be offered by companies that want to conserve their cash. Walt Disney Company issued zero-coupon convertibles to raise funds for their European Disneyland in Paris. These securities were convertible into EuroDisney stock traded on the Bourse in Paris, which, unfortunately for its holders, had been declining in value. This points out the disadvantage of this type of security. When the stock price is depressed and there is a call provision, the zero-coupon convertible will trade close to its call price, which could be less than what investors paid for the security.

Another similar combination security is the *payment in kind,* or PIK. In some respects, PIKs are like zero-coupon securities in that interest (or dividends in the case of preferred stock PIKs) is not paid out in cash in the early years. Instead, interest (or dividends) is paid in the form of additional securities of the underlying issue. For bonds, interest is in the form of more bonds, and for preferred stock, dividends would be additional preferred shares.

PIKs tend to carry higher coupons to entice investors. However, investors need to examine the issuing company's financial status carefully to determine whether the company will be around in future years to make the payoffs in cash. Again, be reminded that there are no free lunches on Wall Street. This is a high-yield security in return for high risk.

SIRENs, or *step-up income redeemable equity notes*, are intermediate convertible bonds with two coupons. The first coupon is below market rates of interest. After a few years, the coupon increases to a higher rate until maturity. These have a convertible provision whereby holders can convert their notes into the common stock of the issuer at a price determined by the issuer (conversion price). As with other convertibles, if the price of the common stock goes up, holders stand to profit. If the price of the common stock goes down, holders of SIRENs have a floor price on their notes, but they will earn less than they would on a similar conventional bond.

The clincher is that these are issued with call provisions which allow the issuer to call the bond at the time of the step-up by paying a slight premium over par. Thus, if the stock price has not risen above the conversion price, investors would not want to convert, as they would have sacrificed a few years of below-market-rate yields on their SIRENs.

## WHAT ARE THE RISKS OF CONVERTIBLES?

As with any debt security, investors are concerned about the *risk of default*. This is especially so for convertible bonds, which tend to be subordinated to the issuing firm's other debt securities. Therefore, convertible bonds are not as safe as the company's senior debt, and in the event of bankruptcy, convertible bondholders stand behind the other bondholders in the collection line. Hence, they may receive only a fraction of their invested principal at best.

In addition to default risk, there is *interest rate risk*. Being a fixed-income security with coupon rates that tend to be lower than conventional debt issues, an increase in market rates of interest will cause a greater decline in the price of convertible issues than of nonconvertible bonds.

Generally, high interest rates tend to depress stock market prices, and the convertible bond is doubly cursed if the issuing company's stock is depressed. Stock prices and stock markets can be both uncertain and volatile, which may not help in the appreciation of the convertible. Thus, there is the risk that if the stock price never rises above the conversion value, there will be no conversion and the convertible bondholder will receive a lower return than on a regular bond. This is due to the lower coupon yields of convertible bonds.

Most convertible bonds have call provisions, so there is always the *risk of call*. When interest rates decline, bonds are generally called by corporations so that they can issue new bonds at lower coupon rates and save money.

## HOW TO BUY AND SELL CONVERTIBLE SECURITIES

Convertible bonds can be bought and sold in the same way as corporate bonds. New issues may be bought through the underwriter or participating syndicate broker, in which case the investor is not charged a fee or markup.

Convertible securities trading on the secondary market may be purchased or sold through full-service brokerage firms, discount brokers, brokerage services offered by banks, and on-line brokers. Most of the convertible bonds are listed on the over-the-counter markets, while convertible bonds of the larger, better-known companies are listed on the New York Bond Exchange. You can find convertible preferred stock listings on the New York Stock Exchange, the American Stock Exchange, and the over-the-counter markets.

Brokerage fees for purchasing convertible bonds are similar to those charged for buying regular bonds. Markups charged per bond can vary, depending on several factors, such as the number of convertible bonds purchased, the total value of the purchase, or the type of broker (full-service or discount). It is important to shop around before buying to find the lowest markups and dealer spreads. Investors will have the same difficulties obtaining prices on convertible bonds that they would on other types of bonds, corporate, agency, municipal, etc.

Fees for convertible preferred stock are similar to those when buying common stocks. They are higher for purchasing in odd lots (less than 100 shares for the higher-priced convertible preferred stocks).

Information on convertible securities can be found in *Value Line Convertibles Report*, a weekly put out by Value Line Investment Survey; the sections on convertible bonds in the *Standard & Poor's Bond Guide* and *Moody's Bond Record*; Standard & Poor's Stock Guide (for convertible preferred stocks); and research information from brokerage companies. Merrill Lynch publishes *Convertible Securities*, a comprehensive monthly report on existing convertible bonds, convertible preferred stock, and many of the combination convertible securities.

## WHAT ARE THE ADVANTAGES OF CONVERTIBLE SECURITIES?

- Experienced investors can use convertible securities to hedge against fluctuations in market prices. Hedging involves buying one security and simultaneously selling short a related security. For example, buying the convertible and selling short the related stock can result in profits at best or at worst, a small loss with fluctuations in the market price of the stock.

- Convertible securities offer the upside potential of capital gains through the appreciation of common stock and downside protection if the market price of the common stock falls below the conversion value, since the convertible will be valued at no less than a straight bond (or preferred stock).

- Interest received on convertible bonds or dividends, in the case of convertible preferred stock, generally exceed the dividends paid by comparable common stock. Some corporations that have convertible securities may not pay dividends on their common stock, and corporations can easily eliminate them if they have a drop in earnings. Failure to pay interest on debt, however, would force the company into bankruptcy.

- Convertible securities offer some protection against inflation, since the market prices of both common stock and convertible bonds rise with inflation. However, if conversion does not take place, that is, if the market price of the common stock does not rise above the conversion value, investors have no protection from inflation because the interest and dividends received on convertible securities are fixed.

## WHAT ARE THE DISADVANTAGES OF CONVERTIBLE SECURITIES?

- Yields on convertible securities are often lower than yields on straight bonds.
- In the event of liquidation, convertible bonds are subordinated to the other debt of the issuing corporation on their claims to assets. Convertible preferred shareholders would be paid after creditors but before common shareholders. Risk depends on the overall strength of the issuing company.
- Convertible securities, like all fixed-income securities, are sensitive to changes in interest rates. The prices of convertible securities fluctuate with changes in market rates of interest.
- When market interest rates fall, there is the increased risk that the convertible bonds will be called by the issuing company. The issuing company can then refinance its convertibles with cheaper debt.
- Investors may face the risk of dilution of the common stock of the company. This occurs when the value of the common stock decreases due to an increase in the number of common shares outstanding brought on by conversion or new issues of common stock.
- In the event of a leveraged buyout of the issuing company, investors may end up with a nonconvertible security, which has a lower yield than the company's other debt.

## CAVEATS

- Do not buy convertible securities unless you would be willing to buy that company's common stock. If the convertible security is never converted to common stock, the interest received on it will be less than if you had invested in a regular bond.

- Be wary of buying convertibles which are trading at high premiums over both the market value of the common stock and/or the callable price of the convertibles.
- Before you buy, check the provisions of the convertibles for the call price, whether there is a sinking fund that will allow the issuing company to redeem a specific number of convertibles each year, and so on.

## ARE CONVERTIBLE SECURITIES SUITABLE FOR YOU?

Convertible securities offer the potential for both appreciation and a steady stream of income, but they may not be the best of both worlds. They certainly allow investors to hedge their bets in both the debt and the equities markets. However, under certain conditions, they are not the best investments, and investors would be better off owning either regular debt or equity.

Generally, convertible securities do well when interest rates are falling and the stock market is rising. This was the case in 1992, when convertible securities outperformed the stock market indices. On an individual basis, however, much depends on the fundamentals of the company issuing the convertible. If investors like the common stock of a particular company but they are not sure if the stock market is going to fall, they can buy the convertible, which will not fall as much in price as the common stock would. The convertible holders then will receive regular income even if the stock price does decline.

However, if the stock price of the company goes up, investors will not do as well with convertibles as they would have had they bought the stock instead of the convertible.

The downside of convertibles is that they can be complicated in structure, with call provisions which can result in holders losing money if they bought the convertibles at a premium. Similarly, if convertibles are not converted into equity, investors generally would have done better with regular bonds, which tend to pay higher coupons.

Convertible securities are suited to investors who have the knowledge of the workings and intricacies of these specialized securities and who can hedge their bets in the bond and equity markets.

## CONVERTIBLE SECURITY MUTUAL FUNDS

Instead of investing in individual convertible bonds, investors can opt for convertible mutual funds. The choices of convertible security mutual funds are not as large as for corporate bond funds, for example. Most mutual fund families tend to offer only one convertible fund. Thus, investors would need to look at and compare the convertible security funds offered by several different fund families.

Since most convertible bonds issued by corporations are unsecured and subordinated debt, the credit quality and risk of default are of a greater concern than they would be for secured, better-quality bonds. However, the diversification achieved by convertible security mutual funds tends to dilute the impact of loss from any potential downgrades in credit quality and the possible default of a few issues.

The risks of a convertible security fund depend on the holdings in the portfolio of investments, the average length of time to maturity, market rates of interest, and the state of the bond and stock markets. Due to the complexities of convertible securities and the fact that their well-being is interdependent with many other factors, investors might be better off in mutual funds, where professional managers can handle the complexities.

## WHAT ARE THE RISKS OF CONVERTIBLE SECURITY MUTUAL FUNDS?

Due to the *lower credit quality* of convertible bonds, investors in convertible security mutual funds need to have a long investment time horizon, at least five years. Share prices of convertible security mutual funds have the potential to be much more volatile than regular bond funds. When interest rates are low and the stock market is in the bull mode, convertible security mutual funds can easily outperform many other types of bond funds as was noted earlier in this chapter in 1992. However, if the stock markets are in a downward spiral, and market rates of interest rate are moving up, convertible security mutual funds may very well underperform other conservative types of investments. Thus, investors in these funds are exposed to the *risk of loss of principal* due to the increased volatility of the underlying securities and the interdependence of the many other factors affecting their prices.

Convertible security mutual funds are subject to *interest rate risk.* Generally, a rise in market rates of interest not only depresses the prices of most fixed-income securities but also those of common stocks. This is the double whammy on convertible securities because the coupon yields on the bonds are lower than conventional bonds, which means that shareholders in these funds are likely to receive lower total returns than if they had invested in regular fixed-income mutual funds. This could prompt fund managers to invest in riskier securities to try and increase their overall returns, and thereby increasing the overall risks of the fund.

## HOW TO BUY AND SELL CONVERTIBLE SECURITY MUTUAL FUNDS

Convertible security mutual funds can be bought directly through mutual fund families or indirectly through brokers, financial planners, and banks. To save on sales commissions, you are better off investing directly with the mutual fund family in no-load funds, especially in light of the increased potential share price volatility of convertible security mutual funds. Figure 9-2 shows an example of the Vanguard convertible security mutual fund, which was printed off their Internet Website, *www.Vanguard.com.* The expense ratio of this fund is 0.73 percent, which is lower than the average 1-percent range of other funds. For example, if a fund earns a yield of 5 percent per annum and the expense ratio is 1 percent, shareholders are essentially paying out 20 percent of their earnings in fees (1% ÷ 5%). Look for low-expense-ratio funds.

A good starting point in determining which convertible security funds to consider is to look at the statistics on different types of mutual funds that are published on a quarterly basis by the financial newspapers and magazines. From the total-return history and expense ratios of the mutual funds listed, investors can determine which of the convertible security mutual funds fit their criteria. By requesting a prospectus from each of the funds you are interested in, you can compare them with regard to:

- The objectives of the fund and the degree of risk tied to the fund managers' latitude to choose lesser-quality securities
- The types of securities in the fund

**FIGURE 9-2**

## Vanguard Convertible Securities Fund Overview

| | | | |
|---|---|---|---|
| **Ticker:** | VCVSX | **Risk Level:** | Moderate |
| **Category:** | Growth and income funds | **Fund Number:** | 82 |
| **Asset Type:** | Stocks | **Inception Date:** | 6/17/1986 |

**Objective**

Vanguard Convertible Securities Fund seeks income and long-term growth of capital.

**Who Should Invest**

- Investors seeking dividend income.
- Investors seeking long-term growth of capital.
- Investors with a long-term investment horizon (at least five years).

**Who Should Not Invest**

- Investors unwilling to accept significant fluctuations in share price.

**Fund Characteristics**

| | |
|---|---|
| **Newspaper Abbreviation** | Convrt |
| **CUSIP** | 922023106 |
| **Quotron** | VCVSX.Q |
| **Fund Assets** | 1/31/1999 $176.55 million |
| **Minimum Initial Investment** | Standard $3,000 IRA $1,000 UGMA $1,000 |
| **Expense Ratio:** | 11/30/1998 0.73% |
| Current Fund Prices | |

**Low Balance Fee**

The fund will deduct a $10 annual fee if your nonretirement account balance falls below $2,500 (below $500 for STAR Fund) or if your UGMA/UTMA account balance falls below $500. The fee is waived if your total Vanguard fund account assets are $50,000 or more. In addition, the low-balance fee does not apply to IRAs and other Vanguard retirement plan accounts.

- Whether the fund charges loads (either front-end or back-end)
- The expense ratios of each fund
- The total returns of the fund

Figure 9-3 shows Vanguard's convertible securities fund portfolio profile page from its November 30, 1998, annual report. An

## FIGURE 9-3

### Annual Report, Fund Profile of Vanguard's Convertible Securities Fund

## FUND PROFILE
### Convertible Securities Fund

This Profile provides a snapshot of the fund's characteristics as of November 30, 1998, compared where appropriate to an unmanaged index. Key elements of this Profile are defined on pages 11 and 12.

**Financial Attributes**

| | |
|---|---|
| Number of Issues | 85 |
| Yield | 4.2% |
| Conversion Premium | 31.1% |
| Average Weighted Maturity | 5.4 years |
| Average Coupon | 3.9% |
| Average Quality | Ba |
| Average Duration | 4.3 years |
| Foreign Holdings | 12% |
| Turnover Rate | 186% |
| Expense Ratio | 0.73% |
| Cash Reserves | 1.7% |

**Distribution by Credit Quality (% of Bonds)**

| | |
|---|---|
| Aaa/AAA | 0.0% |
| Aa/AA | 0.0 |
| A/A | 5.8 |
| Baa/BBB | 14.1 |
| Ba/BB | 18.9 |
| B/B | 30.2 |
| Less than B/B | 1.5 |
| Not Rated | 29.5 |
| Total | 100.0% |

**Volatility Measures**

| | Convertible Securities | S&P 500 |
|---|---|---|
| R-Squared | 0.68 | 1.00 |
| Beta | 0.64 | 1.00 |

**Ten Largest Holdings (% of Total Net Assets)**

| | |
|---|---|
| Comverse Tech, Inc. | 3.0% |
| Jacor Communications, Inc. | 2.9 |
| Network Associates Inc. | 2.9 |
| Office Depot Inc. | 2.7 |
| Union Pacific Capital Trust | 2.4 |
| WMX Technologies Inc. | 2.3 |
| Tower Automotive Inc. | 2.3 |
| Omnicare, Inc. | 2.2 |
| Metamor Worldwide, Inc. | 2.2 |
| Suiza Capital Trust II | 2.1 |
| Top Ten | 25.0% |

**Distribution by Maturity (% of Bonds)**

| | |
|---|---|
| Under 1 Year | 0.0% |
| 1–5 Years | 43.0 |
| 5–10 Years | 55.0 |
| 10–20 Years | 2.0 |
| 20–30 Years | 0.0 |
| Over 30 Years | 0.0 |
| Total | 100.0% |

examination of this page will give potential investors much more information about the fund, and this can be compared with other funds. At 0.64, the beta coefficient of the portfolio indicates that the fund is a little more than half as volatile as the market, which always has a coefficient of 1. What this means is that if the market goes down by 50 percent, the portfolio should only decline by 32 percent. If the market goes up by 50 percent, however, the convertible fund would rise by 32 percent. A beta coefficient greater than 1 indicates that the fund is more volatile than the market.

To determine whether this fund fits your credit risk comfort level, the credit risk for the fund can be compared with other convertible funds by examining the breakdown of the credit quality of the issues.

Interest rate risk can be gauged by examining the length of time to maturity of the issues. As mentioned in the mutual fund chapter, the greater the number of securities with longer maturities, the greater the impact of interest rate risk. The shorter the number of maturities in the fund, the less the impact that changes in market rates of interest will have on the fund.

The yield means that the portfolio earned 4.2 percent of the total net asset value of the fund and the expense ratio is 0.73 percent. The greater the expense ratio, the lower the returns of the fund (interest and dividends) since expenses are paid out of the returns received by the fund.

When you have decided on a fund, to open the account, you just fill out an application form and send it with a check to the address on the form. Each fund offers several different types of account services, which can be chosen by ticking off the appropriate boxes on the application form. These include the payment options for dividends and capital gains (whether you want these sent to you every month or reinvested in the fund), redemption options (by wire, mail), purchase options, and so forth.

## WHAT ARE THE ADVANTAGES OF CONVERTIBLE SECURITY MUTUAL FUNDS?

- Convertible security mutual funds offer shareholders the potential for higher returns than plain vanilla types of bond funds due to the potential appreciation of the common stock and the ability to receive income from the securities that have not been converted.

- Convertible security mutual funds offer shareholders an easy way to own complex securities.
- Because of their diversification, convertible security mutual funds offer shareholders protection against default and the risks of credit downgrades.
- Investing in convertible security mutual funds instead of individual convertible securities spares the investor from having to shop for the best prices.

In addition to these advantages, see Chapter 11, which lists some other advantages that apply to convertible security mutual funds.

## WHAT ARE THE DISADVANTAGES OF CONVERTIBLE SECURITY MUTUAL FUNDS?

- The downside to convertible security mutual funds is that if interest rates rise and the stock market turns down, the returns on these funds will be lower than regular bond funds.
- Share prices of convertible security mutual funds can experience volatile swings due to changes in interest rates and the status of the equity markets. Investors in these funds need long time horizons to weather these swings in share price.

See Chapter 11 for some additional disadvantages of convertible security mutual funds.

## CAVEATS

- If you go with a convertible security mutual fund, invest in one with a low expense ratio.
- Because of the risks and potential volatility of the share price, only a portion of your total investment dollars should be invested in convertible security mutual funds.

## Should You Invest in Individual Convertible Securities or Convertible Security Mutual Funds?

The benefits of investing in individual convertible securities over convertible security mutual funds are summarized in Table 9-3.

With individual convertible securities, you are in control. You know exactly how much interest you will receive and when. You can convert your bonds at your discretion when the stock price rises above the conversion price. This is not so with mutual funds. Also the amount of the monthly dividend payments will vary.

Barring any defaults, individual convertible securities are likely to yield higher returns than mutual funds, which typically pay out up to a percentage point in fees.

Investing in individual convertible securities over mutual funds also gives investors greater control over their tax planning with regard to capital gains. Mutual funds do not pay taxes when they sell securities at higher prices than their purchase prices, so these are passed through to the shareholders in the fund. An investor could conceivably buy into a convertible security mutual fund that had already realized substantial capital gains for the year, and that shareholder would be subject to taxes on those gains, even if they occurred before the investor was a shareholder. There is another tax problem that could affect convertible security mutual funds. With the raging bull market of the past three years, mutual fund managers may have bought convertible preferred stock at higher prices than the current prices. The fall in equity prices will lower the net asset value of the fund, which may result

### TABLE 9-3

Individual Convertible Securities versus Mutual Funds

|                    | Individual | Mutual Fund |
|--------------------|:----------:|:-----------:|
| Control            | ✓          |             |
| Higher return      | ✓          |             |
| Tax planning       | ✓          |             |
| Diversification    |            | ✓           |
| Small investors    |            | ✓           |
| Ease of investing  |            | ✓           |

in unrealized principal losses to shareholders. At the same time, the fund manager may have converted some of the convertible bonds to common stock and then sold the common stock, which would result in capital gains. At the end of the tax year, investors in the fund could face potential capital gains for which they would have to pay the taxes at the same time as seeing paper losses in their principal investments due to share prices of the fund being lower than their purchase prices.

There is another side of the picture that better favors a mutual fund decision. Mutual funds own a diversified portfolio of convertible securities, which cushions the impact of defaults or credit rating downgrades. Investors in individual convertible securities, on the other hand, would have to invest substantial amounts of money to achieve the diversification offered by mutual funds. Therefore, the risk of loss may be greater for individual convertible securities than for mutual funds.

Convertible security mutual funds allow investors to invest with smaller amounts of capital, as opposed to the larger denominations needed to invest in individual convertible securities.

Convertible bonds are complex in their makeup, which requires that investors have the time and knowledge to study the provisions of the indenture before they invest. Investing in convertible mutual funds shifts this focus to the professional managers of the funds, who have more time, knowledge, and expertise to make investment decisions.

# REFERENCES

Bary, Andrew: "Trading Points," *Barron's,* February 8, 1993.

Faerber, Esmé: *Managing Your Investments, Savings, and Credit,* McGraw-Hill, New York, 1992.

Lucchetti, Aaron, and Leslie Scism: "Unusual Convertible Preferred Raises Needed Cash and Risks," *The Wall Street Journal,* September 28, 1998, pp. C1, C7.

Ross, Stephen A., Randolph W. Westerfield, and Jeffrey Jaffe: *Corporate Finance,* McGraw-Hill, New York, 1999.

## CHAPTER 10

# Zero-Coupon Bonds and Zero-Coupon Mutual Funds

## KEY CONCEPTS

- What are zero-coupon bonds?
- The relationships influencing the price of zero-coupon bonds
- The different types of zero-coupon bonds
- What are the risks of zero-coupon bonds?
- How to buy and sell zero-coupon bonds
- The advantages of zero-coupon bonds
- The disadvantages of zero-coupon bonds
- Caveats
- Zero-coupon bond mutual funds
- What are the risks of zero-coupon mutual funds?
- How to buy and sell zero-coupon mutual funds
- What are the advantages of zero-coupon mutual funds?
- What are the disadvantages of zero-coupon mutual funds?

Of all the different types of bonds, zero-coupon bonds are the most volatile. Their prices can soar and plummet like a roller coaster ride with changes in interest rates. There are other aspects of zero-coupon bonds which investors need to be familiar with before investing. These are discussed in later sections of this chapter. The first step is to understand how zero-coupon bonds work.

## WHAT ARE ZERO-COUPON BONDS?

Zero-coupon bonds are debt securities that are issued at deep discounts from their face values. They pay no periodic interest but are
redeemed at face value ($1000) at maturity. For example, a 10-year
zero-coupon bond (with a face value of $1000) yielding 8 percent
would cost about $463 at issuance. In other words, the investor of
this zero-coupon bond will buy it for $463, receive no interim inter-
est payments, and at the end of the tenth year, receive $1000, the
face value of the bond. Since zero-coupon bonds do not pay interest, they do not have a current yield like regular bonds.

The price of a zero-coupon bond is the present value of the
face value of the bond at the maturity date discounted at a particular rate of return. Looked at in another way, the investor's funds
grow from $463 to $1000 in 10 years. The initial price is compounded at a particular rate of interest to equal $1000 in 10 years.

The rate of return, or yield, on a zero-coupon bond can be fig-
ured mathematically or by using compound interest tables or a
financial calculator. The yield equation is:

Zero-coupon bond price $(1+i)^n$ = face value at maturity

where $i$ = yield
$\quad n$ = periods to maturity

In this example, $i$ is 8 percent, so:

$$\$463 \ (1 + i)^{10} = 1000$$
$$(1 + i)^{10} = 1000/463$$
$$i = 8\%$$

Knowing the yield on the bond is helpful not only for federal
tax purposes but also for calculating the price of the bond. Even
though the bondholder receives no interest payments, he or she is
required to pay federal income taxes on the accrued interest as if it
had been paid. For instance, in the example above, the accrued
interest for the first year is $37.04:

$$\text{Interest} = \$463 \times 0.08$$
$$= \$37.04$$

The zero-coupon bondholder will pay taxes on this $37.04,
even though it has not been received, thus creating a negative cash

flow for the investor. In other words, the bondholder pays out-of-pocket cash for the taxes but has not received the $37.04. Instead, the interest is added to the principal price of the zero-coupon bond so that at the end of the first year, the price of the bond increases to $500.04 ($463 + 37.04).

The accrued interest for year two is $40.00:

$$\text{Interest} = \$500.04 \times 0.08$$
$$= \$40.00$$

The adjusted price of the bond at the end of the second year is $540.04 ($500.04 + 40.00). Theoretically, the price will rise with the accrued interest until it reaches $1000 at maturity. This theoretical price structure is illustrated in Figure 10-1. There are other factors that affect the price of the zero-coupon bond. For example, if there is a rise in interest rates, the price of the bond will fall below the theoretical prices shown in Figure 10-1.

Due to the negative cash flows during the life of the bond, the result of paying taxes on accrued (phantom) interest, zero-coupon bonds are better suited in investment accounts which are not subject to taxes. These are pension funds, IRAs (independent retirement accounts), Keoghs, and SEP accounts. In these plans, accrued interest is taxed only when the funds are withdrawn. Municipal zero-coupon bonds alleviate the tax problems of this type of bond.

Advertisements for zero-coupon bonds tout the wonderful growth of investing small sums of money and then receiving larger amounts at maturity. This growth is due to the compounding of interest on interest and principal at the *yield to maturity rate,* 8 percent in the example above. However, the tax disadvantages are not openly disclosed in these advertisements.

Zero-coupon bonds have advantages when purchased for minors because of the low dollar costs of the bonds. However, you need to consider the total income for the child to see if it is worthwhile. Minors may be exempt from the phantom-interest tax payments if their total passive income is less than a threshold amount ($700 in 1998). Phantom interest is taxed at the child's low marginal tax rate for income between certain amounts ($700

**FIGURE 10-1**

Price of a Zero-Coupon Bond from Issue to Maturity

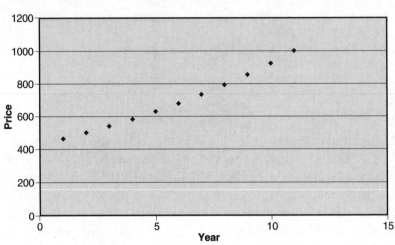

and $1400 for 1998). For higher incomes, the phantom interest on a bond would be taxed at the parent's marginal tax rate, which may make investing in other investments a better alternative. The Internal Revenue Tax Code is constantly changing with regard to these income limits, and investors should keep up with the changes, especially with regard to the effects on the different investment instruments. Consult your tax advisor or accountant for the latest income limits on the "kiddie tax." In certain instances, then, zero-coupon bonds are not advantageous because of the negative cash flows and the complexities of calculating the interest for tax purposes.

## THE RELATIONSHIPS INFLUENCING THE PRICE OF ZERO-COUPON BONDS

The quality of the bond, the length of time to maturity, the call provision, market rates of interest, and the yield all affect the price of a zero-coupon bond. The *quality* of the zero-coupon bond is important, since the return depends on one of two things:

- The issuer's ability to redeem the bonds at maturity
- The investor's ability to sell them before maturity at a higher price than their purchase price

A zero-coupon bondholder has more to lose in the event of a default than the holder of a conventional bond. With the latter, the bondholder would have received some interest payments which could have been reinvested.

The quality of a zero-coupon bond is an assessment of the issuer's ability to pay off the bondholder at maturity. A good-quality zero-coupon bond has less risk of default than a speculative, low-quality one. Investors are willing to pay more for a good-quality bond. Thus, there is a positive relationship between quality and price.

Ratings assigned by the ratings agencies, such as Moody's and Standard & Poor's, are yardsticks as to credit quality, but you should always be aware that changes affecting the issuers of the bonds make these ratings subject to change.

The quality of a zero-coupon bond is also related to the yield. A low-quality zero-coupon bond will offer a higher yield than a good-quality one to entice investors. The flip side of the coin is that investors will pay less for a low-quality than a high-quality zero-coupon bond. Price is, therefore, inversely related to yield.

However, the yield is also related to the length of time to maturity. The longer the maturity, the lower the price and the higher the yield. This is because the zero-coupon bondholder will only get the interest payment at maturity, or an accrued amount built into the sale price before maturity.

Besides the length of time to maturity and the quality of the issue, zero-coupon prices are sensitive to *fluctuations in interest rates.* The purchase price of a zero-coupon bond determines the yield over the life of the security, because interest is only paid at maturity and interest accrues at that fixed yield. If market rates of interest go above the fixed yield of the zero-coupon bond, investors will want to sell their bonds and reinvest at higher rates. This has the effect of depressing the price of the zero-coupon bond more than a conventional bond, which pays interest annually or semiannually. If you recall the concept of duration discussed in Chapter 2, you will see why zero-coupon bonds are more volatile in price than regular, fixed-interest-payment bonds. Zero-coupon bonds will have a higher duration than a conventional bond of similar maturity and yield because the holder does not receive any interest payments until the zero-coupon bond matures. Similarly, when interest rates fall, zero-coupon bonds will appreciate more than existing conventional bonds due to the fixed yield on the zero-coupon bond.

*Market factors* also have a bearing on price. An actively traded zero-coupon bond will be priced differently than an inactively traded one with the same maturity and yield.

## THE DIFFERENT TYPES OF ZERO-COUPON BONDS

Besides the conventional zero-coupon bonds issued by corporations and government entities, there are many different types of zero-coupon bonds. *Derivative zero-coupon bonds* were introduced by several brokerage houses during the early 1980s, primarily for use in retirement accounts. These are called derivative securities because they are derived from another underlying security.

### Stripped Government Securities

In 1982, Salomon Brothers and Merrill Lynch both created *zero-coupon stripped Treasury securities.* To create their respective securities, the brokerage firms bought long-term U.S. Treasury bonds and held them in escrow. They then sold zero-coupon bonds representing an ownership interest in the underlying Treasury bonds and their interest payments. These securities were created by stripping the coupon payments on the U.S. Treasury bonds. An important distinction to make with stripped zero-coupon securities is that they are not backed by the faith and credit of the U.S. Treasury. It is true that Treasury bonds are backed by the faith and credit of the U.S. government, but the zero-coupon securities are merely the products of the brokerage houses.

Salomon's product was marketed under the name CATS (Certificates of Accrual on Treasury Securities), and Merrill Lynch's stripped zero-coupon security went under the name TIGRs (Treasury Income Growth Receipts). Other brokerage firms followed with their stripped zero-coupon securities under other feline acronyms.

The major disadvantage to these stripped zero-coupon securities of the brokerage firms is the lack of liquidity. The securities of one brokerage firm are not traded by competing dealers, and so to improve liquidity of the stripped zero-coupon bonds, a group of primary dealers in the Treasury bond market decided to issue generic securities. These are called *Treasury receipts,* and they are not associated with any of the participating dealers (Fabozzi and Fabozzi, 1989).

In 1985, the U.S. Treasury announced its own STRIP program (Separate Trading of Registered Interest and Principal). Designated Treasury bonds could be stripped to create zero-coupon Treasury bonds. Since these are direct obligations of the U.S. government, they tend to have slightly lower yields than the brokerage firms' stripped zero-coupon securities. Moreover, the Treasury's STRIP securities offer greater marketability than the generics offered by the brokerage firms.

Salomon Brothers created stripped federal agency zero-coupon bonds in the late 1980s. They purchased $750 million FICO bonds, stripped them of their interest, and sold them as zero-coupon FICO strips. FICO was created by Congress to raise money for the financially strapped Federal Savings and Loan Insurance Corporation (FSLIC).

The FICO zeros are not assigned credit ratings by the rating companies, but they are believed to be relatively safe because of Congress's commitment to FICO and the FSLIC. Hence, yields on FICO zeros are slightly higher than those on Treasury strips. FICO strips can be bought through brokers, and they trade over the counter in the secondary market.

## Mortgage-Backed Zero-Coupon Bonds

Mortgage-backed zero-coupon securities were referred to in the CMO section of the chapter on agency bonds. These zeros are backed by Ginnie Mae, Fannie Mae, and Freddie Mac securities as well as the collateral of the real estate on the mortgages. As with other mortgage-backed bonds, these are subject to prepayment risk. That is, these zeros may be paid off before their stated maturities.

## Municipal Zero-Coupon Bonds

These are issued by state and local governments and are advantageous in that the accrued interest is exempt from federal income taxes and generally from state taxes in the state where issued.

Municipal zero-coupon bonds come in two types: the *general obligation zero-coupon bonds* issued by states and *project zero-coupon bonds*, which are issued by highway authorities for highway projects, public power projects, and for sewer systems and other such municipal projects. General obligation issues are backed by the taxing power of the states issuing them, whereas project securities are backed by the revenues generated from the projects. Hence, project zero-coupon bonds are less secure.

You should check the quality of the issue before buying. There are so many good-quality zero-coupon municipal issues that investors need not settle for lower-quality issues. This point is especially relevant for long-term issues (more than 15 years to maturity), for which anything could happen to affect the issuer's ability to repay the bonds. Investors should, therefore, stick to issues with ratings of not less than AA. For better-quality zeros, investors must sacrifice slightly on yields.

Many municipal zero-coupon issues are callable, and investors should check the call provisions before buying. If there is a choice between a callable and a noncallable issue of similar quality and maturity, avoid the callable issue.

The call price and date listed in the bond's indenture are important. For example, the call price could be above par, at par, less than the par price, or it could be at a price that is less than the yield to maturity.

The call provision can be extremely disadvantageous, so it is wise to check it out before buying. Some issues have a serial call, which means that some bonds in the issue can be called earlier than other bonds.

Although municipal zero-coupon bonds are exempt from federal income taxes, investors may want to find out how their states tax the accrued interest on the securities. Some states tax the phantom interest as it accrues, and others tax the interest at maturity or when the securities are sold. Investors can get the information from their particular state's revenue offices. Before selling zero-coupon bonds, investors should consult with their tax advisors or accountants as to the tax consequences of gains and losses.

## Zero-Coupon Convertible Bonds

Zero-coupon convertible bonds were hot products during the late 1980s, but they have become a dying breed in the early 1990s (Mitchell, 1993). These are deeply discounted bonds with conversion provisions. Their yields tend to be lower than those of conventional bonds, and they don't pay out annual interest. Holders are required to accrue interest for federal tax purposes, so like regular zero-coupon bonds, they are suitable for tax-deferred accounts such as IRAs and pension plans.

Like convertible bonds, these can be exchanged into a predetermined number of shares of the issuing corporation's common stock. Some zero-coupon convertibles have put options, which allow the holders to sell their securities back to the issuer at the original issue price plus accrued interest after a certain date (usually five or ten years). These were advertised as terrific investments for investors and were promoted aggressively by the brokerage firms. Merrill Lynch, for instance, called their securities LYONs (liquid yield option notes).

Unfortunately, declining interest rates coupled with the call provisions on many zero-coupon convertible securities have worked to the detriment of investors. Walt Disney's zero-coupon convertible securities scheduled to mature in the year 2005 were called at a price which was lower than what many investors paid in the secondary market. The conversion feature did not help the holders of the Disney convertibles because the securities were tied to Euro Disney stock (traded on the Paris Exchange). The stock price was depressed and trading below the conversion price.

Other companies, such as MCI Communications, Inc., Sonat Co., Carnival Cruise Lines, and Berkshire Hathaway Co., redeemed their LYONS. It was cheaper for these companies to refund the issues and issue new regular bonds due to the sharp decline in interest rates (Mitchell, 1993).

The advantage of zero-coupon convertible bonds is the upside potential for appreciation if the common stock rises above the conversion price. However, if this never occurs, the investor will receive a lower return than similar maturity plain vanilla bonds (regular bonds).

To counter the disadvantage of negative cash flows due to the federal taxation of phantom interest, many municipalities have issued *zero-coupon convertible municipal issues*. These have been sold under different acronyms: FIGS (future income and growth securities); BIGS (bond income and growth securities); PACS (principal appreciation conversion securities); and TEDIS (tax-exempt discount and income securities).

These are much the same as regular zero-coupon convertible securities except for the exemption of accrued interest from federal taxes. However, state taxes may be applicable on the accrued interest, and the quality of the issue is, of course, dependent on the financial position of the issuing municipality. These, unfortunately, may also contain call provisions, and they fluctuate in price in relation to changes in market rates of interest and other factors.

## WHAT ARE THE RISKS OF ZERO-COUPON BONDS?

The *risk of default* depends on the financial position of the issuer and is of great importance to the zero-coupon bondholder. This is because the interest and principal is paid back in a single payment at maturity, and if the issuer is not able to make this single payment, the holder may receive a *large* zero. With regular bonds, the holder would have received some interest payments. Consequently, determining the quality of the zero-coupon bond is an assessment of the likelihood of the issuer's ability to be able to pay off the bondholder at maturity. The risk of default can be lessened by choosing high-quality zero-coupon bond issues or government stripped bonds.

Zero-coupon bonds are also subject to *interest rate risk*. When market rates of interest rise (or fall), zero-coupon bonds, like regular bonds, fall (or rise) in price. However, zero-coupon prices tend to be much more volatile than those of regular bonds. This is tied to the fact that the entire amount that the investor receives is a single payment at maturity, whereas for regular fixed-interest bonds, the price is the discounted cash flows of the interest payments and the principal at maturity. In general, with fixed-interest bonds, the lower the coupon rate of the bond, the greater the price volatility due to changes in market rates of interest. This, then, explains the price volatility of zero-coupon bonds, which have no coupon payments. As a result of different trading activity, quality differences, call features, and length of time to maturity, some zero-coupon bonds are more volatile in price than other similar-yielding zeros.

With the decline in interest rates, many outstanding bond issues have been called. Zero-coupon bonds are no exception. They too have call provisions and many have also been called. This is the lesson many zero-coupon bondholders have learned the hard way. When interest rates decline, higher-yielding zero-coupon bonds appreciate significantly due to the fact that these bonds are locked into an above-market-rate yield. However, the issuers are not thrilled at paying above-market rates, and if their bonds have call provisions, they will call them.

Even issuers of zero-coupon bonds without call provisions tried their luck. Transamerica Finance Corporation issued zero-coupon bonds in 1982 with a yield of 13 percent and maturities from 2007 to the year 2012. Due to the high yield of these zero-coupon bonds in an economic environment with significantly lower interest rates, the bonds appreciated in price. Because the bonds were not issued with call provisions, the most the company could do was send out letters to the bondholders to try and entice them to turn in their bonds. However, Transamerica offered such a low price (they were willing to pay 40 percent of the current market price) that most investors did not fall for the trick. This shows the extent that issuers will go to get rid of higher-yielding bonds. Thus, if zeros have call provisions, they are subject to *call risk,* and because Transamerica's bonds were not callable, they could not redeem them early. To avoid the risk of call, buy noncallable issues (Bary, 1993).

Zero-coupon bonds have no *reinvestment risk* because the yield is determined by the purchase price and then locked in over the life of the bond. With a regular coupon bond, the holder is faced with the uncertainty of having to reinvest the interest payments at fluctuating market rates of interest. Moreover, there is the disadvantage that when interest rates rise, zero-coupon bondholders are locked into their existing lower yields.

If zero-coupon bonds are sold before maturity, there is always the risk of a loss in principal due to the extreme volatility of zero-coupon bonds. They are the most volatile of all bonds. In addition, markups in the pricing of zero-coupon bonds are high, and also they vary from dealer to dealer. This makes zero-coupon bonds expensive to buy and sell.

## HOW TO BUY AND SELL ZERO-COUPON BONDS

Zero-coupon bonds can be purchased in the primary market at issue, in other words, a new issue to the market. Investors who buy these new issues from the brokerage firms underwriting the issue will avoid paying commissions or fees.

Existing zero-coupon bonds trading in the secondary markets can be bought through securities brokers, dealers, and banks, as well as through on-line brokers. Brokers charge fees, which can be relatively high for zero-coupon securities, considering that investors are investing smaller amounts of money (due to the deep discounts) than they would for the same number of regular bonds. These markups vary considerably from broker to broker, and you should not be deceived if your broker announces that his or her firm does not charge a fee or commission. The transaction fees for a small number of zero-coupon bonds can also be considerable.

Some brokerage firms may make a market in certain zero-coupon issues. The prices at which these are bought and sold are determined by the brokerage firm and the conditions on the market. Consequently, the investor does not pay a commission, but the size of the markup will determine whether the investor is getting a break.

It is important to shop around at different brokerage firms for the best prices when buying and selling zero-coupon securities. Many brokerage firms have inventories of different zero-coupon issues, and they may be more competitively priced. If the issue is quoted in the newspapers, you have some yardstick in terms of price. Most zero-coupon issues are traded over the counter, but there are some issues that are quoted on the New York Bond Exchange.

You should be aware that when buying zero-coupon issues from sponsoring brokerage houses at issue, these brokerage houses are not required or obligated to make a market in these issues.

The high transaction costs on zero-coupon issues make them less liquid than other fixed-income securities, and consequently, they are more suited to a buy-and-hold strategy. By holding zeros to maturity, investors will improve their returns.

Rather than buy individual zero-coupon issues, investors may choose to put their money into mutual funds that specialize in zero-coupon bonds. As with all mutual funds, fees are deducted from the earnings (and/or the net assets) of the funds and can be quite high. See the section on zero-coupon mutual funds later in this chapter.

## THE ADVANTAGES OF ZERO-COUPON BONDS

- Zero-coupon bonds appreciate more than conventional fixed-income securities when interest rates decline. Of course, the opposite is true when market rates of interest go up. Prices of zero-coupon bonds will decline more than those of conventional bonds.
- Investments in zero-coupon bonds require less of a capital outflow than other fixed-income securities, since they are sold at a deep discount. For example, a purchase of 10 regular bonds at face value requires an outlay of $10,000, whereas 10 zero-coupon bonds selling at $180 require capital of $1800.
- Investors need not be concerned with reinvestment risk. With zero-coupon bonds, there is no coupon to reinvest at unpredictable market rates of interest.
- Zero-coupon bonds have fixed yields when held to maturity and provide predictable payments. Nearly all zero-coupon bonds have a maturity value of $1000 per bond.
- There are so many existing zero-coupon bond issues on the market to choose from that investors can easily ladder their maturities to provide regular cash flows.
- There are different types of zero-coupon bonds with special features which make them attractive investment vehicles for investors with specific needs.

- Zero-coupon bonds are excellent vehicles for IRAs, Keogh accounts, and pension plans due to their tax-deferred growth and predictable amounts at maturity.

## THE DISADVANTAGES OF ZERO-COUPON BONDS

- Paying taxes annually on accrued (phantom) interest, which is not received until maturity, creates a negative cash flow.
- Zero-coupon bond prices are extremely volatile. When market rates of interest rise, zero-coupon bond prices often plunge significantly, resulting in large capital losses should the investor be forced to sell.
- When interest rates do go up, investors in zero-coupon bonds are not able to benefit because they are locked into a lower rate and there is no coupon interest to reinvest.
- Many zero-coupon bonds have call provisions, which allow the issuers to redeem them before maturity.
- If a zero-coupon bond issuer defaults, investors have more to lose than on conventional bonds because with the latter, they would have received some interest which could have been reinvested.
- Markups tend to be higher on zero-coupon bonds (percentagewise), making them less liquid than other fixed-income securities.
- Certain zero-coupon bonds may not be as marketable as other conventional fixed-income securities.

## CAVEATS

When investing in zero-coupon bonds outside of tax-deferred accounts such as IRAs, Keoghs, and pension accounts, investors should be aware of the tax consequences. They can be quite complicated, and it might be necessary to hire an accountant or tax professional to compute the tax liabilities. The Internal Revenue Service publishes two free guides which are quite helpful in determining the tax liability on zero-coupon bonds. These are IRS

Publication 550, "Investment Income and Expense," and IRS Publication 1212, "List of Original Issue Discount Obligations."

When computing the tax consequences of a zero-coupon bond, you should know what the yield is and when the security was issued. The latter point is important because the computation for the phantom interest will be different for zero-coupon bonds issued before December 31, 1984, than for those issued after that date.

If your tax situation is relatively uncomplicated but you do not think you can cope with figuring the tax liability on your zero-coupon bonds, and need to hire a tax accountant, you would be better off investing in other fixed-income investments.

## ZERO-COUPON BOND MUTUAL FUNDS

Instead of investing in individual zero-coupon securities, investors can invest in zero-coupon mutual funds. Not every mutual fund family offers such a fund. Zero-coupon bond funds differ from other types of bond funds in that they buy securities that all mature at the same date (Thau, 1992, p. 225). At this maturity date, the prices of the bonds reach their par values and the fund distributes the proceeds to the shareholders. Different zero-coupon bond funds will vary in their maturities, either short-, intermediate-, or long-term.

## WHAT ARE THE RISKS OF ZERO-COUPON MUTUAL FUNDS?

The greatest risk facing zero-coupon bond mutual funds is *interest rate risk.* These bonds are much more volatile than other types of bonds when interest rates change. This means that even if you buy into a short-term or an intermediate-term fund, you will still see tremendous volatility in the share price of your mutual fund when interest rates rise and fall.

With the extreme volatility of zero-coupon bonds, there is always the *risk of loss in share price* should investors need to liquidate their zero-coupon bond fund before maturity or at a time when the share price is lower than the purchase price. This risk of loss in share price is minimized if shareholders hold their positions until maturity.

*Credit risk* is a factor that affects the share price of the mutual fund. If the quality of the zero-coupon bonds in the mutual fund portfolio is downgraded, this will have a downward effect on the share price of the fund. However, with the diversification achieved by the fund, a few downgrades in issues will not have as great an effect as it would on a portfolio of individual zero-coupon bonds.

## HOW TO BUY AND SELL ZERO-COUPON BOND MUTUAL FUNDS

Zero-coupon bond mutual funds, which are also called *target funds,* may be bought directly through mutual fund families or indirectly through brokers, financial planners, and banks. To save on sales commissions or loads, look for no-load zero-coupon bond funds and buy directly from the mutual fund family. You can scan the mutual fund tables in the financial newspapers to find those families that offer zero-coupon bond funds. The Scudder mutual fund family, for example, offers a zero-coupon bond mutual fund that matures in the year 2000. In light of the increased potential share price volatility of zero-coupon funds, you can increase your potential returns by investing in no-load funds. Similarly, when comparing the expense ratios of the different funds, look for the low-expense-ratio funds.

Examine the prospectus for the objectives and the degree of risk of the fund, the types of zero-coupon bonds held in the fund, its total returns, and its expense ratio.

## WHAT ARE THE ADVANTAGES OF ZERO-COUPON BOND MUTUAL FUNDS?

- If you hold zero-coupon mutual funds to their maturity dates, you need not be concerned about interest rate risk, credit risk, and reinvestment risk.
- Holding zero-coupon bond mutual funds to maturity provides known returns to shareholders (average yield to maturity of the bonds in the fund minus expenses).
- Zero-coupon bond funds appreciate more than conventional bond mutual funds when interest rates

decline. When interest rates rise, zero-coupon bond mutual funds will decline more than conventional bond mutual funds.

- Zero-coupon bond mutual funds are suitable investments for IRAs, Keogh accounts, and pension plans due to their tax-deferred growth and predictable amounts at maturity.
- Investing in zero-coupon bond mutual funds over individual zero-coupon bonds will likely result in lower transaction costs. Mutual funds pay lower transaction costs than individual buyers.

## WHAT ARE THE DISADVANTAGES OF ZERO-COUPON BOND MUTUAL FUNDS?

- There are tax consequences to owning zero-coupon bond mutual funds. Shareholders have to pay taxes on the accrued interest, which creates a negative cash flow.
- Share prices of zero-coupon bond mutual funds can be extremely volatile when market rates of interest rise.
- If you need to sell your shares before maturity, there is always the risk that you will lose money due to the extreme volatility of this type of mutual fund.

## CAVEATS

Negative cash flows due to phantom interest can be avoided by investing in zero-coupon bond mutual funds for tax-deferred pension and retirement accounts. For regular accounts, you will experience negative cash flows by paying taxes on interest payments that are accrued but not received until maturity.

Because of the volatility of zero-coupon bond mutual funds, you should buy them to hold until maturity.

### Should You Invest in Individual Zero-Coupon Bonds or Zero-Coupon Bond Mutual Funds?

The benefits of investing in zero-coupon bond mutual funds over individual zero-coupon bonds are summarized in Table 10-1.

**TABLE 10-1**

Zero-Coupon Mutual Funds versus Individual Zero-Coupon Bonds

|  | Zero-Coupon Bond Mutual Funds | Individual Zero-Coupon Bonds |
|---|---|---|
| Diversification | ✓ | |
| Ease of investing | ✓ | |
| Ease of determining accrued interest | ✓ | |
| Lower transaction costs to buy securities | ✓ | |
| Control | | ✓ |
| Tax planning | | ✓ |
| Absence of yearly fees | | ✓ |

Mutual funds own a diversified portfolio of zero-coupon securities, which lessens the impact of a default or credit rating downgrade. Those investing in zero-coupon bonds individually would have to invest in many different issues to achieve comparable diversification. Thus, the risk of loss may be greater for holders of individual zero-coupon bonds than for mutual fund shareholders.

Zero-coupon bonds are complex securities, and for individuals who do not have the time or expertise to examine their features, it is easier to invest in mutual funds that employ professional managers.

Zero-coupon mutual funds provide tax information at the end of each year for their shareholders, whereas individual zero-coupon bondholders would have to calculate their accrued interest for tax purposes.

Also, mutual funds purchase large numbers of bonds and pay lower markups than individual buyers. The downside to mutual funds, however, is the annual expense ratio that shareholders must pay. It lowers their returns. Holders of individual zero-coupon bonds don't have to pay annual fees.

Individual zero-coupon bondholders are in control not only of the securities that they choose but also their capital gains and losses. Individuals can sell their bonds when they want to, which gives them some control over their capital gains and losses for tax planning purposes. Individual holders are also able to determine the exact amount of their accrued interest for the year, which is not true for mutual fund shareholders.

# REFERENCES

Bary, Andrew: "Trading Points," *Barron's,* March 15, 1993, p. 57.

Fabozzi, Frank J., and T. Dessa Fabozzi: "Survey of Bonds and Mortgage-Backed Securities," in *Portfolio and Investment Management,* Frank J. Fabozzi (ed.), McGraw-Hill, New York, 1989.

Mitchell, Constance: "Are LYONS Becoming a Dying Breed?" *The Wall Street Journal,* March 8, 1993, p. C1.

Thau, Annette: *The Bond Book,* McGraw-Hill, New York, 1992.

## CHAPTER 11

# Fixed-Income Mutual Funds

## KEY CONCEPTS

- How do mutual funds work?
- The different types of bond funds
- How does performance affect the choice of a mutual fund?
- What is the significance of the prospectus?
- What are the tax consequences of buying and selling shares in mutual funds?
- What are the risks of mutual funds?
- How to buy and sell mutual funds
- What are the advantages of mutual funds?
- What are the disadvantages of mutual funds?
- Should you invest in bond mutual funds or individual bonds?

In some respects, mutual funds have come close to being the ideal investment for millions of investors. Many of these investors are able to move their money in and out of different types of mutual funds just as portfolio managers would when overseeing a large portfolio. Mutual funds have allowed investors who do not have the time, knowledge, or expertise of different financial instruments to invest their money in stock, bonds, and money market funds.

Since the early 1980s, the number of mutual funds has grown rapidly, to the point where quotations of mutual fund prices now occupy more than four pages in *The Wall Street Journal*. The fact that there are more mutual funds than companies listed on the New York Stock Exchange means that investors should be as careful in selecting mutual funds as they are in investing in individual stocks and bonds.

Moreover, the management companies of these mutual funds compete very aggressively for investors' dollars. This is evidenced by all the print advertising in newspapers and magazines as well as the use of television to ensure that the mutual funds are seen and heard about.

This increase in the clutter of "infomercials" coming from mutual fund sponsors compounds the complexity of the investor's decision as to which one to choose. The decision becomes more difficult for investors who take the advertising messages literally, without reading the fine print and stepping back to analyze the investment objectives of the fund.

According to the advertisements, there would appear to be no loser funds, only funds that are "number one" in something, or funds that have had remarkable yields. If you read the fine print, you'll find many of the funds may have achieved that yield for a one-week or one-month period, or achieved a number-one status in some limited way, but this does not assure the fund of a rosy future. For example, the number-one position may have been achieved by an exceptional manager who is no longer with the fund. Results reported by Lipper Analytical Services, Inc., show that even poor-performing funds can sometimes rank as number one at something for a short time. The editor of *Morningstar Mutual Funds*, a Chicago newsletter, supports this finding (Clements, 1993).

A high yield may be only half the picture. A fund can earn a high yield and still have negative total returns because of a decline in the fund's share price.

Nor do the advertisements include the fees charged by their funds. If investors pick a fund that is number one in something and had a wonderful yield once upon a time, they will assume that they have invested wisely. But the fund they chose could be a poor performer. Fees charged by that fund could be higher than those charged by other mutual funds in the same category of investments. Or the fund could rely on riskier investment assets, which would typically make that fund's share price much more volatile.

Many investors are so confused that they turn to one of the many newsletters on the market. The hype from some advertisements of these advisory newsletters can further overwhelm investors and make the choice of a newsletter harder than the choice of a mutual fund. Some newsletters go so far as to predict the returns for certain funds into the future (Savage, 1993).

Of course, the aim is to get investors to subscribe to the newsletter, so the messages promoted by many of them use a combination of hyperbole and fear to move investors in that direction. Implying that investors will choose the wrong fund makes investors even more unsure about choosing a fund. For example, a short time ago, mutual fund advisory letters were touting financial and technology funds, which did outperform all other funds in the first quarter of 1998. But this changed shortly thereafter and financial and technology funds went into a steep decline by the third quarter of 1998. In addition, many newsletters encourage investors to actively trade their mutual funds, but it can be more costly to try to time the markets than to simply buy and hold mutual funds.

For investors who are so confused that they are in a state of paralysis as to how to invest their money, there are *wrap accounts,* which are supposed to answer the concerns of investors who don't know how to manage their money. Major brokerage firms offer these accounts, and for an all-inclusive flat fee, they will manage your investments by diversifying into stocks, bonds, and money market accounts. Sounds ideal!

However, many investors have been jolted into reality by the fees charged for some of these wrap accounts. Some have high annual fees that are not all-inclusive. This means they do not include the management of their cash accounts. An additional fee is charged to manage money market and cash accounts, which in today's economic environment of low interest rates means investors are losing money on their cash funds. Not all investors like to be fully invested in stocks and bonds, and their money in cash accounts may be earning only 2.9 percent per annum. With a 2-percent annual management fee levied, investors' rates of return after paying taxes and adjusting for inflation will be negative.

Performance is another widely touted reason for investing in a brokerage firm's wrap account. However, many of the brokerage firms do not factor their fees into their performance equations. It can make quite a difference and can be disturbing to find you will be earning 2 to 3 percent less than the advertised rate.

The high costs and equivocal performance of many wrap accounts should make investors think twice before jumping into them without careful analysis. Besides cost and performance, investors should also look at potential conflicts of interest in the management of the wrap accounts. For example, does the broker favor securities underwritten by her or his own brokerage firm when choosing investment securities? (Schultz, 1993).

It is indeed confusing for investors to choose a mutual fund, especially when there are more than 7000 of them on the market. Moreover, investors may be equally confused by all the conflicting advice and predictions offered by many of the newsletters. So what do you do? Go back to the basics.

- Understand how mutual funds work.
- Understand the fundamentals of the investments the fund invests in.
- Evaluate the performance of the fund from the prospectus.

By following these steps, investors can narrow the field of funds to choose from. They will then be in a better position to make a final decision on a fund.

## HOW DO MUTUAL FUNDS WORK?

All mutual funds work similarly. A mutual fund makes investments on behalf of the investors in that fund. The money from investors is pooled, which allows the fund to diversify its acquisition of different securities, such as stocks for stock funds and bonds for bond funds. The types of investments chosen are determined by the *objectives* of the mutual fund. For example, if a bond fund's objectives are to provide tax-free income, the fund will invest in municipal bonds. The fund will buy different municipal bond issues to achieve a diversified portfolio, and this will also reduce the risk of loss due to default.

When these securities pay out their interest, fund shareholders get their proportional share. Thus, an investor who invests $1000 will get the same rate of return as another investor who invested $100,000 in the fund.

When the prices of the securities fluctuate up or down, the total value of the fund is affected. These fluctuations in price are due to many different factors, such as the intrinsic risk of the types of securities in the portfolio and economic, market, and political factors. The objectives of the fund are important because they will indicate the type and quality of the investments the fund will choose. From these objectives, investors are better able to assess the risks the fund is willing to take to improve income (return) and/or capital gains. See Table 11-1 for a classification of fixed-income securities by investment objectives.

Investors invest their money in mutual funds by buying shares at the *net asset value* (NAV). The fund's net asset value price of the shares is the total assets minus the liabilities of the fund, divided by the number of outstanding shares.

It is easy for a fund to determine the market value of its assets at the end of each trading day. For instance, if the fund is a balanced fund, which means that it invests in both common stocks and bonds, the investment company would use the closing prices of the stocks and bonds for the day. These prices would be multiplied by the number of shares of stocks and the number of bonds that the fund owns. The resulting totals are added up, and any liabilities that the fund has (accrued fees, for example) are subtracted. The total is then divided by the number of shares outstanding in the fund to give the net asset value price per share. A numerical example illustrates the process:

| | |
|---|---|
| Market value of stocks and bonds | $5,000,000 |
| Minus total liabilities | − 150,000 |
| Net worth | $4,850,000 |
| Number of shares outstanding | 750,000 |
| Net asset value | $6.466/share ($4,850,000 ÷ 750,000) |

The net asset value may change daily due to the market fluctuations of stock and bond prices. The net asset value is important for two reasons:

**TABLE 11-1**

Types of Fixed-Income Funds

| Type | Objectives |
|------|------------|
| Corporate bond funds | Seek high levels of income. Invest in corporate bonds, Treasury bonds, and agency bonds. |
| High-yield bond funds | Seek higher yields by investing in less-than-investment-grade bonds (junk bonds). |
| Municipal bond funds long-term maturities | Seek income that is exempt from federal income taxes. Invest in bonds with long maturities issued by state and local governments. |
| Municipal bond funds intermediate-term maturities | Seek income that is exempt from federal income taxes. Invest in bonds with intermediate-term maturities issued by state and local governments. |
| Municipal bond funds short-term maturities | Invest in municipal securities with relatively short maturities. These are also known as *tax-exempt money market funds*. |
| U.S. government income funds | Invest in different types of government securities, such as Treasury securities, agency securities, and federally backed mortgage-backed securities. |
| GNMA funds | Invest in Government National Mortgage Association securities and other mortgage-backed securities. |
| Global income funds | Invest in the bonds of companies and countries worldwide, including those in the U.S. |
| Money market funds | Invest in money market securities with relatively short maturities. |

1. This is the price that is used to determine the value of the investor's holding in the mutual fund (number of shares held multiplied by the net asset value price per share).

2. It is the price when new shares are purchased or when shares in the fund are sold.

The net asset values of the different funds are quoted in the daily newspapers. Table 11-2 shows how mutual funds were listed in the newspapers several years ago. The current way of listing mutual funds is shown back in Chapter 3. The details of the funds in Vanguard and Westcore families of funds help illustrate the impact of load charges.

## TABLE 11-2

Mutual Fund Quotations

|  | Investment Objective | NAV | Offer Price | NAV Change |
|---|---|---|---|---|
| *Vanguard Group* | | | | |
| STAR | S&B | 13.39 | NL | +0.07 |
| GNMA | BND | 10.53 | NL | +0.02 |
| IG Corp | BND | 9.20 | NL | +0.02 |
| *Westcore* | | | | |
| GNMA | BND | 16.45 | 17.23 | +0.02 |
| ST Govt | BST | 15.87 | 16.19 | ... |

Source: *The Wall Street Journal.*

In the Vanguard Group, the GNMA (Ginnie Mae) fund, which invests only in bonds (as opposed to the STAR fund, which invests in both stocks and bonds), has a net asset value of $10.53 per share. The investment objectives column indicates the types of investments a fund will invest in. NL in the offer-price column signifies that the fund is a no-load fund, which means that investors can buy and sell shares at the net asset value of $10.53. The net asset value change column signifies the change in price from the previous day's closing price. The Vanguard GNMA fund closed $0.02 up from the previous day's closing price.

The two fund examples in the Westcore Group are load funds, since they charge a commission to buy and sell their shares. This is evidenced by the offer price, which is different from the net asset value price. To buy shares in Westcore's short-term government fund, investors would buy at the offer price ($16.19 per share) and would sell their shares at the net asset value price ($15.87). The difference ($0.32 per share) between the offer price ($16.19) and the net asset value price ($15.87) represents the load or commission that investors will pay to buy or sell shares in this fund.

Investors can earn money from their mutual funds in three ways:

**1.** When interest and/or dividends earned on the fund's investments are passed through to shareholders.

**2.** When the fund's management sells investment securities at a profit and the capital gains are passed through to shareholders. If these securities are sold at a loss, the capital loss is offset against the gains of the fund, and the net gain or loss is passed through to the shareholders.

**3.** When the net asset value per share increases. When this happens, the value of the shareholder's investment increases.

Investors in funds are given the option of having their interest and capital gains paid out to them in check form or reinvested in additional shares in the fund.

There are two types of mutual funds, open-end and closed-end. With open-end funds, the investment company of the fund can issue an unlimited number of shares. Investors can buy more shares from the mutual fund company, or they can sell their shares back to the mutual fund company, which means that the overall number of shares will increase or decrease, respectively. Closed-end funds issue a fixed number of shares, and when all are sold, they do not issue more. In other words, they have a fixed capital structure. Closed-end funds are discussed in Chapter 12.

Mutual funds pay no taxes on income derived from their investments. Under the Internal Revenue Code, mutual funds serve as conduits through which the income from the investments is passed to shareholders in the form of interest or dividends and capital gains or losses. Individual investors pay the taxes on the income.

Shareholders receive monthly and annual statements showing the interest, dividends, capital gains and losses, and other relevant data that should be retained for tax purposes. In fact, not only is the interest income important for tax purposes, but when investing in different fixed-income mutual funds, investors should also keep track of the net asset value prices of the shares purchased and sold. This information helps in the computation of gains and losses when shares are redeemed.

## THE DIFFERENT TYPES OF BOND FUNDS

There are many different types of bond funds, and their differences are significant. The overriding difference between the types is that they invest in different sectors of the bond markets. Municipal bond funds are very different from zero-coupon bond funds. Similarly, short-term government funds differ from both municipal bond funds and zero-coupon bond funds. The types of securities that a fund invests in determine the length of time to maturity, the yield of the fund, and the risks of the fund—sensitivity to changes in interest rates, the degree of credit quality, and the risk of default.

Money market funds are the only funds that maintain constant share prices. These are mostly $1 a share, and the investment company will keep the net asset value at $1 per share. Any expenses or short-term losses from the sale of securities are deducted from the revenues to keep the share price constant. This is more easily accomplished for funds that invest in money market securities, which are short-term and don't have that much volatility in the prices of their investment assets.

All the other types of bond funds have share prices, which fluctuate up and down depending on the value of the assets of the funds. Certain types of securities fluctuate more in price than others. For instance, Ginnie Mae securities will be much more volatile to changes in interest rates than similar-maturity Treasury notes and bonds. In order to gauge the extent of the volatility in the mutual fund's price, investors should understand how different bond securities react to changes in interest rates.

A conservative investor should be aware that investing in a bond fund composed of junk bonds (high-yield) can fluctuate as much as 50 percent in net asset value price. During the junk bond sell-off, some funds' prices declined by that much. Similarly, in the past there have been occasional sell-offs in GNMA bond funds (1981 and 1982) and briefly in the municipal bond market (1987). Currently, investors in adjustable rate mortgage funds have seen declines in net asset value prices, even though interest rates have been declining. This is because homeowners have been refinancing their mortgages. These mortgages are paid back to their holders at 100 percent of their face value, but many funds may have paid a premium for these securities. These losses translate into lower net asset value prices.

How individual types of bonds react to changes in interest rates will indicate more or less how the fund prices will react to the same changes. Generally, the higher the risk of the securities, the greater the potential for return, and on the downside, for loss.

As of this writing, interest rates are at historic lows, which means that bond prices as well as bond mutual fund share prices have risen. If market rates of interest decline further, the average price of bond funds will appreciate. However, if market rates of interest go up, there could be a sell-off in bonds, and bond funds of all types would see a decline in price.

To reduce the potential price volatility, investors can invest in shorter-maturity bond funds (three years or less), which tend to fluctuate less than longer-maturity funds (average maturities in the range of 20 years). Money market funds, for example, have an average maturity of 90 days. This is why they are considered to be safe investments. Remember, however, less risk does not mean no risk. During several months in 1992, two top-rated short-term bond funds chalked up large declines in their net asset values. Fund managers are quick to take advantage of changing rates of interest by either increasing or decreasing the maturities of their investments. For instance, when interest rates are on their way down, fund managers will purchase bond issues with longer maturities, which of course increases the yield and the fund's total return.

The credit quality of the investments has an influence on both price volatility and yield. The lower the ratings of the individual bond issues in the fund, the higher the fluctuations in price and the greater the yield potential. Because of the many issues held in a bond fund, credit risk does not affect them in the same way as individual bond issues. For instance, in a typical large fund, each separate issue accounts for less than 2 percent of the total value, which means that a default by a single issuer would not have a significant impact on the net asset value price. This would not be so for an individual investor's bond portfolio, unless it were untypically large. The exception is the high-risk bond fund. This type of fund invests in below-investment-grade bond issues, for which credit risk and the risk of default are of greater concern. For bearing these risks, which also translate into greater net asset value price volatility, investors in these funds are compensated with higher yields.

With market rates of interest currently so low, many bond fund managers have been looking for exotic types of bond investments to boost their funds' yields. Collateralized mortgage obligations (CMOs) were scooped up not only by the mortgage funds but also by funds investing in government and corporate bonds

(Jereski, 1993). Some bond funds held as much as 15 percent of their assets in these instruments. CMOs have the potential of boosting returns for funds, but because of their complexities, they are difficult to price on a daily basis.

Inverse floaters, which were described in the chapter on municipal bonds, were mainly acquired by municipal bond funds to boost their yields. Because of their volatility, these, too, are difficult to price. In fact, Merrill Lynch, which prices most of the mortgage-backed securities in the market, will not price the volatile instruments (Jereski, 1993). How does all this affect shareholders?

At best, most shareholders are unaware of the fund's pricing problems and the fact that many funds use the approximate market values to compute their net asset value prices. This means investors could be buying and selling shares in their bond funds at inexact prices.

By understanding the characteristics of the investments in a fund, shareholders are better able to gauge the extent of fluctuation in the net asset value of the fund. However, if shareholders don't know what the fund is investing in, it becomes harder to anticipate the changes to net asset value prices. Investors don't know what the funds are invested in if it is not clearly spelled out in the prospectus of the fund. The securities that the funds invest in are listed in the prospectus information, but the types of bonds and their characteristics are not fully disclosed. Hence, an investor might see the number of the bond in a mortgage pool with the coupon rate, but other information might not be disclosed. If it is a floating-rate bond or a fixed-rate bond, for example, you might not get the weighted average life of the bond. If it is a CMO, you might not be able to find out which tranche it is in.

Pricing errors may occur much more frequently in the future because of the following factors:

- More complex derivative securities are being held by bond mutual funds.
- Many bond issues are difficult to price, such as thinly traded issues and junk bonds. These are not priced on a daily basis.

Even an error of a few cents in the pricing of the fund's share price can be costly. A few cents multiplied by several million shares outstanding can add up to a significant sum. In November 1992, T. Rowe Price made a mistake in pricing the shares of its International Bond fund, and the company asked some shareholders to pay back the 3-cent-per-share error (Eaton, 1993).

There is not much that investors in bond mutual funds can do about this other than to be aware of the potential glitches that could occur in the pricing of their fund's bond investments.

*Index funds* are the new kids on the block, so to speak. An index bond mutual fund seeks to match the returns of a particular index, such as the Lehman Brothers Aggregate Bond Index, by replicating its holdings with the bonds in the index. The main benefit from indexing is that it does not require active management. After the bonds are purchased, there is no need to actively manage the portfolio. Thus, an index fund will experience lower portfolio trading, which translates into lower transaction costs and lower expense ratios than actively managed bond mutual funds. The annual expense ratio of Vanguard's bond index funds as of December 31, 1998, was 0.20 percent, as compared with an average expense ratio of 1.1 percent for all bond funds (Vanguard Group, February 19, 1999). The aim of an index fund is to match the returns of the index, not to beat the market, as actively managed mutual funds try to do.

Much has been written about hedge funds since the disaster at Long Term Capital Management, a Connecticut hedge fund that had to be bailed out by 14 financial institutions in September 1998. Table 11-3 explains hedge funds. Long Term Capital Management suffered heavy losses due to its positions in Russian bonds and adverse swings in prices on the currency markets. Other hedge funds have also experienced heavy losses, which may result in huge redemptions by investors (Scholl and Bary, October 12, 1998, p. 19).

## HOW DOES PERFORMANCE AFFECT THE CHOICE OF A MUTUAL FUND?

The overall performance of a fund depends on the following:

- Yield
- Total return
- Expenses

## TABLE 11-3

### What Is a Hedge Fund?

Before defining a hedge fund, it is important to state what it is not. A hedge fund is not a mutual fund. Hedge funds are not required to register with the Securities and Exchange Commission (SEC) if they have fewer than 99 investors. However, investors in a hedge fund must be accredited by the SEC. In other words, investors must have at least $375,000 in liquid assets and be able to withstand the risks. The minimum investment in a U.S. hedge fund is generally over a quarter of a million dollars (Strong, 1996, p. 435).

U.S. hedge funds have been in existence for almost 50 years, and they typically take the form of limited partnerships. Hedge funds have numerous investment styles, including market-neutral strategies, in addition to the high- and low-risk strategies. Due to the fact that they are not as heavily regulated as mutual funds, hedge funds do not have the same limits on the types of investments they can make. However, there are limits on how investors can withdraw their funds. Many hedge funds allow investors to withdraw money only at the end of the year. Others may only allow investors to withdraw at the end of each quarter (Scholl and Bary, October 12, 1998, p. 19).

Hedge funds are not allowed to advertise, but information on them can be obtained from a number of publications, among them *Hedge Fund News, Lookout Mountain Hedge Fund Review,* and *Barclay Hedge Fund Report.*

As mentioned at the beginning of the chapter, almost any fund can boast attaining the number-one position in some area of performance at some point in time. Regardless, good past performance may not be indicative of good future performance. Some funds have performed very well in the past and done poorly thereafter. In fact, there are some formerly high-performing funds that are no longer in existence.

It is little wonder that with over 7000 mutual funds on the market vying for investors' savings, many of the messages in their advertisements would lead you to believe that they have attained superhuman performance. Even if funds do well during good times, investors should also examine how these funds have performed during the down markets. Several business magazines track the overall performance records (during up and down markets) of many of the mutual funds, which is a better yardstick than the advertising messages of the mutual funds themselves. *Forbes* magazine publishes annual performance ratings of mutual funds, and from this (or from other publications), investors can see how well bond funds performed in up markets as well as how they protected their capital during periods of declining bond prices.

New funds do not have track records. Therefore, a yardstick on performance during a period of declining prices may not be available. This is especially true for funds that have come into existence during the recent bull markets.

Some organizations, such as Morningstar, rate a mutual fund's performance relative to other funds with the same investment objectives, but this too can be misleading for investors trying to choose a fund (Morningstar's Internet address is *www.morningstar.com*). First, the funds may not be comparable, even though they have similar objectives. One may have riskier assets than another, so a comparison is not appropriate. Second, past performance may not be a reliable indicator of future performance.

In choosing a fund, investors are best off looking at what the fund invests in (as best as can be determined) and trying to determine the volatility in terms of up and down markets.

*Yield* is only one aspect of performance. Yield is defined as the interest and/or dividends paid to shareholders as a percentage of the net asset value price. Money market funds quote yields over a seven-day period. This is an average dividend yield for seven days, and it can be annualized. Long-term bond funds also quote an annualized average yield, but it is generally over 30 days.

Since 1988, the SEC has ruled that funds with average maturities longer than those of money market mutual funds must quote the SEC standardized yield. The *SEC standardized yield* includes the interest or dividends accrued by the fund over 30 days as well as an adjustment to the prices of the bonds for the amount of the amortization of any discount or premium which was paid for the bond assets. The SEC standardized yield makes the comparison of different mutual funds more meaningful. Prior to this rule, comparing the yield of one fund to that of another fund was an exercise in futility if one of them used a formula that inflated its yield (Thau, 1992).

The SEC standardized yield should be used for comparison purposes only, and not as a means to predict future yields. This yield is a measure of the fund's dividend distribution over a 30-day period and is only one aspect of the fund's *total return*. Mutual funds pass on any gains or losses to shareholders, which can increase or decrease the fund's total return.

Another factor which affects total return is the fluctuation in net asset value. When the share price increases by 6 percent, this effectively increases the total return by an additional 6 percent. Similarly, when the net asset value price of the fund declines, the total return will decrease. This explains why funds can have a negative return. It's what happened when the European currencies went into turmoil toward the latter part of 1992 and affected short-term global bond mutual funds. These funds had high yields, but they were diminished by the steep declines in their net asset value prices.

The interest on reinvested dividends is another factor which may be included in the total return. When the monthly interest or dividend paid out by the fund is reinvested to buy more shares, the yield earned on these reinvested shares will boost the overall return on the invested capital.

Therefore, when comparing the total returns quoted by the different funds, you need to make sure that you are comparing the same type of total return.

The total return of a mutual fund, or *cumulative total return*, includes:

- Dividends and capital gains/losses
- Changes in net asset values
- Dividends (interest) on reinvested dividends

When total returns are quoted by funds, you should ask whether all of these are included in the computation. However, there are examples of funds that choose not to advertise a total cumulative return. Some high-yield junk bond funds have at times chosen not to emphasize total returns, since deep declines in junk bond prices caused them to be negative. Instead, they touted their high yields. Thus, basing your choice of fund on yield alone can be misguided, since yields may be easier to manipulate. Investors should, therefore, look at both the yield and the total return of the fund to get a more balanced picture.

*Expenses* are a key factor in differentiating the performance of the different bond funds. By painstakingly looking for funds with the highest yields, investors are only looking at half the picture. A fund with a high yield may also be the one that charges higher expenses, which could put that fund behind some of the lower-cost funds which have lower yields. Fees reduce the total return earned by the funds.

The mutual fund industry has been criticized for the proliferation of fees and charges. Granted, these are all disclosed by the mutual funds, but besides the conspicuous charges, investors need to know where to look to find the less obvious fees.

## Load Funds versus No-Load Funds

Some mutual funds are *no-load funds*, with which the investor pays no commission or fee to buy or sell the shares of the fund. With an investment of $10,000 in a no-load fund, every cent of the $10,000 goes to buy shares in the fund. You can no longer easily identify no-load funds in the newspapers. However, you can easily find out whether the fund that you are interested in is a no-load fund by calling the mutual fund family, looking on their Website, or examining the prospectus.

A *load fund* charges a sales commission for buying shares in the fund. These charges can be front-ended, back-ended, or both, and they can be quite substantial, ranging to as much as $8\frac{1}{2}$ percent of the purchase price of the shares. The amount of the sales charge per share (load) can be determined by deducting the net asset value price from the offer price. See Table 11-2 for an example.

A front-end load is deducted from your funds when you invest. For example, if you are investing $10,000 in a fund with a load of 5 percent, the $500 load charge is deducted from the $10,000. This means that you only have $9500 of your $10,000 to invest.

Some funds give quantity discounts on their loads to investors who buy large blocks of shares. For example, the sales load might be 5 percent for amounts under $100,000, 4.25 percent for investing between $100,000 to $200,000, and 3.5 percent for amounts in excess of $200,000. When buying load funds, you also have to see if they charge a load on reinvested dividends as well.

Some funds also charge a *back-load*, or exit fee, when you sell the shares in the fund. This can be a straight percentage, or the percentage charged may decline the longer the shares are held in the fund.

The ultimate effect of load charges is to reduce the total return. The impact of the load charge is felt more keenly if the fund is held for a short period of time. For instance, if a fund has a yield of 6 percent and there is a 4 percent load to buy into the fund, the total return to the investor for the year is sharply reduced. If there is a back-end load to exit the fund, this could be even more expensive for the investor. If the share price has increased, the load percentage will be calculated on a larger amount.

Why, then, would so many investors invest in load funds when these commissions eat away so much of their returns? I can only speculate on possible answers:

- Investors may not want to decide which funds to invest in, so they leave the decisions to their brokers and financial planners.
- Brokers and financial planners earn their livings from selling investments from which they are paid commissions. These include load funds.
- No-load funds do not pay commissions to brokers and financial planners.

## Do Load Funds Outperform No-Load Funds?

There is no evidence to support the opinions expressed by many brokers and financial planners that load funds outperform no-load funds. According to CDA/Weisenberger, there was no difference between the performance of the average no-load fund and load fund over a five-year period (Clements, 1993). In fact, when adjusting for sales commissions, investors would have been better off with no-load funds. This makes sense when you consider that a load fund would have to outperform a no-load fund for a number of years just to recoup the initial load deducted from the investment amount. Consequently, it makes it much harder for load bond funds to outperform no-load bond funds when the general range of returns earned by bond funds is not that wide.

*12b-1 fees* are less obvious than loads. These are charged by many funds to recover expenses for marketing and distribution. These fees are assessed annually and can be quite steep when added together with load fees. Many no-load funds tout the absence of sales commissions but tack on 12b-1 fees, which are like a hidden load. A 1 percent 12b-1 fee may not sound like very much, but it is $100 less per annum in your pocket on a $10,000 mutual fund investment.

In addition to the above-mentioned charges, funds have *management fees,* which are paid to the managers who administer the fund's portfolio of investments. These can range from 0.5 percent to 2 percent of assets. High management fees also take a toll on the investor's total return.

Thus, all fees bear watching, since they reduce yields and total returns. Critics of the mutual fund industry have cultivated a sense of awareness regarding the proliferation of all these charges. Indeed, investors should not be deceived by funds that claim to be what they are not. Lowering front-end loads or eliminating them altogether doesn't mean a fund can't add fees somewhere else.

Funds have to disclose their fees, which means that investors can find them in the fund's prospectus. Management fees, 12b-1 fees, redemption fees (back-end loads), and any other fees charged are disclosed somewhere in the fund's prospectus. The financial newspapers also list the types of charges of the different funds in their periodic mutual fund performance reviews.

Some guidelines that you may want to follow to help you choose a fund are:

- Examine the performance records of the funds that you are interested in.
- Compare their total expenses and fees.
- Narrow the field to funds you feel will be the best in terms of performance. If there is no difference in the performance of your choices, then go with the fund that has the lowest expenses.

## WHAT IS THE SIGNIFICANCE OF THE PROSPECTUS?

Besides information that can be obtained about the different funds from business magazines, newspapers, and advisory services, essential information is provided by the mutual fund's prospectus. Currently, funds are required to send a prospectus to a potential investor before accepting investment funds. This may change, however, because the SEC has a new proposal that it is testing. The change would allow mutual funds to eliminate sending a prospectus as long as the key points of the prospectus are included in their advertisements. The information in the advertisements would be legally binding; if there were any facts that were not true, investors could sue. However, there is a vast gray area of puffery that has the potential for causing tremendous confusion among investors. Imagine the "clever" letters advertisers of mutual funds could dream up to send as direct mail to potential investors:

---

Dear Potential Investor:


The markets are going to tumble, in addition to...
No need for you to bear these hardships. Invest in XYZ Fund and reap the rewards...
Sincerely,


E.Z. Prey
Chairman, XYZ Fund

---

Although prospectuses are written in a manner that ranks them high on the list of best cures for insomnia, they still provide investors with information about the fund that they may not be able to get anywhere else.

You should look for the following in the prospectus.

## Objectives

The objectives and policies of the fund generally appear somewhere near the front of the prospectus. The objectives describe the types of securities the fund invests in as well as the risk factors associated with the securities. For instance, if the prospectus states that the fund will buy securities which are less than investment-grade, the investor should not be surprised to find that most of the bonds are junk bonds. The objectives will also state whether the fund is seeking current income, stability of capital, or long-term growth.

The investment policies will outline the latitude of the fund manager to invest in other types of securities. This could include trading futures contracts, writing options to hedge bets on the direction of interest rates, and investing in derivative securities to boost the yield of the fund. Many so-called conservative funds, which supposedly hold government securities only, have used derivative securities to boost their returns (Thau, 1992). The greater the latitude in investing in these other types of securities, the greater the risks if events backfire.

## Selected Per Share Data and Ratios

The selected per share data and ratios table in the prospectus summarizes the fund's performance over the time period shown. Table 11-4 gives an example of such a table. Although these will vary in detail from fund to fund, the format will be similar.

The investment activities section shows the amount of investment income earned on the securities held by the fund, and this generally is passed on to the mutual fund shareholders. In Table 11-4, for instance, all of the 1998 net investment income of $0.37 was distributed to the shareholders (line 4), but in 1997 only $0.30 of the $0.31 of net income was paid out to shareholders. That year, the $0.01 which was not distributed to shareholders increased the net asset value (line 7) in the capital changes section. (The capital loss and distribution of gains were reduced by this $0.01 that was not distributed.)

Capital gains and losses also affect the net asset value. Funds distribute their realized capital gains (line 6), but the unrealized capital gains or losses will also increase or decrease the net asset value.

Changes in the net asset value from year to year give you some idea of the volatility in share price. For instance, for the year 1997, the net asset value decreased by $1.01, which is a 9.17 percent decrease. How comfortable would you feel in the short term if you invested $10,000 knowing it could decline to $9082.65 (this is a 9.17 percent decline)?

Using the following formula, and taking into account the three sources of return (dividends distributed, capital gains distributed, and the changes in share price), investors can calculate an average total return.

Average total return =

$$\frac{\text{(dividend + capital gain distributions)} + \dfrac{\text{ending NAV} - \text{beginning NAV}}{\text{number of years}}}{\text{ending NAV} + \text{beginning NAV}}$$

## TABLE 11-4

### Selected Per Share Data and Ratios

|  |  | 1998 | 1997 | 1996 |
|---|---|---|---|---|
| Net asset value (NAV) beginning of the year |  | $10.02 | $11.01 | $10.73 |
| *Investment Activities* |  |  |  |  |
| line 1 | Income | .40 | .35 | .55 |
| line 2 | Expenses | (.03) | (.04) | (.05) |
| line 3 | Net investment income | .37 | .31 | .50 |
| line 4 | Distribution of dividends | (.37) | (.30) | (.47) |
| *Capital Changes* |  |  |  |  |
| line 5 | Net realized and unrealized gains (losses) on investments | $1.00 | (.75) | 1.50 |
| line 6 | Distributions of realized gains | (.70) | (.25) | 1.25 |
| line 7 | Net increase (decrease) to NAV | .30 | (.99) | .28 |
|  | NAV beginning of year | 10.02 | 11.01 | 10.73 |
|  | NAV at end of year | 10.32 | 10.02 | 11.01 |
|  | Ratio of operating expenses to average net assets | .45% | .46% | .84% |
|  | Portfolio turnover rate | 121% | 135% | 150% |
|  | Shares outstanding (000's) | 10,600 | 8451 | 6339 |

$$\text{Average total return for 1998} = \frac{(.37+.70) + \left(\dfrac{10.32 - 10.02}{1}\right)}{\dfrac{10.32 + 10.02}{2}}$$

$$= 13.50\%$$

Having calculated this simple yield of 13.5 percent indicates that an investor in this fund would have received double-digit returns, resulting mainly from realized gains and increases in the NAV share price. The more volatile the net asset value of the fund, the greater the likelihood of unstable returns. Thus, when considering whether to invest in a particular fund, don't go by the advertised yield alone. Look at the total return.

The ratio of operating expenses to average net assets is fairly low in this hypothetical fund (close to one-half of 1 percent). This is the aggregate of the expenses in the fund, which is expressed as a percentage of the assets in the fund. Investors should be interested in this ratio because they are paying for it through its direct deduction from the earnings of the fund. Look for funds with expense ratios of less than 1 percent.

The portfolio turnover rate indicates how actively the assets in the fund are turned over. Bond funds tend to have high turnover rates, and 150 percent is not uncommon. A turnover rate of 100 percent indicates that all the investments in a portfolio would change once a year (Thau, 1992).

## Annual Expenses

Although annual expenses are shown in the Selected Per Share Data and Ratios section, mutual fund prospectuses will also have a separate table with a breakdown of expenses. This typically shows the different load charges, redemption fees, shareholder accounting costs, *12b-1* fees, distribution costs, and other expenses.

By examining the prospectuses of the funds you are interested in, you will be able to make a more informed choice than if you merely go by the advertised messages of the funds.

# WHAT ARE THE TAX CONSEQUENCES OF BUYING AND SELLING SHARES IN MUTUAL FUNDS?

Tax reporting on mutual funds can be complicated. Even if you buy and hold shares in a mutual fund, there are tax consequences. Dividends, which are paid to investors on a monthly basis, may be automatically reinvested in the fund to buy more shares. At the end of the year, the mutual fund will send a Form 1099 to each mutual fund shareholder showing the amount of dividends and capital gains received for the year. Dividends and capital gains are taxable to the shareholder regardless of whether they are reinvested in additional fund shares or paid out in cash. Therefore, these dividends and capital gains need to be added into the cost basis when the investor sells the shares in the fund.

For example, suppose an investor invested $10,000 in a fund two years ago and has received a total of $2000 in dividends and capital gains in the fund to date. The investor sells all the shares in the fund and receives $14,000. The investor's cost basis is $12,000 (not $10,000), and the gain on the sale of the shares is $2000 ($14,000 − $12,000).

When investors sell only a part of their total shares, the procedure is different and may be tricky. This is further complicated when investors actively buy and sell shares as if it were a checking account. In fact, many mutual funds encourage investors to operate their funds like a checking account by providing check-writing services. However, every time an investor writes a check against a bond fund, there is a capital gain or loss tax consequence. This does not include money market funds, which have a stable share price of $1. This action either causes a nightmare for the investor at tax time or produces extra revenue for the investor's accountant for the additional time spent calculating the gains and losses.

The most important thing in an actively traded bond mutual fund (or any mutual fund for that matter) is to keep good records. For each fund, keep a separate folder and store all the monthly statements showing purchases and sales of shares, dividends, and capital gain distributions.

By keeping records of all transactions, investors will be able to determine the cost basis of shares sold. This can be done using an average cost method, on a FIFO basis, or using the specific identification method. FIFO is first in, first out, which means that the cost of the first shares purchased in the fund will be used first as the shares sold. Table 11-5 illustrates the FIFO method of calculating capital gains or losses on the partial sale of shares in a mutual fund. The example shows that the earliest shares purchased are the first to be used in the sale of shares. After all the shares of the invested funds are sold, the basis of the dividends and capital gains shares will be used to determine any gains or losses.

Several funds provide the gains and losses on an average cost basis when investors sell shares in these funds. The *average cost method* allows shareholders to average the cost of the shares in the fund. Moreover, there is the *single-category method* and the *double-category method*. The former includes all the shares held in the fund. The double-category method involves separating the shares in the

**TABLE 11-5**

## Calculation of Gains/Losses on the Sale of Shares

### Summary of GNMA Bond Fund

| Date | Transaction | Dollar Amount | Share Price | No. of Shares | Total No. of Shares |
|------|-------------|---------------|-------------|---------------|---------------------|
| 06/14 | Invest | $10,000 | $10.00 | 1000 | 1000 |
| 11/26 | Invest | 4,500 | 9.00 | 500 | 1500 |
| 11/30 | Redeem (sell) | 12,000 | 10.00 | (1200) | 300 |
| 12/31 | Income, dividends | 1,000 | 10.00 | 100 | 400 |

### To Calculate Gain/Loss on an FIFO Basis

Sold 1200 shares at $10.00 per share        **Sale Price**        $12,000

**Cost Basis**

| | | |
|---|---|---|
| 06/14 | 1000 shares at $10.00 | $10,000 |
| 11.26 | 200 shares at $9.00 | 1,800 |
| | Total cost | $11,800 |
| | Gain | 200 |

### GNMA Bond Fund after Sale

| Date | Transaction | Dollar Amount | Share Price | No. of Shares | Total No. of Shares |
|------|-------------|---------------|-------------|---------------|---------------------|
| 11/26 | Invested | $2,700 | $ 9.00 | 300 | 300 |
| 12/31 | Income, dividends | 1,000 | 10.00 | 100 | 400 |

fund into short-term and long-term holdings and calculating average prices for these two categories. Redemptions use the short-term or long-term average price. The average cost basis can get quite complex with additional sales and purchases of shares. Hence, some bond funds don't allow their shareholders to write checks against their accounts.

The *specific identification method* allows shareholders to identify the specific shares that they wish to sell. Investors can minimize their gains by choosing to sell first shares with the highest cost basis.

To minimize any potential tax hassles, investors are better off not writing checks from their bond funds for their short-term cash needs. This only creates gains or losses where the investor would have been better off investing the money needed for short-term purposes in a money market fund, which alleviates these tax problems.

Whether you trade actively or not, the solution to tax computations is to keep good records. If you can't determine the cost basis of your shares, an accountant will be able to do so, provided you keep good records. If you don't have all the records of your purchases and sales, you may not be able to prove your cost basis to the Internal Revenue Service if it is disputed.

## WHAT ARE THE RISKS OF MUTUAL FUNDS?

The major risk with bond mutual funds is the *risk of loss of funds invested* due to a decline in net asset value. The longer the maturity of the fund, the greater the possibility of a decline in the net asset value. This is because of interest rate risk. When interest rates rise, bond prices (and net asset values of bond funds) decline. Similarly, when interest rates go down, bond prices (and the net asset values of bond funds) appreciate.

*Credit risk* affects those funds that invest in below-investment-grade bonds such as junk bonds. When there is nervousness about defaults in junk bonds, a major sell-off in the junk bond market is provoked, which in the past has resulted in steep declines in junk bond prices and the net asset values of related bond funds. However, as explained earlier in this chapter, credit risk may not be as significant for bond funds as it is for individual bonds. This is because funds are large and diversified, with many different issues. In general, the loss from the default of one or two issues would have a small overall impact on a fund.

As a result of some bank failures and the shaky financial status of some savings and loan associations, some investors are naturally concerned about the *risk of insolvency* of mutual funds. There is always the risk that a mutual fund could go under, but the chances of this happening are small. The key distinction between banks and mutual funds is the way that mutual funds are set up, which reduces the risks of failure and loss due to fraud. Typically, mutual funds are corporations owned by shareholders. A separate management company is contracted by the shareholders to run the fund's daily operations. The management company oversees the investments of the fund, but it does not have possession of these assets (investments). The assets are held by a custodian such as a bank. Thus, if the management company gets into financial trouble, it cannot get access to the assets of the fund.

Another safeguard is that the shareholders' accounts are maintained by a transfer agent. The transfer agent keeps track of the purchases and redemptions of the shareholders. In addition, management companies carry fidelity bonds, which are a form of insurance to protect the investments of the funds against malfeasance or fraud perpetrated by their employees.

Besides these safeguards, there are two other factors which differentiate mutual funds from corporations such as banks and savings and loan associations:

1. Mutual funds must be able to redeem shares on demand, which means that a portion of the investment assets must be liquid.
2. Mutual funds must be able to price their investments at the end of each day, known as *marking to market*.

Hence, mutual funds cannot hide their financial difficulties as easily as banks and savings and loans.

In addition to these checks and balances, mutual funds are regulated by the SEC. Therefore, it is unlikely that investors in mutual funds will have to worry about losing money due to the financial collapse through fraud. However, investors should be aware that they can lose money by purchasing a fund whose investments perform poorly in the markets.

See also the specific risks that pertain to the different types of bonds covered in the different chapters.

## HOW TO BUY AND SELL MUTUAL FUNDS

Buying and selling shares in bond mutual funds can be accomplished in several ways, depending on whether the fund is a load or no-load fund.

Investors can buy into no-load mutual funds by dealing directly with the mutual fund. Most, if not all, funds have (800) telephone numbers. Mutual funds will send first-time investors a prospectus along with an application form to open an account. The prospectus and application form can also be downloaded from a fund's Website on the Internet. Once investors have opened accounts with the fund, they can purchase additional shares by sending a check along with a preprinted account stub detached from the account statement. As mentioned earlier, there are no sales commissions with no-load funds and so they are not sold by brokers. Shares in no-load funds are bought and sold at their net asset values.

Load funds are sold through brokers and salespeople, who charge commissions every time new shares are bought. Some funds also charge a redemption fee, which is a back-end fee, or reverse load, for selling shares. If the percentages for loads are the same (for front- or back-end), it may be preferable to go for a reverse load rather than a front load because all the money is invested immediately with the back-end load (Faerber, 1992).

Financial planners, brokers, and salespeople may try to convince you to buy load funds, claiming they perform better than no-load funds. There is no evidence to support this premise. In fact, according to a study by Morningstar, a Chicago firm that tracks mutual funds, no-load bond funds consistently outperformed load funds over three-, five-, and ten-year periods through March 31, 1993 (McGough, 1993). However, there may be some truth to the claim that no-load bond funds are much more volatile than load funds during expanding and contracting markets.

Banks and discount brokerage firms have also entered the mutual fund arena, and they too sell mutual funds. This, of course, further complicates the choice process, but investors who feel confident enough to choose their own funds are better off with no-load funds. The difference saved may be minimal over a short period of time, but this difference can grow substantially over a 10-year period due to the compounding of interest (time value of money).

A good source of information on mutual funds is a reference book called *Investment Companies*, available in most libraries. In it, you can review the long-run performance of the funds you are interested in.

Information can also be obtained from the individual mutual fund companies' Websites, as well as from other Websites on the Internet. One such Website is *www.fundsinteractive.com*.

Table 11-6 summarizes the information you should consider in selecting one mutual fund over another.

**TABLE  1 1 - 6**

Criteria to Consider When Choosing a Mutual Fund

- Select funds with low costs.
- Don't overrate past performance. Top-performing funds can lose their edge over time.
- Use past performance data to see the range of performance and the risks of the fund.
- Don't buy too many funds, as you will become overdiversified.
- Define your long-term objectives and risk tolerance, and then stick with the funds for the long term.

# WHAT ARE THE ADVANTAGES OF MUTUAL FUNDS?

- Mutual funds offer small investors the opportunity to own a fraction of a diversified portfolio. For instance, investing $2500 in a bond fund gives the investor a share of an excellent cross section of bonds. Investors would need to invest at least $150,000 in individual bonds to have a diversified portfolio.

- Mutual funds provide administrative and custodial services: recordkeeping of all transactions, monthly statements, information for tax purposes, as well as the safekeeping of all securities.

- Mutual funds are professionally managed. Many investors do not have the time or the expertise to manage their bond portfolios.

- Mutual fund companies redeem shares on demand. In the case of no-load funds, they are redeemed at net asset value.

- Investors have the option of being able to reinvest dividends and capital gains automatically for more shares in the fund or have them paid out on a monthly basis.

- Investors in a family of funds can switch from one fund to another as market conditions change. For example, when interest rates are going up, investors can switch money from their bond funds to money market funds.

- Levels of risk, return, and stability of income and principal vary with the type of fund chosen. Most families of mutual funds offer a range of different types of bond funds with various characteristics.
- Mutual funds distribute dividends on a monthly basis, whereas individual bonds only pay interest on a semiannual or annual basis.

## WHAT ARE THE DISADVANTAGES OF MUTUAL FUNDS?

- Professional management does not guarantee superior performance. Many funds underperform the market over long periods of time.
- When load charges and fees are included, total returns may be significantly less than if investors bought individual bonds and held them to maturity.
- Investors have no control over the investment decisions that portfolio managers make.
- Investors have no control over the distribution of hidden capital gains, which can upset very careful tax planning. Since investment companies do not pay taxes, income and capital gains are passed through to the shareholders.
- Dividend income from mutual funds fluctuates from month to month.
- Mutual funds do not have maturity dates.

## CAVEATS

- Choose a mutual fund family which has a wide range of different funds. This allows you greater flexibility to transfer from one fund type to another.
- Avoid funds which have high sales charges, redemption fees, and management and expense ratios.
- Keep all the records of income and capital gains distributions as well as the dates, amounts, and share prices of all purchases and redemptions of shares. This can alleviate a potential nightmare at tax time.

- Avoid buying into a mutual fund towards the end of the year because you could be increasing your tax burden. Before buying into a fund, investigate whether the fund has accumulated any capital gains distributions, which they have not yet distributed to shareholders. This occurs when fund managers sell investments at higher prices than they purchased them at which results in capital gains. These gains are passed onto shareholders at the end of the year through a capital gains distribution, even if the shareholders did not own the fund when the capital gains were incurred.

## SHOULD YOU INVEST IN BOND MUTUAL FUNDS OR INDIVIDUAL BONDS?

Bond mutual funds have been very popular among investors. As of March 1993, a record $622 billion was invested in bond mutual funds, according to the Investment Company Institute (Herman, 1993). This amount was more than for both stock mutual funds and money market funds.

As stated earlier, the advantages of bond mutual funds include professional management, diversification, being able to invest small amounts of money, and ease of buying and selling. For many investors, these advantages outweigh the disadvantages of mutual funds. Mutual funds may be the most practical way for investors to buy many bond types, for example, bonds that sell in high denominations, such as certain mortgage-backed bonds, certain agency bonds, and some municipal issues. Another factor in favor of mutual funds involves the complexity of certain types of bonds. The complexities of mortgage-backed bonds, zero-coupon bonds, convertible issues, and derivative securities may exclude most investors from buying them as individual bonds. Mutual funds, therefore, allow investors to own even these complex types of bonds.

It certainly makes sense to invest in junk bond mutual funds rather than individual junk bonds. The diversification achieved by mutual funds minimizes the impact from any unexpected defaults. Professional managers of these funds have quicker access to information about the different issues as well as greater expertise than most average investors. Mutual funds will also pay lower transaction fees for buying and selling bonds than individual investors.

However, there is a strong argument for buying individual bonds over mutual funds in certain cases. Rates of return on individual bonds are often greater than those earned from mutual funds. This is true even for no-load funds, because in addition to sales commissions, there are other fees which eat into the returns of mutual funds (12b-1 and operating fees, for instance). By investing in individual bonds, investors avoid these fees.

The second powerful argument for individual bonds is that if they are bought and held until maturity, interest rate risk is avoided. Changes in interest rates affect the prices of both individual bonds and bond mutual funds. However, if investors have a set time for which they will not need their money, they can invest in individual bonds with maturities corresponding to their needs and not worry what happens to interest rates. This does not apply to bond mutual funds. If interest rates go up, there will be a decline in the net asset value of share prices of bond funds. That's because mutual funds never mature.

Bonds such as Treasury securities are easy to buy, and by owning these Treasury securities individually, investors can eliminate many of the fees that mutual funds charge, thereby increasing their returns. Moreover, when these are bought directly from the Federal Reserve Banks or branches, investors do not pay any commissions. Buying and holding Treasury securities makes more sense than investing in Treasury bond funds. However, if investors do not plan on holding the bonds through maturity, funds may be a better alternative.

Buying U.S. Treasury notes requires minimum amounts of $1000 and $5000 for different issues. Investors with less than these minimums are precluded from buying Treasury securities. For example, if an investor has only $4980 to invest, individual Treasury notes are out of the question until that investor has the other $20. Similarly, if an investor has $5950, only $5000 could be used to buy individual Treasury notes, whereas that investor could invest all of the proceeds in a U.S. government bond mutual fund. Once investors have opened a fund account, they can invest in increments of as little as $100 in many funds.

Thus, bond mutual funds offer investors a convenient way to invest small amounts as well as large amounts of money.

Investors could, of course, buy individual U.S. Treasury notes for the minimum amounts and invest any marginal dollars in bond mutual funds.

Investing in bond mutual funds is good for investors who do not have enough money to diversify their investments and who also do not have the time, expertise, or inclination to select and manage individual bonds. In addition, there is a wide range of different bond funds, which offers investors the opportunity to invest in types of bond securities that would be difficult to buy on an individual basis.

The advantages of individual bonds versus mutual funds are summarized in Table 11-7.

### TABLE 11-7

Individual Bonds versus Mutual Bond Funds

|  | Individual Bonds | Mutual Funds |
|---|---|---|
| Loss of principal | None, if held to maturity | Yes, if share price declines |
| Diversification | No, unless a large number of bonds are purchased | Yes |
| Ease of buying and selling | No, except for Treasury securities | Yes |
| Fixed amounts of interest | Yes | No |
| Professional management | No | Yes |
| Tax planning | Yes | No |

# REFERENCES

**Clements, Jonathan**: "The 25 Facts Every Fund Investor Should Know," *The Wall Street Journal*, March 5, 1993, p. C1.

**Eaton, Leslie**: "Price Fixing, Costly Mistakes in Valuing Shares," *Barron's*, April 19, 1993, p. 35.

**Faerber, Esmé**: *Managing Your Investments, Savings, and Credit*, McGraw-Hill, New York, 1992.

**Herman, Tom**: "Bond vs. Bond Mutual Funds: Which Are Better for You?" *The Wall Street Journal*, April 30, 1993, p. C1.

**Jereski, Laura**: "What Price CMOs? Funds Have No Idea," *The Wall Street Journal*, April 12, 1993, p. C1.

**McGough, Robert**: "Banks vs. Brokers: Who's Got the Best Funds?" *The Wall Street Journal*, May 7, 1993, p. C1.

**Savage, Stephen**: "Refrigerator Rules, ABCs for Today's Complex Fund Climate," *Barron's*, February 15, 1993, p. 43.

**Scholl, Jaye, and Andrew Bary**: "A Lousy New Year," *Barron's*, October 12, 1998, p. 19.

**Schultz, Ellen**: "How to Unwrap a Wrap Account," *The Wall Street Journal*, February 5, 1993, p. C1.

**Strong, Robert A.**: *Practical Investment Management*, Southwestern College Publishing Co., Cincinnati, 1996.

**Thau, Annette**: *The Bond Book*, McGraw-Hill, New York, 1992.

**Vanguard Group**: "Sage Online" Hosts Vanguard's Index Bond Chief, *www.vanguard.com*, February 19, 1999.

## CHAPTER 12

# Closed-End Funds

## KEY CONCEPTS

- What are closed-end funds?
- What are unit investment trusts?
- What are the risks of closed-end bond funds and unit investment trusts?
- How to buy and sell closed-end funds and unit investment trusts
- What are the advantages of closed-end funds and unit investment trusts?
- What are the disadvantages of closed-end funds and unit investment trusts?
- Are closed-end funds and unit investment trusts suitable for you?

## WHAT ARE CLOSED-END FUNDS?

Closed-end funds bear similarities to open-end mutual funds, but there are some significant differences. Table 12-1 summarizes the differences. As pointed out in the previous chapter, open-end mutual funds issue an unlimited number of shares, and they will redeem shares from shareholders when they want to sell. When investors buy more shares in an open-end fund, more money is available to the fund manager to buy more investment assets.

Closed-end funds have a fixed number of shares outstanding, and after these are sold, the fund does not issue any new shares. Shares of closed-end funds are traded on the stock exchanges or on the over-the-counter market. Most closed-end funds are traded on the New York Stock Exchange, some on the American Stock Exchange, and a few on the over-the-counter market.

Since the number of shares in a closed-end fund is fixed, investors who want to invest in an existing fund (as opposed to a new fund) have to buy shares from shareholders who are willing to sell their shares on the market. Consequently, the share price of the closed-end bond fund fluctuates depending on the supply and demand for the shares and other factors, such as the return of the fund, average maturity of the assets of the fund, net asset value, and so forth.

## TABLE 12-1

### Closed-End Funds versus Open-End Funds

| Closed-End Funds | Open-End Funds |
|---|---|
| 1. Issue a fixed number of shares, which are sold to original shareholders. | 1. Issue an unlimited number of shares. |
| 2. Shares (after issue) are traded on the stock exchanges. | 2. Shares, including new shares, may be bought and sold from and to the fund. |
| 3. Shares may trade at, above, or below net asset values. | 3. Shares trade at net asset values. |
| 4. Share prices depend not only on the fundamentals but also on the supply and demand for the shares. | 4. Share prices depend on the fundamentals of the assets in the fund. |
| 5. Closed-end funds do not mature. Unit investment trusts do. | 5. Open-end funds do not mature except for zero-coupon funds. |

Like open-end mutual funds, the net asset value is important in the valuation of the share price. Unlike open-end funds, however, share prices of closed-end funds can be above or below their net asset values. For example, when interest rates decline, there may be heavy demand for closed-end bond funds, and that can drive their share prices above their net asset values. Hence, these funds would trade at a premium. Similarly, when interest rates go up, shares of closed-end bond funds could trade at significant discounts to their net asset values. For example, a closed-end bond fund could have a net asset value of $9 per share and be selling at $7.50 per share (a $1.50 discount per share). At times, the discounts to net asset values of closed-end funds can be as much as 20 to 30 percent.

The types of assets held in the fund and their maturities also affect the share price. The longer the maturities, the greater the volatility in share prices.

As with open-end funds, there are many different types of closed-end funds. There are stock funds, bond funds, international funds, and specialized funds. Among the bond funds, there are corporate bond funds, municipal bond funds, government bond funds, international bond funds, and balanced funds. Balanced funds invest in both stocks and bonds.

Depending on the investment objectives of the closed-end fund, the professional managers (of the fund) will invest in different financial assets to make up a diversified portfolio. Even though closed-end funds do not issue new shares to expand their capital structure, their portfolio assets can and do change. Existing bond issues may be sold and new ones bought for the portfolio. Thus, when bond issues mature, the proceeds received are used to buy new issues. Closed-end funds, like open-end funds, never mature.

Net asset values for closed-end funds are calculated in much the same way as for open-end funds. The total assets minus any liabilities equal the net worth of the fund, which is divided by the fixed number of shares to give the net asset value per share.

Occasionally, closed-end funds become open-end mutual funds, and the net asset value becomes the price that the shares trade at through the mutual fund, that is, if it becomes a no-load fund. For a load fund, there will be an additional commission added to the net asset value.

## WHAT ARE UNIT INVESTMENT TRUSTS?

In the closed-end bond fund market, unit investment trusts have become very popular. Brokerage firms such as Merrill Lynch, Bear Stearns, Nuveen, and Van Kampen and Merritt all sponsor unit trusts.

Unit investment trusts have been seductively marketed as the investment which earns high current income as well as returning investors' entire investment when the trust assets mature. Theoretically, this is possible, but in practice, it may not always be the case. By examining how unit trusts work, the difficulty of living up to those lofty promises becomes apparent.

A unit investment trust, like a closed-end fund, will sell a fixed number of shares. For instance, assume that the trust sells one million shares at $10 per share for a total of $10 million. Sales commissions of $500,000 would be deducted, leaving the unit trust $9.5 million to invest in different bond issues (the same as for a closed-end bond fund). The trust will then remit the earnings on the investments, minus management fees, to the shareholders. When the different investments mature, the trust will pay back the proceeds from the investments to the shareholders. (Closed-end funds differ in that when issues mature, the proceeds are reinvested in other issues). This is basically how unit investment trusts and closed-end funds work.

However, before looking at the factors that could make it difficult for the trust to live up to its promise of high income and the full return of principal, let's take a quick look at some of the differences between unit trusts and closed-end funds.

In general, with unit investment trusts the portfolio of investments does not change after purchase. In other words, no new bonds are bought and no existing bonds are sold. Theoretically, as the bond issues approach maturity, the prices of the individual bonds will rise toward their par prices. Also, theoretically, management fees should be lower on unit investment trusts than on closed-end funds, since the portfolio remains unmanaged. In fact, there should be no management fees on a unit investment trust, but in most instances this is not the case. With closed-end bond funds, the portfolio changes as issues are bought and sold.

Shares of unit investment trusts, like those of closed-end bond funds, trade on the secondary markets. Under certain conditions, however, shares in unit investment trusts can become illiquid. This happens when interest rates are rising and new investors do not want to buy into a trust with bond investments that are locked into lower yields. Hence, existing unit trust shareholders might have difficulty selling their shares due to this illiquidity.

## WHAT ARE THE RISKS OF CLOSED-END BOND FUNDS AND UNIT INVESTMENT TRUSTS?

Both closed-end bond funds and unit investment trusts are subject to *interest rate risk.* When market rates of interest rise, prices of the bond issues held in both the portfolios of unit trusts and closed-end bond funds will go down. This, of course, means that the share prices will fall.

Moreover, if there is selling pressure on the shares, the decline in share prices will be even greater than the decline in the net asset values. The opposite is true as well. If interest rates fall, there will be appreciation in the assets and, of course, in the share price.

Interest rate risk has another effect on unit investment trusts. Because the assets in the portfolio remain the same, the yields of the fixed-coupon bonds will theoretically remain the same despite changes in interest rates. On the other hand, with closed-end bond funds, when the assets mature or are sold, new issues with higher (or lower) coupons are bought, so yields on closed-end bond funds will fluctuate more than those of unit investment trusts. If, however, unit investment trusts invest in mortgage securities and interest-only strips, a reduction in interest rates would cause a reduced return for shareholders. Interest-only strips fall in price when interest rates decline. This happened to some of the Hyperion Trust funds, which had negative rates of return on some trusts and poor returns on others (Bary, May 1993).

Many unit investment trusts have used leverage to increase their yields. Leverage is where the trusts use borrowed money to supplement amounts invested by shareholders to invest in portfolio assets. Currently, this has worked well for many trusts because of the yield curve, which is the relationship between long-term and short-term rates. Currently, short-term rates are lower than long-term interest rates. Therefore, trusts have been borrowing on a short-term basis and investing the funds in long-term issues, which yield higher returns. This strategy works well as long as short-term rates are lower than long-term rates.

However, this is a risky strategy. If interest rates bottom out and begin to rise, not only will borrowing costs climb and cut into the yields paid to shareholders, the prices of the different bond securities held in the portfolio will decline, which, of course, translates into lower share prices. Thus, the use of leverage adds further risks when combined with changes in interest rates.

For both closed-end funds and unit investment trusts, there is the *risk that share prices will fall way below net asset values* due to excess selling pressure in the stock markets. Then, of course, the danger arises of not being able to recoup the original price paid for the shares when selling.

Unit investment trust shareholders have the added risk that they may not get back the full amount of their original investment. This can be caused by a number of factors. For one thing, bond issues may be called before maturity, with the call price being less than the face value. The composition of the trust's assets, commissions, high management fees charged to the trust, the dividend yields, and as mentioned earlier, the use of leverage are all factors that can add to the risk of loss of principal.

In many cases, the managers of unit investment trusts and closed-end bond funds charge generous annual fees in addition to their up-front commissions on the original sale of the shares. These funds will not only have to earn spectacular returns so that the managers can collect their fees without eroding yields significantly, they will also have to rake in some capital gains to be able to recoup the sales commissions and be able to return to shareholders their entire investment amounts at maturity. This explains why many investment trusts use leverage and resort to derivative securities to try and boost their returns.

When interest rates fall, there is always the risk that bond issues will be called, causing *reinvestment risk*. This means that shareholders of unit trusts will get their money back, which is reinvested at lower rates of interest, which reduces overall returns. Note: this return of funds includes the shareholders' principal, so it should be reinvested and not spent as if it were interest.

The types of investments that the fund or trust holds will have a marked effect on the net asset value and the volatility of the share price. Unfortunately, for the original shareholders of closed-end bond funds and unit investment trusts, there is no way of knowing the investment composition of the portfolio when they first subscribe. That's because only after the original shareholders invest their money to buy the shares do the managers of the fund or trust buy the investment assets. Thus, shareholders may not be able to evaluate the levels of risk of the assets until the portfolio has been constituted. The composition could include low-quality bonds or complex derivative securities for the purpose of boosting the yields of the portfolio. If the low-quality securities deteriorate or interest rates change in an unanticipated direction, this strategy could backfire and send the prices of these funds and trusts into a steep decline. Investors trying to exit would experience losses from the decline in share price.

What you see with advertised yields is not always what you get. Certain funds will incorporate capital gains as well as returns of principal from mortgage-backed securities to boost their yield figures. The only true yield for a closed-end fund is the current yield: the net investment income per share (after management fees) divided by the price per share. For closed-end funds, for which there is no maturity, a yield to maturity calculation is not meaningful. The total return for closed-end funds depends on the yield of the investments and the fluctuations in share price.

With unit investment trusts, the sales pitch often features a high yield. In a low-interest-rate climate, many trusts will disregard the risks of high-yielding lower-quality securities for their portfolios. This happened to many unit investment trusts that loaded up on Washington Public Power Securities before they defaulted, resulting in losses which fell to the shareholders (Thau, 1992).

In summary, investors in unit investment trusts should look beyond the advertised yield and scrutinize the makeup of the portfolio of investments. In reality, shareholders of unit investment trusts have no protection against either the deterioration of the quality of the investments in the portfolio or interest rate risk (Thau, 1992). Similarly, if there is an exodus of shareholders from unit investment trusts and closed-end funds, they may find it difficult to sell their shares without taking large losses. When selling shares of a unit investment trust, it is done through a stock broker back to the sponsor of the trust. The sponsor of the trust is not legally obligated to repurchase the shares. Generally, the sale price is the net asset value minus a spread or commission. When selling closed-end funds, the shareholders sell their shares at the market prices quoted on the exchanges where the funds are listed.

## HOW TO BUY AND SELL CLOSED-END FUNDS AND UNIT INVESTMENT TRUSTS

When closed-end funds and unit investment trusts are newly issued, the shares are underwritten by brokerage firms and sold by brokers. Brokerage fees can be as high as 8 percent, which means that the investor's investment is immediately reduced by that amount. For instance, if a fund or trust sells one million shares at $10 per share for $10 million, it will have only $9.2 million to invest after deducting the $800,000 (8 percent) for brokerage commissions. This means that after shareholders have paid $10 per share to invest in the new fund or trust, the shares will drop in value and trade at a discount. This is a quick erosion in capital and is a well-documented phenomenon for closed-end funds and unit investment trusts. This will not be a topic of conversation brought up by the brokers who stand to earn high commissions from the sale of these shares. Many brokers assert that closed-end funds are sold commission-free. This is a play on words; it may be commission-free, but in its place is a hefty underwriting charge which is absorbed by the shareholders. Investors would do better to wait until the funds or trusts are listed on the stock exchanges than to buy them at issue and see the shares drop in price.

Another reason not to buy closed-end funds or unit investment trusts at issue is that the portfolio of assets has not yet been constituted, so investors do not know what they are getting, and they most certainly won't know what the yields will be. Unit investment trust sponsors do not like to see the shares of their trusts fall to discounts, and so they often advertise above-market yields to keep the shares from trading at discounts to their net asset values.

The advice from expert Thomas Herzfeld, who follows closed-end funds and unit investment trusts, is to pay attention to the prices of the funds that you are interested in and to buy them when the discount is 3 percent wider than the normal discount for the fund (Thau, 1992).

Common sense suggests that besides the attractiveness of buying into a fund when its shares are selling below their net asset values, there are other factors to consider:

- The yield is important, particularly if investors are buying into the fund in order to get the income. Examine the yield, total return, and expense ratios before investing.
- The frequency with which dividends are paid (semiannually, quarterly, or monthly).
- The composition of the assets and the credit quality of the assets.
- The average length of time to maturity of the portfolio investments.

Information on closed-end funds can be found in Thomas J. Herzfeld Advisors' annual *Encyclopedia of Closed-End Funds, Value Line Investment Survey, Standard & Poor's Record Sheets, Moody's Finance Manuals,* and Wiesenberger's *Investment Companies* (in most public libraries).

Share prices of the listed closed-end funds and unit investment trusts can be found in the stock exchange sections of the daily newspapers. For example, the following is a quote from *Barron's* October 19, 1998, of the Black Rock Municipal Trust 2008 listed on the New York Stock Exchange.

| 52-Wk | | | | | | | | Week's | | | |
|---|---|---|---|---|---|---|---|---|---|---|---|
| Hi | Low | Name | Tick Sym | Div Amt | Vol 100s | Yld | P/E | High | Low | Last | Net Chg |
| $16\frac{7}{16}$ | $14\frac{5}{8}$ | BlkrkMuni2008 | BRM | .80 | 994 | 4.9 | ... | $16\frac{3}{16}$ | $15\frac{13}{16}$ | $16\frac{3}{16}$ | $+\frac{5}{16}$ |

Reading from left to right:

- The first two columns indicate the year's high of $16\frac{7}{16}$ per share and low of $14\frac{5}{8}$ per share.

- The name of the stock is the Black Rock Insured Municipal Trust, with a maturity in 2008.
- The ticker symbol for this fund on the New York Stock Exchange is BRM.
- The dividend is $0.80 per share.
- The sales volume indicates the number of shares traded that week, which was 99,400 shares.
- The yield percentage is 4.9 percent, which is the dividend divided by the last price of the day ($0.80 \div 16^3/_{16}$).
- The high, low, and last indicate price "extremities." $16^3/_{16}$ was the high price for the week. $15^{13}/_{16}$ was the low price for that week's trading. And $16^3/_{16}$ was the last, or closing price.
- The change column indicates that the share price closed up $^5/_{16}$ of a point from the previous week's close.

*Barron's*, the weekly financial newspaper, has a separate section which includes a comprehensive list of closed-end funds, including unit investment trusts. For example, the information provided on Black Rock Insured Municipal Trust 2008 from the *Barron's* closed-end bond fund section for the week ending October 19, 1998, provided different information from that offered in the stock columns of the same financial newspaper:

| Fund Name (Symbol) | Stock Exchange | NAV Price | Market | Prem/ Discount | 12 Month Yield 9/30/1998 |
|---|---|---|---|---|---|
| BlckRk Ins 2008 (BRM) | N | 17.18 | $16^3/_{16}$ | −5.8 | 5.2 |

- Black Rock Insured Municipal Trust 2008 trades on the New York Stock Exchange.
- The net asset value as of the week's close was $17.18 per share.
- The closing market price for the week was $16^3/_{16}$ per share.
- The minus sign indicates that the stock was trading at a discount of 5.8 percent to the net asset value $(16.1875 - 17.18) \div 17.18 = -5.8\%$. A plus sign would indicate that the fund or trust was trading at a premium to its net asset value.

- The 52-week return for Black Rock Insured Municipal 2008 Trust is 5.2 percent.

By combining the information in the stock market columns with that provided by *Barron's*, investors can better follow the closed-end funds that they are interested in buying or selling. Shares listed on the exchanges are sold through brokers.

Before buying closed-end funds or trusts, ask your broker or call the fund sponsor for the annual or quarterly report.

## WHAT ARE THE ADVANTAGES OF CLOSED-END FUNDS AND UNIT INVESTMENT TRUSTS?

- Investors can buy into closed-end funds and trusts trading at discounts to their net asset values, which may offer the potential for capital gains and increased yields. The downside of this strategy is that it could lead to capital losses if the discount to the net asset value widens.
- The shares of the larger, more actively traded closed-end funds and trusts can easily be bought and sold on the stock exchanges. The less actively traded funds will not be as liquid. For income-seeking investors, most unit investment trusts pay dividends on a monthly basis.
- Unit investment trusts have maturities, at which time investors will have all (or most) of their capital returned to them.

## WHAT ARE THE DISADVANTAGES OF CLOSED-END FUNDS AND UNIT INVESTMENT TRUSTS?

- Both closed-end funds and unit investment trusts are subject to interest rate risk. Unit investment trusts have no protection against a rise in interest rates because their portfolio of investments is fixed.
- There is the risk that the share prices of funds and trusts can move independently of the value of the securities that are held in their portfolios. More investors exiting the fund

or trust than buying will have the effect of driving the price down despite the fact that the assets in the fund are doing well. It often represents a buying opportunity when a fund's or trust's shares are trading at a deep discount to its net asset value.

- Brokerage commissions and management fees can be high, which eats into the yields of closed-end funds and unit investment trusts.
- Some of the shares of the smaller, less actively traded funds and trusts may be illiquid.
- Buying into funds and trusts when they are first offered to shareholders means that these shareholders are investing into an unknown portfolio of assets. This is of particular significance for unit investment trusts in that investors cannot gauge the level of risk in the composition of the assets and whether the trust will use leverage to try and increase yields.
- Since their portfolios are fixed, unit investment trusts offer no protection against the credit deterioration of their assets.

## CAVEATS

- Investors should avoid investing in closed-end bond funds and unit investment trusts when they are first offered to the public because a percentage of their initial funds will go toward paying underwriting fees and selling commissions. For example, if investors pay $10 per share and $0.80 goes toward these expenses, net asset values will fall to $9.20 directly after issuance.
- Compare the long-term performance of closed-end funds and unit investment trusts before investing. Some have not performed well, and investors may want to avoid those with poor long-term track records.
- Examine the fees charged before buying into closed-end funds and unit investment trusts. They can be high.
- When bonds are called or sold early in unit investment trusts, the principal and any interest is returned to

investors. If this is spent, you are spending part of your principal investment.

## ARE CLOSED-END FUNDS AND UNIT INVESTMENT TRUSTS SUITABLE FOR YOU?

Under certain conditions in the past, closed-end funds and unit investment trusts have provided investors with profitable returns. According to Herzfeld Closed-End Averages (based on closed-end equity funds), at a point late in 1998, closed-end funds were trading at an average discount of 9 percent to their net asset values (*Barron's*, October 19, 1998, p. MW91). This means that investors were paying on average $0.91 for every $1 of assets to invest in closed-end funds (not taking into account brokerage fees to buy the shares). If the coupon yields of the bond investment holdings are higher than current rates of interest, some closed-end bond funds and unit investment trusts can trade at premiums to their net asset values. Unit investment trusts, which do not buy and sell their bond holdings, will retain the higher yields to maturity as interest rates fall. If the bonds are called, the trust will return the principal to the shareholders. With closed-end bond funds, the manager of the fund will take the proceeds and invest in new bonds with lower coupon yields, thus lowering the average total yield of the fund.

It is often advantageous for investors to buy into closed-end funds and unit investment trusts when they are trading at discounts to their net asset values. In fact, many investment advisors recommend buying closed-end funds and unit investment trusts when they are trading at large discounts, by historical standards, to their net asset values and then selling them when they have small discounts or premiums. A caution on this strategy is that these fixed-income closed-end funds and unit investment trusts are sensitive to changes in interest rates. When market rates of interest rise, the prices of these funds and trusts will go down, which may push the discounts even lower. Closed-end bond funds and unit investment trusts were much more desirable to investors seeking income when interest rates were relatively high, around 8 percent in the early 1990s.

Another buying opportunity may occur when closed-end funds are to be converted to open-end funds. If the shares of these funds are trading at discounts to their net asset values, they will rise to their net asset value price at the date of conversion.

Because of their inherent characteristics, unit investment trusts need to be examined carefully before buying. They have maturity dates. Therefore, investors will have their principal returned to them at a specified time. Whether they get all of their principal back is questionable. If interest rates continue to go down and the unit investment trust benefits from the use of leverage, shareholders should get close to if not all of their original principal back. However, if interest rates rise and borrowing costs climb, the return of their entire principal would be jeopardized.

With both closed-end funds and unit investment trusts, share prices fluctuate due to supply and demand for the shares on the stock market. Thus, if investors cannot find closed-end funds or unit investment trusts that are trading at discounts and they do not want the added risk of further fluctuations in price over net asset values, they should consider open-end mutual funds.

## REFERENCES

**Bary, Andrew**: "Whom Do You Trust?" *Barron's,* February 8, 1993, pp. M8–M9.
**Bary, Andrew**: "Father Knows Best? How Lew Ranieri's Bond Funds Fared So Poorly," *Barron's,* May 17, 1993, pp. 14–15.
**Clements, Jonathan**: "Bargains in Closed-End Funds Are Tougher to Find These Days," *The Wall Street Journal,* April 5, 1993, p. C1.
**Thau, Annette**: *The Bond Book,* McGraw-Hill, New York, 1992.

## CHAPTER 13

# Managing Your Portfolio

## KEY CONCEPTS

- Investor objectives
- Investor characteristics
- Allocation of assets
- Selection of individual investments
- Management of the portfolio
- Management of interest rate risk

Managing a portfolio can mean different things to different people. For some, it means buying the most conservative investments and holding them through maturity or indefinitely. At the other extreme, there are those investors who change their investments on a regular basis as if they were disposable napkins.

Managing a portfolio has some analogies to managing your health. Eating healthy foods, exercising regularly, and eating an apple a day works well for people who are in good health. For a person who has a major illness or something chronically wrong, the apple a day, exercise, and good health regimen alone won't rectify the overall problem.

Similarly, managing a portfolio of investments means assembling those investment securities which will perform together to achieve the investor's overall objectives. When this has been accomplished, the investor can sit back and eat an apple a day while monitoring the securities in the portfolio. If, however, the investment assets are haphazardly chosen and the investor has not set objectives or goals for the portfolio, there is no way of telling how well or badly this portfolio is doing. It can be likened to a walk in space. You don't know where you are drifting to, which means that you will not have a clue as to where you will end up.

Knowing what you want to accomplish from your investments allows you to manage your portfolio effectively. Buying and selling investments are relatively easy tasks, but knowing what to buy and sell is more difficult. In essence, the choice of assets to hold is determined by the investor's objectives and personal characteristics.

## INVESTOR OBJECTIVES

The investor's objectives will determine the purpose and time period for the investments. For instance, one investor may be saving for retirement in five years, and another may be saving for retirement in thirty years. Although their objectives may be the same (saving for retirement), the time period and elements of risk tolerance are very different.

The first step in any plan is to determine long-range, medium-range, and short-term objectives. For example, a young family with small children may have the following objectives:

Short-term
- Set up an emergency fund
- Buy a new car
- Save for a vacation

Medium-term
- Save for a downpayment on a house

Long-term
- Save for children's education
- Save for retirement.

Once objectives have been developed, it becomes easier to see what you can expect to get from the portfolio. Before setting a strategy to achieve these objectives, investors should examine their personal circumstances, which will serve as a guide in the selection of the portfolio assets.

# CHARACTERISTICS OF THE INVESTOR

Marital status: Single, married, widowed

Family: No children, young children, teenage children, empty nest

Age: Under 25, 25–39 years, 40–60 years, over 60

Education: High school graduate, college degree, graduate degree

Income: Stabile and level, future growth prospects

Job/profession: Skills and expertise, ability to improve level of earnings

Net worth/size of portfolio: Level of income, assets, and net worth will determine the size of the portfolio

The variables in the above list will determine the types of investments and the level of risk that can be absorbed in the development and management of the portfolio. For example, a non-working widow who is dependent entirely on income generated from her investments will not be able to tolerate the high risks of investments in junk bonds, collateralized mortgage obligations, inverse floaters, or newly issued public offerings of common stocks. Her portfolio of assets would need to generate income but not at the expense of capital preservation.

Likewise, the sole breadwinner of a young family may be risk-averse, but circumstances may allow for more emphasis on growth assets than purely preservation of capital. A prosperous litigation lawyer can withstand more risk in the hope of expanding capital (net worth) without having to generate current income.

Depending on the investor's characteristics, there will be a tradeoff between assets generating current income and assets seeking capital appreciation. To the degree you opt for capital appreciation, you will probably sacrifice on current income.

A portfolio of assets is created based on the investor's characteristics and steered by the investor's objectives.

# ALLOCATION OF ASSETS

Asset allocation is a plan to invest in different types of securities so that the capital invested is protected against adverse factors in the market. This, in essence, is the opposite of putting all your eggs in one basket. Imagine an investor with $200,000 to invest investing it all in the stock of Schlumberger at the beginning of 1998 at $85 per share. The value of the portfolio as of this writing would be cut almost in half, as Schlumberger is trading in the low $40s per share.

Developing a portfolio is generally based on the idea of holding a variety of investments rather than concentrating on a single one. This is to reduce the risk of loss and to even out the returns of the different investments.

The latter point can be illustrated with the following hypothetical example of a portfolio:

|  | Investment |
| --- | --- |
| Assume the investor buys: | |
| 1000 shares of XYZ Co. at $50 per share | $50,000 |
| 100 convertible bonds of ABC Co. at $1000 per bond | 100,000 |
| Total | $150,000 |
|  | Investment |
| A year later, the portfolio is valued as follows: | |
| 1000 shares of XYZ Co. at $70 per share | $70,000 |
| 100 convertible bonds of ABC Co. at $800 per bond | 80,000 |
| Total | $150,000 |

The investor has spread the risks of loss by owning two different types of securities and therefore averaging the returns of the two types of investments. Certainly the investor would have done much better had he invested totally in XYZ shares, but hindsight always produces the highest returns. The fact that we are not clairvoyant points to the benefits of diversifying across a broad segment of investments. In other words, diversification seeks a balance between the risk-return tradeoff discussed in Chapter 2.

Classifying some of the different types of investments on a continuum of risk, we see that common stocks are considered to be the most risky (in terms of variability in share price), followed by long-term bonds, with the shorter maturities on the low-risk end. Bear in mind that there are many other types of investments which are riskier than common stocks, such as commodities and futures contracts. Similarly, there is a great variation of quality among common stocks. The common stocks of the well-established "blue chip" companies are considered to be less risky than the bonds of highly leveraged companies with suspect balance sheets.

| Common Stock | Long-Term Bonds | Intermediate Bonds | Short-Term Bonds | Money Market Securities |
|---|---|---|---|---|

High-risk (aggressive)                                                               Low-risk (conservative)

Common stocks are considered to be the most risky due to the volatility of stock prices. However, over long periods of time, during which the ups and downs of the stock market can be averaged out, stocks have provided higher returns (see Chapter 2). Common stocks provide the growth in a portfolio and should be included among the investment assets to accomplish long-term growth goals. The percentage allocated to common stocks will depend on the investor's objectives and personal characteristics. As mentioned earlier, a retired widow who is dependent on the income generated from the investments in the portfolio may not have any common stocks in the portfolio. However, if the portfolio generates more than a sufficient level of income for the widow's current needs, a small portion of the portfolio could be invested in common stocks to provide some growth in the portfolio for later years.

Bonds are sought by investors primarily for their ability to generate a steady stream of income. However, an often overlooked fact is that long-term bonds (15- to 30-year maturities) can also be quite risky. Although 30-year U.S. Treasury bonds are safe investments in that the U.S. government is not liable to default on the interest and principal payments, they can be quite volatile in price due to changes in interest rates. Corporate and other types of long-term bonds will be more volatile than Treasuries, due to the increased risk of default.

Investors would have to weigh the advantages of taking on the greater risks of investing in other types of long-term bonds over Treasuries by examining their coupon yields. If the yields are significantly greater than those of long-term Treasuries, investors may want to contemplate purchasing these other types of long-term bonds. Besides coupon yield, a second consideration is that interest on Treasury securities is exempt from state and local taxes.

Total return includes transaction costs, which are very much less for Treasuries, particularly if these are bought directly through the Federal Reserve Bank or branches. If these bonds are held to maturity, there will be no transaction costs.

Some of the price volatility of bonds may be reduced by shortening maturities to intermediate-term bonds. Even though returns may be diminished by shortening the length of time to maturity, intermediate-term bonds offer investors greater flexibility. For instance, say an investor's characteristics change, and that investor is no longer dependent on current income from investments. Intermediate-term securities are generally much more liquid than longer-term bonds and can more easily be changed to growth-oriented investments.

Low-risk, low-return securities such as certificates of deposit, Treasury bills, and money market funds should account for the percentage of the investor's portfolio that will serve liquidity and emergency fund purposes. Many investors keep too large a percentage of their portfolios in these low-risk, low-return assets.

Conservative investors who do not feel comfortable keeping only an amount necessary to meet liquidity and emergency needs should increase the percentage. However, the returns from these low-yielding investments often do not even keep pace with inflation, let alone the effects of taxation on the interest.

There isn't a rigid formula for asset allocation. Rather, it is a good idea to think about the concept as a guideline when investing money. Some investors may tilt toward an aggressive portfolio, while others require a conservative portfolio. The mix of investment assets depends primarily on the levels of risk that investors are willing to take and their time horizons. The percentage allocated to the different types of assets can always be changed depending on circumstances. As individual circumstances change, so will the investor's objectives. If the emphasis shifts, for example, to greater income generation and preservation of capital from capital growth, the percentage of the investments in the portfolio can be changed accordingly.

Table 13-1 includes some questions that can assist investors in determining their asset allocations. See Table 13-2 for asset allocation models. The most *conservative portfolio* is not one that consists entirely of bonds and money market securities. This is because the bond and stock markets do not always go up and down in tandem. There are many times when the two markets go in opposite directions. According to Roger Gibson, a Pittsburgh investment advisor, over the past 70 years a portfolio consisting of 23 percent stocks and 77 percent bonds has the same risk pro-

## TABLE 13-1

### Investor Questionnaire to Determine the Types of Assets for a Portfolio

1. Do you have an emergency fund consisting of at least three months' salary?

   No

   Yes, but less than three months

   Yes

   **Investment Planning:** These investment funds should be invested in liquid assets (money market securities) to avoid any loss in principal before the money is needed. The first step is to establish an emergency fund; after that, an investment fund can be established.

2. When will you need the investment funds (over and above your emergency fund) that you have invested?

   Within 1 year

   Within 5 years

   Between 5 and 10 years

   Longer than 10 years

   **Investment Planning:** If you need the money within one year, you need to invest in liquid investments. Money needed within a five year time frame should be invested in short-term securities. Investments with longer than a five year time frame can be invested more aggressively, such as long-term bonds and stocks, depending on your circumstances and your risk tolerance.

3. What percentage of your total investment funds is in retirement accounts?

   Below 25 percent

   Between 25 and 50 percent

   Between 51 and 75 percent

   Above 75 percent

   **Investment Planning:** The lower the percentage in retirement funds, the more aggressively you can invest.

4. How stable is your income from employment likely to be over the next five years?

   Likely to decrease

   Likely to stay the same

   Likely to keep pace with inflation

   Likely to increase above inflation

   **Investment Planning:** If there is uncertainty about future earnings, you may have to withdraw funds from your investments, which means that a corresponding amount should be invested conservatively. If there is a good chance that employment earnings will increase in the future, you can invest more aggressively.

**TABLE 13-1** (Continued)

---

5. How many dependents do you have?

   None

   1

   2

   More than 2

**Investment Planning:** The greater the number of dependents, the greater the responsibilities. Generally, this may require being a little more conservative in your investment approach.

6. What percentage of your earnings goes toward paying off debts, including a mortgage?

   Less than 10 percent

   Between 10 and 25 percent

   Between 25 and 50 percent

   Over 50 percent

**Investment Planning:** The higher the percentage of your earnings that goes toward paying off debts, the greater the likelihood that you will need to dip into your investment account, which would suggest a more conservative approach.

7. With regard to your investment assets, where would you feel comfortable on the scale below?

| I am willing to invest aggressively for the maximum possible growth, even if there is the potential for losses due to market fluctuations. | I am comfortable with some level of fluctuations in my funds in order to achieve reasonable levels of growth | I am uncomfortable when my investment funds go down in value due to market fluctuations. |
|---|---|---|

**Investment Planning:** Your appetite for risk will determine whether you can invest aggressively, somewhere in the middle, or conservatively.

8. If you could increase your potential returns by taking on more risk, would you feel comfortable?

   Yes

   No

**Investment Planning:** If yes, you can be a little more aggressive in your investments. If no, you should invest in those assets that you feel comfortable with.

**TABLE 1 3 - 1** (Continued)

9. What rate of return do you expect to earn from your investments?

Keep ahead of inflation, while seeking stability of principal.

Earn returns which are greater than inflation, even if there is some potential for loss in principal.

Earn high returns regardless of the increased potential for loss in principal.

**Investment Planning:** Your acceptance of the risk of loss in principal will determine whether you should invest aggressively, conservatively, or somewhere in the middle.

10. What do you need from your investment assets?

Investment Income

Long-term capital growth

**Investment Planning:** If you need investment income, the investment assets should be allocated more toward bonds. Long-term capital growth can be obtained from diversified investments in common stocks.

file as a 100 percent bond portfolio, but has earned 2 percentage points higher per year. At the other end of the risk spectrum is a 100 percent stock portfolio. The stock market cannot always be counted on when you need to withdraw funds, and as was pointed out in Chapter 1, there have been many shorter periods of time when bonds outperformed stocks. Thus, an *aggressive portfolio* would consist of 90 percent stocks and 10 percent bonds (Clements, November 10, 1998, p. C1).

An example of asset allocation for a newlywed couple with no children, both of whom are employed professionals, might look like this:

80% common stocks with emphasis on growth

10% intermediate-term municipal bonds

10% money market securities

However, if the wife decides to give up her career to stay home to bring up a child, the couple might want an asset allocation that would provide for greater income generation. The portfolio might be altered to look like this:

40% long-term bonds

10% intermediate-term municipal bonds

20% money market securities

**TABLE 13-2**

Asset Allocation Models

An evaluation of your answers to the questions in Table 13-1 will assist you in your allocation of investment assets.

A *conservative portfolio* is one in which the investment goals are to preserve capital with some growth. The weighting is geared toward high-quality bonds and some common stocks for growth.

**Asset Allocation for a Conservative Portfolio**

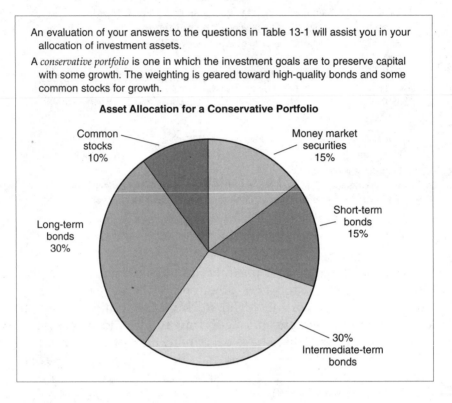

30% common stocks, half invested in blue chip companies, the rest in growth stocks

What may work for one couple or family may not work for another. Asset allocation is dependent on the investment objectives and the personal and financial situation of each investor.

The most important aspect of investing is having an asset allocation plan which outlines the broad mix of assets to strive for. Once these broad categories are determined, the individual assets may be purchased.

## SELECTION OF INDIVIDUAL INVESTMENTS

In order to match individual objectives with the specific investments, you need to identify the characteristics of the different investments and their risks. Funds for immediate needs and

**TABLE 13-2** (Continued)

Asset Allocation Models

A *balanced portfolio* includes a greater percentage of common stocks, which provides the capital growth, and keeps a large percentage of assets in fixed-income securities, which provide income.

**Asset Allocation for a Balanced Portfolio**

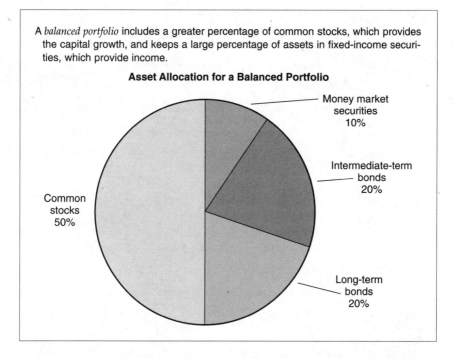

emergency purposes should be liquid, in investments that can be converted easily into cash without a loss in principal. These would be money market mutual funds, checking accounts, and savings accounts. These are readily convertible into cash. By increasing the time horizon from immediate needs to short-term needs, investors can marginally increase their rates of return by investing in certificates of deposit, Treasury bills, and commercial paper. Of these, however, only Treasury bills are marketable, which means that they can be sold on the secondary market before maturity.

These individual investments—savings accounts, certificates of deposit, money market mutual funds, Treasury bills, and commercial paper—provide some income, which is taxable, are liquid but not marketable, except for the Treasury bills, and do not provide much possibility for capital gains. Although investors will not lose any of their principal by investing in this group of investments, there is a risk that the returns from these investments will not keep up with inflation.

## TABLE 13-2 (Continued)

### Asset Allocation Models

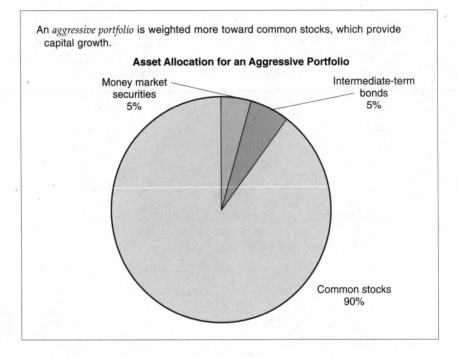

An *aggressive portfolio* is weighted more toward common stocks, which provide capital growth.

**Asset Allocation for an Aggressive Portfolio**

Money market securities 5%

Intermediate-term bonds 5%

Common stocks 90%

The financing of intermediate-term objectives requires investments that are relatively safe. These objectives stretch several years into the future, and include things like the purchase of a car, house or appliance; the funding of a child's education; and emergencies that may crop up in the future. These investments would need to produce a greater rate of return than leaving the money in a savings account or in short-term money market securities. Short- to intermediate-term bonds offer increased rates of return over money market securities as well as the possibility of capital gains or losses if the investor needs the money before maturity. Although investors will get increased rates of return from intermediate-term securities, these are not as liquid as short-term securities. Treasury notes and bonds have no credit risk or risk of default. This means that with Treasury notes and bonds, there is no need to diversify, whereas with corporate bonds, it is a good idea for investors to spread the risks of default (and call) by buying the bonds of different issuers. Similarly, it is a good idea to diversify when investing in municipal bonds and some of the smaller agency bonds.

Financing a child's education in five years requires an investment that is relatively safe. Most people would not gamble with the money earmarked for their children's education. Thus, the credit quality of the issuer is important. Similarly, if the yield differential between Treasuries and other types of intermediate bonds is not significant, it is probably advantageous to stick with Treasury securities. This is not only because they are free of default risk, but their interest payments are tax-free at the state and local levels of government. However, if the yield differential of other types of bonds (agency bonds, corporate bonds, and municipals) over Treasuries is large, investors should invest in these other bonds. Again, choosing a diversified portfolio is more important than investing all the intermediate-term funds in the securities of one issuer. Federal taxes and changes in the individual tax rates may steer the choice towards municipal bonds.

Long-term objectives, such as saving for retirement or an infant's college education in 18 years, require investments that offer long-term growth prospects as well as greater returns. The level of risk that can be withstood on these investments will depend on the individual investor's circumstances.

A more conservative long-term portfolio would consist of long-term bonds, blue chip stocks, and conservative growth stocks. The emphasis of this strategy is to invest in good-quality bonds and the stocks of established companies, which pay dividends and offer the prospects of steady growth over a long period of time. Securities offering capital growth are important even in conservative portfolios. They provide some cover against any possible erosion in future purchasing power because of inflation.

A more speculative portfolio in which the investor can absorb greater levels of risk and strive for greater growth and returns would include growth stocks, stocks of small emerging companies, convertible bonds, junk bonds, real estate, options, commodities, and futures. Including the last three types of investments does not mean they should play a major role in a portfolio. For a speculative investor who understands the nuances of these investments, these securities should account for no more than 5 percent of the total portfolio. Casino gambling is not an investment strategy! The other assets mentioned offer the investor the opportunity for large gains, but the risks of loss are also greater. Foreign bonds and stocks should also be considered, but investors should do their homework first so that they understand the risks fully. International mutual funds may be more helpful to spread some of the risk, although there will always be currency risk when investing in off-shore investments.

Some investors may not feel comfortable buying bonds and stocks individually, and they should stick with mutual funds. Investors willing to make their own investment decisions on individual securities can eliminate the fees and expenses charged by mutual funds. However, they still need to make sure that the brokerage commissions charged are discounted and competitive. Many full-service brokers will discount their commissions if they know that the investors have done their homework and they will lose them to discount brokers if the commissions are not matched. On-line investing can reduce commissions significantly.

When considering the different types of securities to choose for a portfolio, investors should weigh the characteristics of the type of investment along with the risks to assist them in their overall choice. See Table 13-3 for a summary of strategies to reduce the different types of risks.

## MANAGEMENT OF THE PORTFOLIO

Investors need to be continually aware not only that their objectives and individual characteristics change over time, but that their investments need to be monitored due to changing financial conditions and markets. Companies change and their securities may no longer fulfill the criteria that they were purchased for. For example, Schlumberger, the largest oil service equipment company, has seen its stock price go up and down along with the underlying commodity price of oil per barrel. Not all investments in a portfolio will realize their projected returns, so investors managing their portfolios will need to sell these and replace them with other investments. This does not mean that all or most of the investments in the portfolio should be continuously turned over. Only those that are not likely to achieve the goals specified should be liquidated.

The management of bond portfolios does not generally require as much attention as stock portfolios. In fact, bonds are much more conducive to a passive management style, since they pay a fixed stream of income and mature at a specified date. By selecting a convenient maturity date for the issue, the investor can wait until the issue matures to get back the principal. Not only does

**TABLE 13-3**

## Summary of Strategies to Manage Risk

| Investment | Risk | Strategy |
|---|---|---|
| Common stock | Market Risk | Invest for a long period of time |
| | Financial risk | Diversification |
| | | Invest in companies with low leveraged balance sheets |
| Bonds | Interest rate risk | Interest rate management strategies |
| | ■ When market rates are declining | Increase the maturities of the bond issues |
| | ■ When market rates are increasing | Shorten maturities |
| | | Ladder maturities in the portfolio |
| | Credit risk | Invest in higher-quality issues (above investment grade) |
| | | Shorten maturities |
| | Purchasing power risk (when inflation increases) | Shorten maturities |
| | | Requires active portfolio management |

this strategy minimize transaction costs, but it also makes fluctuations in the value of the issue before maturity meaningless. However, if the investor needs the money for any reason before maturity, the current market value would be important. Table 13-4 summarizes what you can do to increase your rate of return.

Many investors follow a more active management style than the buy-and-hold strategy. Such a strategy involves replacing existing bonds in the portfolio with new bonds. This is referred to as *bond swapping*. This strategy may be used for tax purposes, to reduce capital gains taxes. At the end of the tax year, if an investor has capital gains from other transactions, the investor can sell some bonds whose prices have declined for a loss to offset some or all of the capital gains. (If the investor only has bonds in the portfolio that have not declined in price, this strategy cannot be used.) The proceeds from the sale of the bonds are used to buy similar type bonds (same maturity and quality). By swapping one set of bonds for another set of similar bonds, the investor has benefited by generating a tax loss, which brings about tax savings.

## TABLE 13-4

Strategies to Increase Returns

Increase the **maturities** of your bonds, particularly if the yield curve indicates that long-rates will remain higher than intermediate-term and short-term bond rates. Bear in mind that the longer the maturity of the bond, the greater the potential volatility.

Increase your holdings of **lower-quality** bonds. Before doing so, you should examine the spread between the yields of good-quality bonds and lower-quality bonds to see if the returns are worth the risks. Moving from Treasuries to good-quality corporate bonds with higher yields may cause fewer sleepless nights than a move from Treasuries to corporate junk bonds. If junk bonds are too risky, move up the spectrum to medium-quality bonds. The move to lower-quality bonds comes with the prerequisite that you can tolerate the increased risks.

If you are in the higher tax brackets, consider municipal bonds to increase **after-tax returns.** Calculate the taxable yields of the municipal bonds so that they can be compared with the equivalent taxable bond yield. This can be done by dividing the tax-free yield of a municipal bond by 1 minus the marginal tax rate. For example, a 4.5% yield on a municipal bond is equivalent to a 7.45% taxable yield for an investor in the 39.6% tax bracket. If the after-tax yields are greater than what you can get from taxable bonds, you should consider municipal bonds.

Other reasons for swapping bonds could be to improve yields (a lower-yielding bond swapped for a higher-yielding bond) or to take advantage of price differentials between different types of bonds, for example, selling agency bonds and replacing them with higher-yielding corporate bonds.

Anticipation of changes in interest rates could prompt investors to swap bonds with different maturities. If higher market rates of interest are anticipated, the investor would swap existing bonds for shorter maturities. Anticipation of lower rates of interest would lead to swapping bonds for longer maturities.

## MANAGEMENT OF INTEREST RATE RISK

Instead of trying to anticipate market rates of interest, investors could pursue a number of strategies which allow for changes in interest rates.

Using a *matching strategy,* an investor determines the holding period or time frame for the investments and then selects a bond portfolio with a duration equal to the holding period. For instance, if the holding period is seven years, a bond portfolio with a duration equal to seven years is selected. Duration, which was discussed more fully in Chapter 2, is a measure of the average time that it takes for the bondholder to receive the interest and principal.

The duration value is determined by three factors:

- The maturity of the bond
- The market rates of interest
- The coupon rate

Duration has a positive correlation with maturity (the longer the maturity, the greater the duration) and a negative correlation with coupon rates and market rates of interest (the larger the coupon rate, the lower the duration, and similarly duration moves in the opposite direction to interest rates). By matching the duration to the time period when the funds will be needed, interest rate risk is minimized. If interest rates rise, the value of the bonds in the portfolio will go down, but the interest payments received will be reinvested at higher rates of interest. Similarly, if interest rates decline, the bonds in the portfolio will increase in price, but the interest payments will be reinvested at lower interest rates. Through the use of duration, a portfolio can be protected against the changes in market rates of interest.

The *laddering strategy* is another method to cope with changes in market rates of interest. It is a passive strategy which entails constructing a portfolio of bonds with different maturities over a time period. For example, a 10-year laddered portfolio would have 10 percent of the bond issues with a maturity of one year, another 10 percent of the bond issues with a maturity of two years, and so on. When the first year's bonds mature, the investor can reinvest the funds (if they are not needed) in issues with a 10-year maturity to maintain the original laddering structure.

The advantages of laddering are:

- Funds become due on a yearly basis to provide for any short-term needs.
- Short-term bonds generally earn more than leaving funds in money market securities.
- The impact on the valuations of the portfolio is reduced because of the fluctuations in interest rates.

The disadvantage of laddering is that if the investor anticipates a change in interest rates, the investor would have to sell most of the bond issues in the portfolio to react fully to the anticipated changes. For instance, in the 10-year laddering example, if interest rates go up, the investor would want to replace 90 percent of the portfolio with higher-coupon shorter-maturity investments. The same would be true for lower anticipated interest rates. The investor would want to replace most of short-term maturities with longer-term higher-yielding coupon issues.

The *barbell* or *dumbbell strategy* is used to counter the major disadvantage of laddering (having to liquidate a large percentage of the portfolio to take advantage of anticipated changes in interest rates). A barbell strategy involves using only short-term and long-term bonds. By eliminating intermediate-term bonds from the portfolio, the investor is better positioned to take advantage of anticipated changes in interest rates. If half the portfolio is invested in short-term bonds and lower rates are anticipated, the investor would sell the short-term bonds and reinvest in long-term bond issues. The opposite happens when higher market rates are anticipated—the long-term bonds are swapped for short-term bonds.

The advantages of the barbell strategy are:

- By eliminating intermediate-term bonds from the portfolio, investors get increased liquidity from the short-term bonds and increased returns from holding long-term issues.
- Only half the issues need to be swapped in the event of anticipated changes in interest rates.
- If market rates of interest are correctly anticipated, the impact of the changes will be reduced.

However, the major disadvantage is that if interest rates are incorrectly anticipated the investor could experience greater losses.

These strategies—matching, laddering, and barbell—are attempts to eliminate the effects of changes in interest rates on a portfolio. However, a key ingredient for the successful management of a bond portfolio is accurate forecasting of interest rates.

# REFERENCES

Clements, Jonathan: "Portfolios for the Conservative and the Bold," *The Wall Street Journal*, November 10, 1998, p. C1.

**Accrued Interest**   Interest that has been earned but not yet paid.

**Active Management**   The portfolio manager frequently changes the components of the portfolio.

**Adjustable Rate Mortgage**   A mortgage with an interest rate that changes periodically to reflect the movement of a specified index of current interest rates.

**Annual Report**   A published report of a publicly traded company that contains audited financial statements, auditor's report, chairman's report, review of the company's operations, and future prospects.

**Ask Price**   The price at which a dealer is willing to sell a security.

**Asset Allocation**   Dividing investment funds among different types of investment assets.

**Average Cost Method**   A method of accounting for capital gains or losses on a mutual fund by using the average cost of the shares.

**Back-End Load**   A fee charged by an open-end mutual fund to investors when they sell their shares back to the mutual fund.

**Balance Sheet**   A financial statement that indicates the wealth of a company at a point in time.

**Bankers' Acceptance**   A short-term debt instrument. The acceptance is a draft drawn on a bank for approval for future payments.

**Barron's Confidence Index**   A ratio of *Barron's* average of 10 high-grade corporate bonds to the yield on the more speculative Dow Jones average of 40 bonds. It shows the yield spread between high-grade bonds and more speculative bonds.

**Barbell Strategy**   A bond portfolio strategy with investments concentrated in short-term and long-term maturities.

**Basis Point**   One basis point is equal to .01 percent. It is a measure of change on interest-bearing securities.

**Bid Price**   The price at which a dealer is willing to purchase a security.

**Bid-Ask Spread**   The difference between the price that a dealer is willing to buy a security at (bid price) and the price at which a dealer is willing to sell a security (asked price).

**Blue Chip Stock**   The common stock of a large established company.

**Bond**   The borrower of funds issues a security, or bond, which stipulates the amount of the payments to the lender.

**Bond Rating**   A rating given to a bond as a measure of the likelihood that the issuer of the bond will default on the interest and principal payments.

**Bond Swap**   The selling of a given bond and the immediate replacement with another bond of similar characteristics to improve portfolio performance or yield or to take advantage of tax losses.

**Business Risk**   Refers to the uncertainty about a company's sales, profits, and rate of return.

**Call Premium**   The price above the par value that the issuer will pay bondholders for retiring their bonds when called.

**Call Provision**   A provision in the bond indenture that allows the issuer to retire bonds before maturity.

**Call Risk**   The uncertainty associated with the call provision of a bond.

**Certificate of Deposit**   A time deposit issued by banks and savings and loan associations.

**Closed-End Fund**   A mutual fund with a fixed number of shares.

**Collateral Trust Bond**   A bond that has the backing of other financial assets.

**Collateralized Mortgage Obligations**   A debt security based on a pool of mortgages, which pay monthly interest and principal.

**Commercial Paper**   An unsecured IOU of a large corporation.

**Commodity-Backed Bonds**   Bonds whose coupons or maturity values are indexed to a specific commodity, such as gold, silver, or oil.

**Conversion Price**   The price at which a convertible security can be exchanged for common stock.

**Conversion Ratio**   The number of common shares received for each convertible security at conversion.

**Conversion Value**   The value of the common stock represented by the convertible security (conversion ratio multiplied by the market price of the common stock).

**Convertible Security**   Convertible bonds or preferred stock that can be exchanged for a specified number of common shares of the issuing company at the option of the convertible holder.

**Coupon Rate**   The fixed rate of interest paid on a bond. The dollar amount of the interest payment is expressed as a percentage of the par value of the bond.

**Credit Risk**   The uncertainty associated with the financial condition of a company.

**Currency Risk**   The uncertainty that a particular currency may lose its value relative to another currency.

**Current Yield**   The dollar amount of a bond's coupon payments divided by the market price of the bond.

**Debenture**   An unsecured bond.

**Default Risk**   The uncertainty that some or all of the investment will not be returned.

**Derivative Security**   A security whose value depends on the price of an underlying security or asset.

**Diversification**   Investing in different securities as opposed to concentrating on only one.

**Duration**   The weighted average number of years that the bondholder receives interest and principal payments.

**Eurobond**   An international bond denominated in a currency not native to the country in which it is issued.

**Expense Ratio**   The total expenses of a mutual fund as a percentage of the assets of that fund.

**Face Value (Par Value)**   The nominal value of a bond; the amount repaid to bondholders at maturity.

**Fed Funds Rate**   The rate at which banks can borrow or lend reserves.

**Financial Risk**   The uncertainty associated with the way a company has financed its assets.

**Fiscal Policy**   The government's use of taxation, spending, and debt management to attain economic goals.

**Flower Bonds**   A particular Treasury bond that can be redeemed at face value to settle federal estate taxes.

**Front-End Load**   The sales charge paid to buy shares in a mutual fund.

**General Obligation Bond**   A municipal bond backed by the full faith, credit, and taxing power of the issuer.

**Global Fund**   A mutual fund that invests in both U.S. and non-U.S. securities.

**Graduated Payment Mortgage**   A mortgage whose payments increase over the life of the loan.

**Growth Fund**   A mutual fund whose primary objective is capital appreciation.

**Growth Stock**   The common stock of a company that is growing faster than the norm.

**High-Yield Bond (Junk Bond)**   High-risk, low-rated speculative bonds.

**Immunization**   A bond portfolio management strategy using duration. It allows an investor to be able to meet a stream of cash outflows despite changes in interest rates.

**Income Bond**   Debenture bond on which interest payments are made only if funds are earned.

**Income Statement**   A financial statement that shows revenues and profits over a period of time.

**Indenture**   A legal document which spells out the provisions of a bond issue.

**Index Fund**   A mutual fund that seeks to match the portfolio composition of a particular index.

**Inflation**   The increase in the prices of goods and services in an economy.

**Inflation-Indexed Savings Bonds**   Savings bonds issued by the U.S. Treasury Department whose returns are tied to the inflation rate.

**Initial Public Offering (IPO)**   The initial offering of shares to the public.

**Interest Rate Risk**   The uncertainty of returns on investments due to changes in market rates of interest.

**International Fund**   A mutual fund that invests in non-U.S. securities.

**Inverse Floaters**   Derivative securities which reflect the changes in price of the underlying bonds sold with them.

**Investment Companies**   Companies that sell shares in diversified portfolios of investments to investors.

**Investment-Grade Bond**   Bonds whose ratings are BBB and above (by Standard & Poor's).

**Junk Bond**   Speculative bond with ratings below investment grade.

**Keogh Plan**   A retirement pension plan that can be used to shelter self-employment income.

**Ladder**   A technique used to construct a portfolio with different maturities over a time period.

**Liquidity**   The ability to convert an investment into cash with minimum capital loss.

**Listed Security**   A security that is traded on an organized security exchange.

**Load Charge**   A sales commission or fee charged by load mutual funds when investors buy or sell shares.

**Load Fund**   A mutual fund that charges a load fee.

**Low-Load Fund**   A mutual fund that charges a relatively low load when investors buy and sell shares in the fund.

**Margin**   The amount of cash an investor puts up to invest in a security, with the balance borrowed from the brokerage firm.

**Market Risk**   Uncertainty over the movement of market prices of securities.

**Marketability**   To be able to sell an investment quickly.

**Monetary Policy**   The regulation of the supply of money and credit to affect the country's economic growth, inflation, unemployment, and financial markets.

**Money Market**   The financial market where assets with maturities of one year or less are traded.

**Money Market Funds**   Mutual funds that invest in money market securities.

**Mortgage-Backed Security**   A debt security backed by a pool of home mortgages.

**Mortgage Bond**   A bond that has specific mortgage assets pledged as collateral.

**Municipal Bond**   A debt security issued by a state, county, city, or local government to finance public needs.

**Mutual Fund**   An investment company that manages the funds for the shareholders who buy shares in the fund.

**Net Asset Value**   The total market value of the securities in a fund, less any liabilities, divided by the number of shares outstanding.

**No-Load Fund**   A mutual fund that does not charge a sales commission to buy shares in the fund.

**Notes**   Intermediate-term debt securities with maturities between one and ten years.

**Open-End Fund**   A mutual fund that has no limit on the number of shares that it can issue.

**Original Issue Discount Bond**   A bond that is issued with a coupon that is below prevailing market yields and is sold at a discount.

**Passive Management**   Portfolio management approach in which the manager buys and holds securities in the fund rather than actively trading them.

**Portfolio Turnover Rate**   A measure of the trading activity of a fund.

**Premium (Convertible Security)**   The difference between the market price and the conversion value on a convertible security.

**Primary Market**   The market for the sale for the first time of securities by the issuer to the public.

**Prospectus**   A condensed version of the registration statement filed with the SEC for a new bond issue. It is designed to provide information to prospective investors.

**Purchasing Power Risk**   The uncertainty associated with inflation.

**Put Feature**   A provision that allows the investor to sell the security back to the issuer at a specified price.

**Recession**   A decline in the gross domestic product for two consecutive quarters.

**Refunding**   A provision in a bond indenture which allows the issuer to call the bonds with a higher coupon rate and pay the holders with the proceeds from a newly issued lower-coupon-rate bond issue.

**Registered Bond**   A bond whose ownership is registered with the issuer.

**Reinvestment Risk**   The uncertainty related to the rate at which interest payments received on a bond will be reinvested.

**Revenue Bond**   A municipal bond that is backed solely by the revenues from a particular project, authority, or agency.

**Secondary Market**   The market in which already existing securities are bought and sold.

**Serial Bond**   A bond issue with portions maturing at different dates.

**Series EE Bond**   A U.S. savings bond that pays a market-based interest rate which is a market average for five-year Treasury securities.

**Series HH Bond**   A U.S. savings bond that pays semiannual interest.

**Sinking Fund**   A provision in a bond that allows an issuer to allocate funds to repay the principal or purchase the bonds on the market and retire them before maturity.

**Subordinated Debenture**   An unsecured bond whose claims are junior to other bonds of the same issuer in the event of bankruptcy.

**Substitution Swap**   A bond swap where an investor exchanges one bond for another bond with a higher yield.

**Syndicate**   A group of investment bankers who share the underwriting and distribution responsibilities in an offering of securities to the public.

**Tax-Exempt Bond**   A security whose income is not taxable by the federal government.

**Term Bond**   A bond issue in which all the bonds have the same maturity date.

**Trade Deficit**   An imbalance in which a country's imports exceed its exports.

**Treasury Bill**   A short-term security issued by the U.S. Treasury.

**Treasury Bond**   A fixed-income security issued by the U.S. Treasury with a maturity of over 10 years.

**Treasury Note**   A fixed-income security issued by the U.S. Treasury whose maturity ranges from one to 10 years.

**Treasury Indexed Inflation Securities**   Treasury bonds issued by the U.S. Treasury whose returns are pegged to the rate of inflation.

**Unit Investment Trust**   A type of investment company that has a finite life and raises funds from investors to purchase a portfolio of investments.

**Variable Rate Note**   A debt security whose coupon rate fluctuates with a specified short-term rate.

**Yankee Bond**  A bond issued by a foreign company or government but sold in the U.S. and denominated in U.S. dollars.

**Yield Curve**  A curve showing interest rates at a particular point in time for securities with the same risk but different maturity dates.

**Yield to Call**  The return on a bond if it is held from a given purchase date to the call date.

**Yield to Maturity**  The annualized rate of return on a bond if it is held until the maturity date.


**Zero-Coupon Bond**  Bonds that are sold at a deep discount and pay no interest until maturity.

# INDEX